American Art Since 1970

Painting, Sculpture, and Drawings
from the Collection of the
Whitney Museum of American Art, New York

Richard Marshall

This exhibition and catalogue are sponsored by the National Committee of the Whitney Museum of American Art, with additional support from the National Endowment for the Arts.

Exhibition Itinerary

La Jolla Museum of Contemporary Art, California
March 10–April 22, 1984

Museo Tamayo, Mexico City
May 17–July 29, 1984

North Carolina Museum of Art, Raleigh
September 29–November 25, 1984

Sheldon Memorial Art Gallery, University of Nebraska, Lincoln
January 12–March 3, 1985

Center for the Fine Arts, Miami
March 30–May 26, 1985

Some of the works illustrated in this catalogue will not be included in the traveling exhibition because of prior loan commitments.

This publication was organized at the Whitney Museum of American Art by Doris Palca, Head, Publications and Sales; Sheila Schwartz, Editor; and Amy Curtis, Secretary/Assistant.
Curatorial assistance and research: Nancy Cohen, Sue Felleman, Sue Marlieb, Anne Todorchev.

Photograph credits:
All photographs are by Geoffrey Clements with the exception of eeva-inkeri: Garet; Steven Sloman: Graham, Zakanitch; Jerry L. Thompson: Arneson, Hunt; Zindman/Fremont: Baldessari

Cover: Elizabeth Murray, *Children Meeting*, 1978 (detail).

945 Madison Avenue
New York, New York 10021

Library of Congress Cataloging in Publication Data

Whitney Museum of American Art.
American art since 1970.
Catalog of an exhibition.
Bibliography: p.
1. Art, American—Exhibitions. 2. Art, Modern—20th century—Exhibitions. 3. Whitney Museum of American Art—Exhibitions. I. Marshall, Richard, II. Title. N6512.W532 1984
709'.73'07401471 83-27422

ISBN 0-87427-043-X

Designer: Michael Glass Design, Inc.
Typesetter: Michael and Winifred Bixler
Printer: Eastern Press, Inc.

Foreword

The Whitney Museum of American Art, throughout its history and especially during the 1970s, has actively supported living American artists through a vigorous program of acquisitions and exhibitions. The Museum has always considered collecting the art of its own time to be one of its primary purposes. This dedication to the work of living artists, which began with the efforts of Gertrude Vanderbilt Whitney as early as 1908 and has continued since the Museum was founded in 1930, has led to the formation of the most comprehensive collection of twentieth-century American art. As a result, the Museum is one of the few public institutions in the world able to present an overview of American art of the last decade with works from its own Permanent Collection.

Since the Whitney Museum began accepting gifts of artworks in 1948, many people committed to American art have helped us in innumerable ways. Each work in this exhibition credits the donors or the acquisition committees which represent them. Public patronage for twentieth-century American art is a relatively new phenomenon, and I am pleased to acknowledge it through the outstanding works presented in this exhibition.

The National Committee of the Whitney Museum of American Art, formed in 1980, sponsors a project each year to make the resources of the Museum available to a wider public. The Committee consists of thirty-eight members from nineteen states, and the two exhibitions the Committee has sponsored to date will be seen in eleven states. "American Art Since 1970" is the Committee's most ambitious project and provides an exhibition which many institutions might not have been able to organize on their own. We are grateful to the National Committee and to the National Endowment for the Arts for their assistance in presenting this material to an audience outside New York City. Moreover, we are extremely pleased that they have recognized the importance of exhibiting the work of living artists so that the public can become familiar with these artistic achievements and with the fabric of our culture as it is being formed.

TOM ARMSTRONG
Director

American Art Since 1970

American art of the past thirteen years is a large and complex topic to cover in one exhibition, one publication, and through the collection of one museum. Yet the Permanent Collection of the Whitney Museum of American Art, which numbers over 10,000 works, contains approximately 350 produced since 1970, reflecting the Museum's commitment to collecting the art of its own time. The fifty-two objects selected here offer a compact view of the period. Each one represents a significant aesthetic attitude and a varying form of its expression. What this survey of major artists and developments conveys is a sense of the vitality, richness, and importance of American art of the past decade. The exhibition includes art produced by artists of all generations, from Alice Neel, born in 1900, to Jedd Garet, born in 1955. But the largest concentration of artists belongs to the generation that reached artistic maturity during the 1970s.

To use 1970 as a point of demarcation is, of course, somewhat arbitrary, but it does create a temporal framework for discussion and generalization. With the historical perspective now attained on the period, it is possible to perceive gradual shifts in style, emphasis, and intent that began to occur in the late 1960s and developed into the 1970s.

The art of this period is most frequently described as "pluralistic," implying a variety of styles, media, forms, and ideas that seem fractured and disjointed, with no single expressive mode dominating. One way of approaching the early and mid-1970s is to view it as an explosion of fragments, each containing different ideas, materials, intents, and forms, all flying away from the reductive, rigid, restrictive, and seemingly impersonal aspects of Minimalism. In 1982, Roberta Smith cast a perceptive look back at the 1970s:

> . . . the 1970s seem to be gaining the reputation as the decade which never got off the the ground, an undistinguished period short on both genuine innovation and neat, packageable trends which remained, in effect, rather unformed.
>
> Actually the first two-thirds of the 1970s were a time of crisis, of mourning, and of growth, during which the foundations for what has been happening in the last three or four years were slowly and painfully laid. By the early seventies, the sequential, orchestrated flow of one school or movement into another, each more reductive than its predecessors, seemed to have reached an end point in Minimalism, an art of pure form, and its dialectical opposite, Conceptualism, an art of pure idea. . . . Conceptualism in particular brought art to the brink of extinction, but, by focusing almost exclusively on subject matter, it also broke the grip of reductivism, reversing the "disappearing act" of advanced art (*Joel Shapiro*, exhibition catalogue. New York: Whitney Museum of American Art, 1982, p. 11).

As reductivism lost its grip, it yielded to those apparently pluralistic fragments. But the diversity is deceptive, for much post-Minimalist art had the same goal: to put personal content, meaning, and imagery back into art. By the end of the 1970s and in the early 1980s, the fragments of expression started to exhibit features of an implosion—a concentration of related ideas and styles that seem to show a more unified and cohesive grasp of the means employed to achieve the goal.

Following the movement from explosion to implosion requires a discussion organized chronologically, but with frequent overlaps and backtrackings, examining groups of artists who are vaguely related in intent, content, and style, and who illustrate the often slow and experimental evolution of artistic forms.

Like many artistic evolutions, much of the art of the 1970s initially emerged as a response to prevailing aesthetics—to Pop, Conceptualism, and Minimalism. In the case of Minimalism, individual Minimalist works may differ in appearance, but they share a singular desire to rid art of personal reference, subjective expression, and allusion to representational imagery. However, as with all strict definitions of an art movement, the terms soon become more restrictive than the art itself. Under close scrutiny, it is clear that during the course of the seventies, Minimalism began to exhibit subtle shifts away from impersonality and nonreferential forms.

A comparison of Dan Flavin's *Untitled (for Robert, with fond regards)* (1977) and Sol LeWitt's *Lines to Points on a Grid* (1976) reveals just how subtle some of these shifts were. Flavin's work—despite the personal allusion of the title—is "pure" Minimalism. In a grid of twelve commercially produced fluorescent tubes situated diagonally across a corner, three horizontal pink tubes and three yellow ones face the viewer, while six vertical red tubes face the corner. All of them emanate light that envelops the viewer and fills the site. The dematerialized matter—pure light—is the artwork. LeWitt's wall drawing also interacts with its environment. But although it is a realization of the rigid, logical formula described in the title, it displays the irregularities and imperfections of both the wall on which it is drawn and the human hand that executed it. Agnes Martin's *Untitled #11* (1977) displays an even more personalized geometry. A delicate pencil-line grid creates rectangles that fill the entire surface. Yet the reductiveness of straight lines drawn on canvas is secondary: the primary visual impact of the drawing is the artist's touch. Rather than making the work coldly objective and rigid, the delicate line grid gives a soft, hypnotic, and reflective effect.

Al Held's *South Southwest* (1973) offers another approach to a personalized geometry. Here it is the surface that is tangible. A layer of white paint was applied, then sanded down, and additional layers were applied by the same process until the surface was thick enough for the overlapping black lines to physically cut into it. Moreover, the outlines and overlays in disjunctive perspectives create a confusion of space. There is no apparent system of geometric logic at work—the forms are manipulated by the artist according to his own sensitivity to balance and movement, so that even though his hand has been removed, his thought is apparent.

Like Martin and Held, Robert Ryman attempts to purge painting of extraneous elements and deal with only its inherent components, paint and support. However, what emerges in *Carrier* (1979) is a Minimalist attitude that is an expression of the act of painting and a homage to the objectness of a painting—revealed in the romantic and contemplative application of white paint strokes on the surface. Like Ryman, Robert Mangold presents the most reduced elements of painting—shape, geometry, color, surface, line—and investigates how each element reinforces the other. The title *Three Red X Within X* (1981) is descriptive of the three shades of red used on each of the three separate panels that form an X, a shape then reiterated with a drawn line centered on the two crossing arms of the X. Mangold's work emphasizes the objectness of the painting, the totality of our perception of it, and the importance of the edge. In addition to the outer, physical edges of the stretched canvas, the internal, drawn line also becomes an edge, superimposing symmetry on an asymmetrical configuration.

A slightly younger generation of artists, including Mel Bochner, Barry Le Va, and John Baldessari, takes a conceptual approach to reductivism and signals a move away from a purely restrictive mode. Similar to LeWitt's wall piece, drawn according to a preconceived formula, Mel Bochner's arrangement of stones on the floor, *Ten to 10* (1972), is a visualization of concepts related to theory and problem solving. Barry Le Va's *Installation Study for Any Rectangular Space: Accumulated Vision: Boundaries Designated (Configurations Indicated)* (1977) is a schematized plan for a project in three dimensions that would occupy any rectangular room, with objects indicating designated locations. Le Va's plan, however, is not systematically plotted according to fixed rules, and thus allows for the interjection of personal interpretation and response.

Richard Serra and Brice Marden, also somewhat younger than the first-generation Minimalists, are aesthetically linked to that movement, but they too begin to reintroduce emotion and allusion into their work. The massive wedge shape in Serra's *Untitled* (1972) is executed in such a gesturally powerful manner that the form itself becomes both the statement and the emotional content. Marden's *Summer Table* (1972) is likewise elemental in its geometric configuration of three equal-sized panels of grayed blues and yellow. The layers of clear, soft encaustic color have an expressive impact—subliminal yet present—that evokes nature, light, and romance.

In the 1960s, John Baldessari and other Conceptual artists had explored ways of presenting information, language, notes for a painting, and ideas as formal artworks. Baldessari also began using photographs and commercially produced pictures as the media with which to visualize conceptual structures, procedures, and narratives. These works remained governed by a Minimalist aesthetic, but they validated and opened the way for a subsequent generation of artists to infuse recognizable images and subject matter into an art previously expunged of these qualities. The title of a recent Baldessari work, *Ashputtle* (1982), refers to the original German name for Cinderella. He chose existing black-and-white photographic stills from movies, then enlarged and cropped them to a standardized size and grid arrangement. However, Baldessari employs the images not to illustrate the story or represent a sequential narrative, but to evoke an association or a metaphor—an approach that imposes diverse and ambiguous interpretations on a pre-set physical and conceptual structure. Alexis Smith uses texts and images in a similar way, but with a more direct narrative sense. *Beauty and the Beast* (1977) is arranged in a long strip of standard-sized paper sheets that contain typed text, collaged reproductions, and small objects, all designed to be read from left to right. The text relates to and includes sections of Jean Cocteau's screenplay for *Beauty and the Beast*, in addition to collaged elements that symbolically illustrate the written words. Both Baldessari and Smith appropriate words and images from others to create works that comment on the idea of transformations: Ashputtle into a princess, the beast into a prince, fairytales into movies, and dislocated forms of expression into art.

A more substantial break away from the reductive, abstract, and monochromatic aspects of Minimalism began in the late 1960s with a generation of artists born around 1940. This post-Minimalist expression first emerged in sculpture, which apparently offered more options for experimentation in materials and forms. At that moment, painting seemed far too restrictive, and was proclaimed to be dead by many of its own practitioners and to have been reduced to the ultimate by the previous generation. Sculpture of the early 1970s elicits a sense of searching, of seeking avenues out of Minimalism and trying to open up new areas of exploration. Of primary importance was the apparent need to re-infuse sculpture with allusions to something outside itself.

John Duff and John Torreano both created red, totemic shapes that combine aspects of painting and sculpture in a way that injects hints of subjective feeling. Duff's *Two Part Column* (1973), a freestanding rectangular form cast in fiberglass in a wooden mold, has shafts cut through to confound its being read as a single element. This ambivalence and the tactile surface of the piece—sensuous, textured, translucent—counteract the severe geometry of the form by encouraging layers of vague associations. Torreano's *Red Column* (1974) is a cigar-shaped, three-dimensional painting mounted on the wall. His attention to surface relates to Robert Ryman's concern with the painting as an object, but Torreano's use of reflective glass jewels imbedded in the thickly painted surface sets up a confrontation with the viewer. The jewels serve a dual function: internally, they define the painting as a decorated object; externally, they provoke responses in the viewer because they are perplexing, attractive, repulsive, and ironic at the same time. Lynda Benglis' *Bravo 2* (1975–76) is also a wall-mounted object, but here the references are more pronounced, although remaining vague and subtle. The knot form is manipulated while in a flexible state and then secured with layers of sprayed metal and finished with a coating of sprayed copper. There is great attention to the process and materials, but the final object begins to suggest indirect anthropomorphic associations—body movement, posture, gesture of hands or legs—and creates a striking dramatic presence through the dichotomy of a soft form that has been frozen by a cold, industrial finish.

Jackie Winsor's *Cement Piece* (1976–77) is, like John Duff's *Two Part Column*, an ordinary geometric form; like Lynda Benglis' *Bravo 2*, it reveals the process of its construction—an assemblage of lathes, cement, and nails—so as to draw attention to the temporal element that makes the fabrication visible. The weighty cement cube has small square openings on each of its six sides that pull the viewer into a perceptual experience of the interior. Winsor uses a minimal form—the cube—but manipulates it for maximum readings. Weighty, solid, hollow, unfinished, and rough, it urges the viewer to indulge in personal associations.

Of the sculptors of his generation, Joel Shapiro has most dramatically infused sculpture with meaning. Using a simple geometric shape—a rectangle topped by a triangle—and casting it in bronze, Shapiro created a small-scale shape of a house: not a description of a house, but a form that suggests a house and all the various connotations a house might have. Shapiro chose a house as a metaphor for his own experience, a form psychologically charged with recollections of family, childhood, and security—or the absence of them. In *Untitled* (1975–76), he places the house form in the center of a broad expanse of bronze, and elevates it on a table-like base. In this way, the house becomes even further removed and isolated, creating a physically compacted and psychically charged atmosphere.

Bryan Hunt and Steve Keister, two slightly younger sculptors working in a post-Minimalist vein, retain abstract forms but insist on representational references. Hunt's *Step Falls* (1978) presents a tall, elongated strip of bronze that appears to be a frozen fall of water minus the surrounding rock that channels the flow and creates a step in the fall. Hunt maintains a close relationship between the properties of bronze and the image being depicted, but emphasizes and abstracts the essence and nature of a waterfall while exploring formal sculptural considerations. Keister, too, explores surface, color, mass, and balance in an eccentric three-dimensional geometric object. *U.S.O. #68* (1981)—the title means "Unidentified Suspended Object"—is made of two intersecting and interlocking hollow wooden hexahedrons that are covered with zebra skin, including the animal's mane. The startling incongruity resides in the presentation of a sharply angled, boxy structure covered with curving fur stripes that refer to a severely abstracted animal form. The walls of the sculpture are cut open (like the Duff and Winsor pieces), allowing visual entry into the brightly painted chartreuse and green chambers, dematerializing the mass of the object by revealing the internal structure. In addition, light entering the suspended piece from above causes the entire interior to emanate an eerie glow which contradicts the earthy, animalistic association.

These sculptors' rejection and violation of Minimalist tenets—pure geometric form, purity of materials, process-oriented techniques, flat monochromatic color, and lack of subject matter and imagery—also emerge in American painting in the early 1970s, again among artists born in the early 1940s. Their work, like that of the sculptors, simultaneously borrows and rejects Minimalist modes. They draw on various aspects of Minimal, Pop, Conceptual, and cinematic art forms in order to re-introduce subject matter into painting, while maintaining allegiance to desired Minimalist attributes. Among the first painters to signal new options were Richard Artschwager, Chuck Close, and Joe Zucker. Artschwager, who is also a sculptor, made a number of paintings, such as *The Bush* (1971), which comment on the art and act of painting, and, ironically, on the idea of personal choice in subject matter and painting style. For *The Bush*, Artschwager chose a photograph of an unpeopled, quasi-modern interior and re-created the image in thin washes of paint on a commercially produced paperboard with a textured surface mechanically impressed into it. While giving the appearance of a personalized image executed in an expressionistic, grisaille technique, the picture is actually a found composition, painted on a found surface. Thus the artist seems to have violated at least two taboos of Minimalism—recognizable imagery and personal gesture—without actually having done so. Chuck Close also approaches the problems of imagery with an impersonal process and technique. His first series of paintings of colossal heads, done in 1968–69, was governed by a strict adherence to a grid format and a systematic and rigid technique. The process of making a painting consisted of superimposing a grid over a black-and-white photograph of a friend or acquaintance, and then transferring with an airbrush each square of the photograph to a 9 x 7-foot canvas, retaining the exact look of the photograph, including out-of-focus areas. In a later work, *Phil/Fingerprint II* (1978), the artist's fingerprints—one print per square—replace the airbrush. As a result, this portrait of the composer Philip Glass emphasizes the process and manner of depiction rather than the physical features of the sitter. This same emphasis on process characterizes Joe Zucker's work. Zucker builds paintings with color-saturated cottonballs that create both gesture and line, and always maintains a tight relationship between the subject and the process. *Merlyn's Lab* (1977) depicts the famous magician working in his laboratory, attempting to turn lead (Pb) into gold (Au), while, having put his finger to his nose, he magically begins to disappear. Merlyn can be seen as a metaphor for the artist, attempting to turn pigment and cotton into a painting. Merlyn's disappearing powers are also analogous to the way that the images in the painting dissolve and emerge from its agitated surface.

A number of other artists were striving to reconcile formalist considerations with their concern for personal subject matter and emotionalism. Jennifer Bartlett's *Falcon Avenue, Seaside Walk, Dwight Street, Jarvis Street, Greene Street* (1976) reflects the artist's self-imposed guidelines on the formal aspects of the painting. She restricted the support to an arrangement of twelve-inch steel plates; restricted the colors to red, green, blue, and black; and restricted the manner in which paint was applied to a dotted application, a measured stroke, or a freehand gesture. Bartlett, like Joel Shapiro, then selected a simple geometric configuration (a square topped by a triangle), which forms a house—a container of memory and feeling. The five contiguous sections correspond to the five streets in California, Connecticut, and New York where the artist has lived since childhood. Each of the sixteen-plate sections depicts the house in different painting styles that refer to psychological states associated with those periods of her life.

Bartlett's work reduces the formal elements of painting and imposes on them a system of personal symbolic significance. This conjunction of form and content typifies the situation of painting in the mid-1970s: the attempt to wed formal aspects of painting to emotional, autobiographical expression. Vija Celmins—like Close, Zucker, and Bartlett—created work that is both personal and impersonal, simple and complex, abstract and representational. Her finely detailed and tightly controlled graphite drawing *Ocean* (1972–73) depicts seven sequential views of the same detail of the water's surface; the views become progressively darker in each section. On one level, the picture is a formal exploration of composition, movement, and sequence; but on another level, these same features are open to personal associations—by the artist and the viewer. These associations are encouraged by the ambiguities inherent in the drawn patterns, which could also be read as a close-up of a dry desert landscape or an aerial view of a mountainous region. The use of abstracted yet symbolic imagery is also apparent in the paintings of

Pat Steir and Lois Lane. Onto the grid structure of *Line Lima* (1973), Steir paints lima bean pods —three-dimensionally and in the form of flat, broken lines. The beans thus function like the nonrepresentational markings; the message is not about beans, but about how a line can become a lima. The painting reads as a diagram for the possibilities inherent in the making of marks, of paintings, and of meanings.

Lois Lane's forms are more clearly personal and emotive. *Untitled* (1978) presents simplified silhouettes of a bird, a dress, and a pair of pants painted in flat black against a Minimalist-derived, monochromatic, indigo background. The entire canvas is bisected horizontally by a yellow line that these objects seem to perch on or hang from. Lane's are identifiable images, rich in potential associations, but ones that defy specific interpretation. For Robert Moskowitz, the monochromatic, Minimalist field also becomes a receiving ground for iconic forms. *Swimmer* (1977) depicts a head and arm both immersed in and emerging from a sea of deep blue-violet pigment. The application of paint in rolling, agitated strokes and waves mimics the characteristics of water.

In the late 1960s and early 1970s, Neil Jenney produced a series of paintings that were among the first intentionally naive, seemingly poorly painted subjective works of the decade. They presented childlike depictions of paired images on a loosely painted, gestural background reminiscent of Abstract Expressionism. Jenney's use of large, black, architectural frames also draws attention to the traditional concept of a painting as a window onto an idealized reality. *North America Abstracted* (1978–80) is one of a group of recent Jenney paintings that strive to be more intentionally detailed and realistic. The abstract formal values of color, structure, and line are employed to render a realist subject. As the boldly visible title painted on the frame suggests, the work is an abstracted view of an unidentified area of North America in winter. Moving from the immediate foreground to the distant space, we see a frozen pond that is being fed water from a small brook running across slabs of slate thrusting from the snow at the lower right. In the middle ground is a severely geometric, stylized stand of evergreen trees, and behind them, a dark hill above which hover dark, heavy, wedge-shaped cumulonimbus clouds partially illuminated by the setting sun. High in the stratosphere, a bright, orange sky displays dramatically aligned strands of cirrus clouds. As with his earlier paintings, Jenney creates a unique and personal brand of realism that broadens the possibilities for painterly expression.

Other painters during the 1970s continued to explore a geometrically based structure that included organic references and nonspecific allusions with emphasis on surface texture and paint application. Elizabeth Murray's *Children Meeting* (1978) best exemplifies the combination of geometry with organic referential forms, painted in high key colors on an active and textured surface. The large purple and green amoebic shapes that stretch and press across the surface suggest the children of the title. At the same time, forms, lines, and bolts of color crisscross in front of and behind each other, creating an extremely active interplay that replaces the Euclidean space of Minimalism with a more psychologically derived space. Frank Stella's *Silverstone* (1981) makes the spatial depth and overlapping of forms physical. In this three-dimensional relief, the collage of French curves, circles, angles, waves, and cutouts has been commercially fabricated in honeycomb aluminum and individually embellished in an energetic and exuberant application of drawn, scribbled, and painted color areas. This dense and excessively painted surface—as dense as the physical forms themselves—counteracts the rigidity of the hard-edged forms. The entire work dissolves into one overall visual experience. The effect of the painting is loud, aggressive, and additive, but its basic intent is a reductive exercise: isolating and accentuating specific painterly elements of form, shape, edge, depth, support, and objectness. In contrast, Bill Jensen's *The Meadow* (1980–81) has an abstracted organic form as the central element, employed for its emotive and subjective properties. With a heavy paint application and worked surface, a central, seed-like form dominates the painting and alludes to vegetative, human, and cosmic life. This quiet, thoughtful painting works on a psychological and subconscious level, and is subject to a variety of interpretations and readings.

By the mid- and late 1970s, painting had moved further away from the confines of the Minimalist approach—even from a negative reaction to it—and the artists already discussed had inaugurated new ways to treat subject matter and meaning. Other American artists continued to develop more additive, externalized, and emotional aspects of painting, and sought a maximal rather than minimal saturation of imagery, references, and impact. They sought out and drew upon a wider and broader range of inspiration and source material. All art, of every definition, style, and period became available as a source—not only the art that immediately preceded. There emerged a move against an insular, elitist attitude toward art and what it is, should be, or must be. American artists strove to widen the definitions and possibilities of art —to make it more ambitious and expressive of a larger realm of feeling. In addition to the autobiographical and psychological sources for content, artists began to look at a more diverse visual repertory: comercial art, advertising, fashion, television and movies, popular culture, the decorative arts, rugs, religion, ancient artifacts, and Middle Eastern cultures.

Robert Kushner's *French Tart* (1978) presents a stylishly dressed woman (originally seen in a newspaper photo of a fashion model) in mirror image. The two outside panels are of a second woman, split down the center and sewn to both sides to frame the central panels. The figures are painted in strong, often lurid, colors—pinks and purples, greens and oranges—with a fluid and energetic line that recalls Matisse and Picasso. The painting, on unstretched canvas secured directly to the wall, has an informal character reminiscent of hanging fabrics. This manner of presentation, combined with the references to fashion, posing, and decoration, are intended to diminish the pretensions of fine art. Robert Zakanitch also draws upon nontraditional sources for imagery, in an effort to make an unabashedly beautiful and decorative painting. In the central panel of *Angel Feet* (1978), the open petals and angled stems of oversized, floating flowers hover over an active blue field of swirls and patterns. The surface is richly painted in shades of pink, blue, and cream that emphasize the sensuousness of paint application and the layering of images. Feathery, leafy forms in the two narrow side panels reinforce the implications of the title. Zakanitch appropriated a variety of unexpected visual sources, including floral and vegetative patterns from American linoleum of the 1940s, and stylized fleur-de-lis stencils used for wall, floor, and furniture decoration. The introduction of these sources in painting heralds a wider cross-cultural and multi-disciplined approach to image making.

Philip Guston is one of the oldest artists discussed here and one whose impact on art since 1970 has been profound. His career transcends the generational guidelines that often describe art movements because his approach to and idea of what painting could or should be was in sync with—or sometimes even preceded—those of a much younger group of artists. Guston established a career and reputation as an Abstract Expressionist painter in the 1950s, but by the late 1960s felt constrained by a nonrepresentational mode and embarked on an exploration of a figurative, symbolic, narrative style. *Cabal* (1977) is from a body of work begun in 1969 that occupied Guston until his death in 1980. These paintings drew heavily on the life of the imagination, and on art, with undercurrents of social or political commentary. *Cabal* renders a pile of bodyless heads with large gaping eyes, crude eyelashes and ears, all resting on an undefined surface. The images are rough, sketchy outlines, quickly painted in red and black, which impart a great sense of urgency and violence. While the title suggests intrigue, visually the painting conjures up dark feelings of despair and depression; it seems to make a comment on the human condition.

Guston's paintings primarily provoke questions rather than offer answers. In a related way, Susan Rothenberg's *For the Light* (1978–79) presents a familiar, but mysterious and undefined, vision from the imagination: a frontal view of a horse shape roughly outlined in black, with awkward posturing and ungainly proportions. Any effort to read the horse form rationally is thwarted by the bone-like shape thrusting out from its head. The horse therefore fluctuates between the representational and the abstract, a condition that frees the artist to explore the emotive qualities of paint application, drawing, and gesture.

Jonathan Borofsky's subject matter derives from dreams or images born in the unknown, subconscious areas of the psyche. He makes rough sketches of these visions at the time they occur, and such preliminary, diaristic notations then become part of the pictorial vocabulary he uses to create large-scale drawings on paper, directly on the wall, or on canvas. *Self-Portrait at 2668379 and 2670098* (1979–80) presents two superimposed and strangely surreal self-portraits. The foreground figure is of a full, oddly proportioned body, uncomfortably postured, with tall, pointed ears. With a curved, scythe-like object in hand, the figure stares intently at the viewer. Surrounding this figure is a flattened profile of the artist, wide-eyed and open-mouthed, as if screaming or singing. The profile is painted in loose, gestural, and explosive strokes of black, blue, and white that only partially fill the drawn outline of the head. At the lower right, where the artist's signature might ordinarily be placed, are two numbers. In 1969 Borofsky began counting from one to infinity, and as images appear and are recorded, they are assigned a number that corresponds to their position in the counting progression. In this way, he can ally two different, and somewhat opposite, aspects of his expression: the linear, regimented, logical act of counting with the emotional, intuitive aspect of image making.

Equally surreal and unsettling is Jedd Garet's *Precarious Notoriety* (1982). Painted in black, gray, and white with a free, nonchalant, but deliberate application, the image is extremely cerebral, threatening, and perverse. The twisted amoebic figure displays intertwined limbs as if it could re-form or transform itself. Shiny and reflective, it rests on a white drape that floats inside a shallow, undersized alcove. The painting evokes a stage-like, artificial mood, enhanced by the hard lighting and shadows and by the imitation-marble veining of the shallow, boxy space. Garet's work comments on the stylistic stereotypes of modern art, recalling Picasso, Arp, and Henry Moore. The title is self-referential, alluding to the precarious position of an artist in the manipulations and fads of the current art market.

William T. Wiley's *Harpoon for the Dreamer* (1981) visualizes dream states through cryptic signs and symbols. The painting combines drawing, painting, writing, and sculpture in an amalgam of styles, media, and techniques. The vast unstretched canvas is dominated by a large triangular shape of swirling saturated paint, emanating from an eyeball, which intersects half of a yellow sphere that suggests a setting sun. The specter at right, and the inscription above ("One Scythe Fits All Comers") refer to the death of H.C. Westermann, whom Wiley admired, while the shark fins and the ship in the centered window are motifs found in Westermann's work. In addition, the painting incorporates numerous images and symbols from Wiley's personal iconography to create a painting that is dense, suggestive, but often uninterpretable.

Another work equally rich in imagery, paint, and references is Julian Schnabel's *Hope* (1982). The painting draws upon many sources—art history, mythology, memory, and reality —combining images without regard for continuity of scale or narrative. The large, central figure is a self-portrait, with paintbrushes in hand, which recalls Matisse's sketch *Male Model* (c. 1900) in drawing style and posture. To the left is a crouching figure with head on knees borrowed from a William Blake engraving of 1793; and to the right is a figure, cut off at the knees, with a mask-like face, who appears to be striding. At upper right, a headless torso in a loincloth stretches his arms out like a Christ on the cross. To further confuse and confound the density of the surface, the images are painted on overlapping pieces of blue and yellow velvet fabric, which add another visual and textural experience. This layering of images, textures, colors, brushstrokes, and references—this overload of visual stimuli—challenges the viewer to penetrate the imagery and meaning.

In their search for more diverse and eclectic subject matter, artists also looked to popular culture and topical and political events. It is here that Pop Art of the 1960s reemerges as a pronounced influence. Pop Art, like Minimalism, was essentially a reductive form of expression even though it was representational. Moreover, its imagery was impersonal, public, and specific. In the art of the 1970s, subjects also come from the public domain, but are more often chosen for their secondary and tertiary meanings. Ed Paschke's *Violencia* (1980) is an eerie, hallucinatory depiction of three aggressive figures, painted in sharp, acid greens and yellows, partially out of focus, with double images and wavy interference lines running horizontally across the canvas. The images seem to be broadcast from a malfunctioning television screen, and they are the violent images so often seen there. The content of Kim MacConnel's *Formidable* (1981), a bold, colorful, and direct painting, is paradoxically weighty and serious. The four component sections depict pink, green, and yellow chemistry vials and beakers; an open hand and fingers (symbolizing the Indian god of destruction and rebirth); top-hatted and tuxedoed men on a red background; and a colorful, geometric repeated pattern illustrating the Pythagorean theorem. The panels are painted individually on cotton sheeting in a cartoon-like and naive manner reminiscent of outdoor murals and advertisements in India and Mexico. The painting hangs loosely on the wall—a method consistent with the artist's concern for a nontraditional presentation. In actuality, *Formidable* makes a political comment on the threat of business and government interests (top-hatted capitalists), which use and abuse logistical thinking (the Pythagorean theorem) and scientific research (chemical vials) to lead us to destruction and oblivion (the hand).

Eric Fischl's two-paneled painting *A Visit To/A Visit From/The Island* (1983) also contains strong sociopolitical content. The left panel presents an idyllic scene of vacationing sunbathers relaxing in an inviting ocean under clear blue skies. The right panel is a grim, dark scene of anguished rescuers and drowned figures on a beach. For them the ocean is cruel and violent. Although the painting was inspired by a newspaper photograph of a recent incident of Haitian emigration, it makes a more universal statement—about refuge and jeopardy, escapism and escaping, and the social realities that underlie each condition.

In David Salle's diptych *Splinter Man* (1982), the two panels do not relate narratively, but are independent compositions chosen for their pictorial qualities and representative styles of picture making. The left panel depicts the back of a nude woman and her mirror reflection, painted in black and then washed with a strong red that saturates and softens the image and enhances its spatial depth. The right panel is a flat, two-dimensional illustration of fantastic comic-book characters rendered in sharply contrasting black and white. Both images are derived from commercially produced pictures—the nude from a photograph in a 1950s pulp magazine and the other from a printed drawing in a comic book. These "reproductions of reproductions" attest to the acceptability of media-produced images in a "fine art" context. Moreover, Salle is proclaiming, there already exists such a wealth and variety of images that there is no need for an artist to invent new ones. The work questions the meaning of painting as a form of expression, and draws attention to types of representation and reproduction—of sophisticated versus common, abstract versus realistic, subjective versus objective, personal versus public, and emotional versus logical—all issues that have characterized the major developments in American art since 1970.

The developments in painting and sculpture during the 1970s were not limited exclusively to reactions against Minimalism or the influence of Pop. Two of the most traditional and ongoing forms of expression—realism and portraiture—continued to show great strength and variety in the artistic mainstream, but assimilated the aesthetic mood of the decade. Artists exploring a realistic, rather than abstracted or symbolic, approach to depicting the human figure sought out forms that suggested the psychological, as well as the physical, attributes of the subject. Alice Neel's *Andy Warhol* (1970) is a direct, raw, and unflattering portrait of the most celebrated Pop artist: seated on a couch, with eyes closed, and shirtless so that the scars resulting from the 1968 shooting attempt on his life are painfully visible. Neel's portrait is not romanticized or idealized. Its honesty is reflected in the immediacy of her painterly gesture and in the unfinished look of the canvas. In contrast to Warhol's own remote and unemotional painting style and persona, Neel's depiction is human and warm. Nicholas Africano's approach to portraiture involves intense interaction between specific figures. His idiom deals with real responses rather than accurate physiognomic details or settings. *An Argument* (1977) depicts the artist and his father as small, condensed figures in profile, painted in low relief in an awkward, rudimentary fashion. The figures are isolated on a large, flat expanse of bland-colored paint that suggests an anonymous but ordinary locale, so that all attention is focused on the human drama.

Alex Katz renders likenesses in a simplified "modern" style. In *Place* (1977) the features and clothing of his five friends are strongly lit and flatly painted in broad areas of light and dark to bring the entire group close to the picture plane. This reinforces the artificial quality of the painting, while the dramatically cropped, oversized heads recall movies, advertising, and billboards. Katz's concern is not with emotional narrative, but with portraiture style—with giving the traditional genre of a posed portrait an expansive, contemporary look. Robert Graham, working in three dimensions, also pursues a classical approach to portraiture. *Stephanie and Spy* (1980–81) are precise and anatomically detailed effigies of an actual woman and a horse named Spy. The artist uses a traditional method, modeling clay in front of his models; he also uses photography and videotape to capture minute details and subtle nuances of gesture and attitude. The final piece is then cast in bronze, by the lost-wax method, and bases and pedestals are designed for each piece. The statues are smaller than life size, a format that enables the viewer to become more intimately engaged in observing on a somewhat voyeuristic level. Stephanie is an intriguing, motionless classical beauty, distant and self-absorbed. There is no suggestion of interaction with the horse, Spy, and we are confronted by two independent yet related portraits.

Robert Arneson and James Surls create self-portraits that exhibit the influence of Dada and Surrealism. Arneson's *Whistling in the Dark* (1976) is one of a number of oversize, ceramic portrait heads in which he abuses his own likeness. The punning title suggests several meanings: it is a description of his puckered lips in the act of whistling (or blowing out hot air), and of the dark, unglazed clay. The title is also a vernacular phrase describing a state of uncertainty that Arneson uses as a humorous metaphor for the situation of the artist. James Surls' *Me and the Butcher Knives* (1982) takes a less humorous and more macabre approach to self-portraiture. Surls has hewn a full-scale figure from oak branches and then thrust sixteen knives through the entire body. The wooden figure is also burned and scorched in places, evoking the look of animal skin markings and primitive and folkloric motifs. The portrait is menacing and imposing, with suggestions of aggression and violence that are intended to provoke responses.

Urban landscape is another aspect of contemporary realism that continued to develop during the 1970s. Drawing on the stylistic and conceptual concerns of Pop Art, many artists chose the city environment, and its architecture and advertising, as subject matter. Roger Brown's *The Entry of Christ into Chicago in 1976* is more surreal than real, with its pervasive sense of artificiality and incongruity. Against a stylized and abstracted view of the Chicago skyline, Christ is being driven down the main street on a flat-bed truck toward a parade stand of visiting dignitaries, rock musicians, and a priest. The title and subject allude to James Ensor's *The Entry of Christ into Brussels* (1888), but Brown has updated and modernized the locale and the painting style. The buildings and people are done in a silhouetted illustrational manner, with flat, unmodulated color areas, hard edges, and sharp lighting and shadows. The painting makes historical, biblical, and contemporary references in an irreverent and satirical style, leaving discovery, interpretation, and meaning to the imagination of the viewer.

Robert Cottingham's *Radios* (1977) represents a more extreme approach to a realist cityscape. The painting is photographically real—the artist used a photograph as the source and painted it in a style that mimics the look of a photograph. This kind of realism in the art of the 1970s is an extension of Pop Art of the previous decade, but without Pop's underlying irony. In Cottingham's cropped, dislocated, and disjointed detail of a store front, great technical expertise is exhibited in the sharply focused, super-real composition of objects, reflections, and perspective. The work is reductive and nonemotional, relaying visual information in a public and generalized manner that does not strive to elicit personal or emotional associations. Richard Estes' *Ansonia* (1977) is also a photographically real urban environment derived from photographs, here taken by the artist. The title refers to the Ansonia Hotel on upper Broadway in New York City. All areas of the image have been given equal attention in detail, clarity, and reflections, with a strong central vertical break dividing the composition. Although clearly intended to be starkly realistic, the clean, calm, unpeopled scene is a somewhat romanticized and idealized conception of the city.

In just over a decade, a dramatic shift and realignment have occurred in the intent, content, and style of American art. The change has not been as unfocused and aimless as is often thought or suggested. The gradual, and often tentative, drift away from the austere rigor of Minimalism toward an expressive, aggressive, and subjective expression reflects a profound and deliberate rethinking of the purpose, function, and capabilities of art. As this review has illustrated, American art since 1970 has been an extremely rich, varied, and productive body of work that continues to expand and develop.

RICHARD MARSHALL
Associate Curator, Exhibitions

Nicholas Africano
Robert Arneson
Richard Artschwager
John Baldessari
Jennifer Bartlett
Lynda Benglis
Mel Bochner
Jonathan Borofsky
Roger Brown
Vija Celmins
Chuck Close
Robert Cottingham
John Duff
Richard Estes
Eric Fischl
Dan Flavin
Jedd Garet
Robert Graham
Philip Guston
Al Held
Bryan Hunt
Neil Jenney
Bill Jensen
Alex Katz
Steve Keister
Robert Kushner
Lois Lane
Barry Le Va
Sol LeWitt
Kim MacConnel
Robert Mangold
Brice Marden
Agnes Martin
Robert Moskowitz
Elizabeth Murray
Alice Neel
Ed Paschke
Susan Rothenberg
Robert Ryman
David Salle
Julian Schnabel
Richard Serra
Joel Shapiro
Alexis Smith
Pat Steir
Frank Stella
James Surls
John Torreano
William T. Wiley
Jackie Winsor
Robert S. Zakanitch
Joe Zucker

Nicholas Africano

Born in Kankakee, Illinois, 1948
Studied at Illinois State University, Normal (B.F.A., 1970; M.A., 1974; M.F.A., 1975)
Lives in Normal, Illinois

I want my paintings to be about something, as opposed to being about nothing or being about themselves. Their reference is human experience, so they are figurative and narrative. I don't assume a rhetorical posture as a painter and I don't want my work to reiterate rhetorical assumptions—I want something to mean something, in a cogent and revealing way, because I want to be purposeful, even useful. So I regard subject matter as my primary concern as an artist.

Quoted in Richard Marshall, *New Image Painting*, exhibition catalogue (New York: Whitney Museum of American Art, 1978), p. 14.

Selected One-Artist Exhibitions

1976
Nancy Lurie Gallery, Chicago

1977
Fine Arts Center, University of Rhode Island, Kingston
Nancy Lurie Gallery, Chicago
Sheldon Memorial Art Gallery, University of Nebraska, Lincoln
Holly Solomon Gallery, New York

1978
Walker Art Center, Minneapolis

1979
Asher/Faure Gallery, Los Angeles
Galerie Farideh Cadot, Paris
Mayor Gallery, London
Holly Solomon Gallery, New York

1980
Holly Solomon Gallery, New York

1981
Asher/Faure Gallery, Los Angeles
Middendorf/Lane Gallery, Washington, D.C.
Holly Solomon Gallery, New York

1982
American Graffiti Gallery, Amsterdam
Dart Gallery, Chicago
Greenberg Gallery, St. Louis
Holly Solomon Gallery, New York

Selected Group Exhibitions

1976
Illinois State University, Normal, "Illinois Artists 76"

1977
P.S. 1, Institute for Art and Urban Resources, Long Island City, New York, "A Painting Show"
San Francisco Art Institute, "First Annual Exhibition"
Sarah Lawrence College, Bronxville, New York, "Painting 75 76 77" (traveled)
Whitney Museum of American Art, New York, "1977 Biennial Exhibition"

1978
Indianapolis Museum of Art, "Painting and Sculpture Today"
Institute of Contemporary Art, Boston, "Narration"
Whitney Museum of American Art, New York, "New Image Painting"

1979
Aspen Center for the Visual Arts, "American Portraits of the 60s and 70s"
Philadelphia College of Art, "Words and Images"

1980
Contemporary Arts Center, Cincinnati, "Chicago/Chicago"
Neue Galerie, Sammlung Ludwig, Aachen, West Germany, "Les Nouveaux Fauves—Die Neuen Wilden"
United States Pavilion, 39th Venice Biennale, Italy, "Drawings: The Pluralist Decade" (traveled)
Whitney Museum of American Art, New York, "The Figurative Tradition and the Whitney Museum of American Art: Painting and Scuplture from the Permanent Collection"
Whitney Museum of American Art, New York, Downtown Branch, "Painting in Relief"

1981
The Squibb Gallery, Princeton, New Jersey, "Aspects of Post-Modernism: Decorative and Narrative Art"
University Art Museum, University of California, Santa Barbara, "Contemporary Drawings"

1982
Indianapolis Museum of Art, "Painting and Sculpture Today, 1982"

Selected Bibliography

Delahoyd, Mary. *Painting 75 76 77* (exhibition catalogue). Bronxville, New York: Sarah Lawrence College, 1977.
Hills, Patricia, and Roberta K. Tarbell. *The Figurative Tradition and the Whitney Museum of American Art: Painting and Sculpture from the Permanent Collection* (exhibition catalogue). New York: Whitney Museum of American Art, 1980.
Kardon, Janet, ed. *Drawings: The Pluralist Decade* (exhibition catalogue). Texts by John Hallmark Neff, Rosalind Krauss, Richard Lorber, Edit deAk, John Perreault, Howard N. Fox, and Nancy Foote. Philadelphia: Institute of Contemporary Art, University of Pennsylvania, 1980.
Marshall, Richard. *New Image Painting* (exhibition catalogue). New York: Whitney Museum of American Art, 1978.

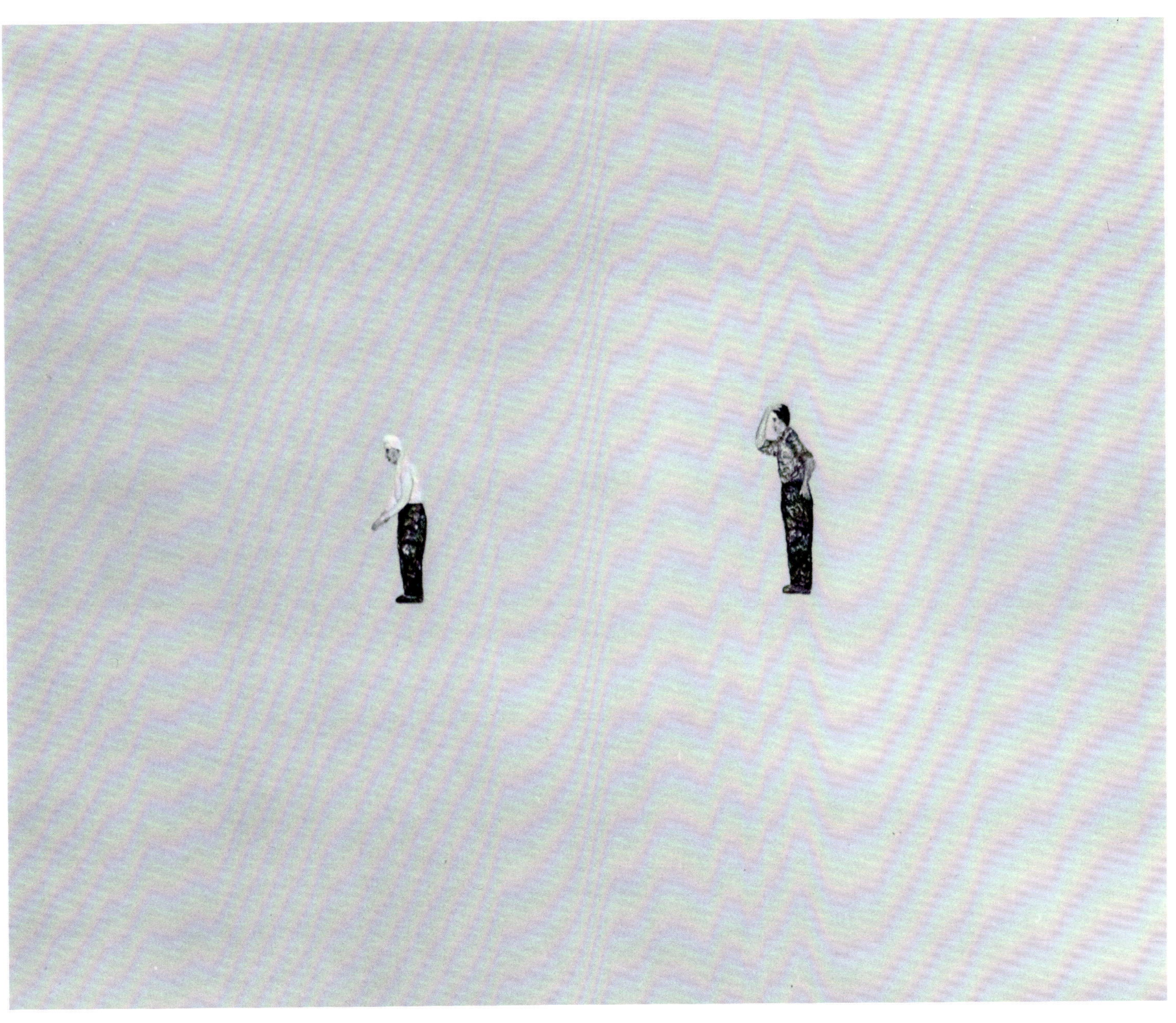

An Argument, 1977
Acrylic, oil, wax on canvas, 69 x 85½″ (175.3 x 217.2 cm)
Gift of Mr. and Mrs. William A. Marsteller
77.68

Robert Arneson

Born in Benicia, California, 1930
Studied at College of Marin, Kentfield, California (1949–51); California College of Arts and Crafts, Oakland (B.A., 1954); Mills College, Oakland (M.F.A., 1958)
Lives in Benicia, California

I like art that has humor, wit, irony and playfulness. I want to make "high" art that is outrageous while revealing the human condition, which is not always high . . . . For about the past ten years I've been modeling oversized portrait heads of myself (and other infamous artists) in clay and glazing them colorfully. I like to work with faces that talk back to you dead in the eye. After all, faces are what most of us mortals relate to—certainly I do. The human face, unlike the frog's or monkey's, is a window on the mind.

Quoted in Henry Hopkins, *50 West Coast Artists* (San Francisco: Chronical Books, 1981), p. 24.

Selected One-Artist Exhibitions

1960
The Oakland Museum

1964
Cellini Gallery, San Francisco
Allan Stone Gallery, New York

1969
Hansen Fuller Gallery, San Francisco

1970
Hansen Fuller Gallery, San Francisco

1972
Hansen Fuller Gallery, San Francisco

1973
Hansen Fuller Gallery, San Francisco

1974
Hansen Fuller Gallery, San Francisco
Museum of Contemporary Art, Chicago (traveled)

1975
Allan Frumkin Gallery, New York
Hansen Fuller Gallery, San Francisco

1976
Fendrick Gallery, Washington, D.C.
Hansen Fuller Gallery, San Francisco
Memorial Union Art Gallery, University of California, Davis

1979
Allan Frumkin Gallery, New York
Moore College of Art Gallery, Philadelphia

1980
Hansen Fuller Gallery, San Francisco

1981
Allan Frumkin Gallery, New York

1982
Fuller Goldeen Gallery, San Francisco

Selected Group Exhibitions

1963
Museum of Contemporary Crafts of the American Crafts Council, New York, "Creative Casting"
The Oakland Museum at Kaiser Center, "California Sculpture"

1966
Museum West, American Craftsmen's Council, San Francisco, "Ceramics from Davis"

1967
University Art Museum, University of California, Berkeley, "Funk"

1968
The Museum of Modern Art, New York, "Dada, Surrealism, and Their Heritage" (traveled)

1969
National Collection of Fine Arts, Smithsonian Institution, Washington, D.C., "Objects: USA—The Johnson Collection of Contemporary Crafts"
Whitney Museum of American Art, New York, "Human Concern/Personal Torment: The Grotesque in American Art"

1970
Whitney Museum of American Art, New York, "1970 Annual Exhibition: Contemporary American Sculpture"

1971
Museum of Contemporary Crafts of the American Crafts Council, New York, "Clayworks: 20 Americans"

1972
San Francisco Museum of Art, "A Decade of Ceramic Art, 1962–1972: From the Collection of Professor and Mrs. R. Joseph Monsen"

1974
Lang Art Gallery, Scripps College, Claremont, California, "The Fred and Mary Marer Collection: 30th Annual Ceramics Exhibition"
Whitney Museum of American Art, New York, Downtown Branch, "Clay"

1976
San Francisco Museum of Modern Art, "Painting and Sculpture in California: The Modern Era" (traveled)

1978
Everson Museum of Art, Syracuse, New York, "Nine West Coast Clay Sculptors, 1978" (traveled)

1979
Everson Museum of Art, Syracuse, New York, "A Century of Ceramics in the United States, 1878–1978" (traveled)
Stedelijk Museum, Amsterdam, "West Coast Ceramics"
Whitney Museum of American Art, New York, "1979 Biennial Exhibition"

1980
San Diego Museum of Art, "Sculpture in California, 1975–1980"
San Francisco Museum of Modern Art, "Twenty American Artists"

1981
Whitney Museum of American Art, New York, "Ceramic Sculpture: Six Artists" (traveled)

Selected Bibliography

Armstrong, Richard. *Sculpture in California, 1975–1980* (exhibition catalogue). San Diego: San Diego Museum of Art, 1980.
Clark, Garth, and Margie Hughto. *A Century of Ceramics in the United States, 1878–1978* (exhibition catalogue). New York: E.P. Dutton in association with Everson Museum of Art, Syracuse, New York, 1979.
Coffert, Beth. *Robert Arneson: Self-Portraits* (exhibition catalogue). Philadelphia: Moore College of Art Gallery, 1979.
Foley, Suzanne. *A Decade of Ceramic Art, 1962–72: From the Collection of Professor and Mrs. R. Joseph Monsen* (exhibition catalogue). San Francisco: San Francisco Museum of Art, 1972.
Hopkins, Henry T. *Painting and Sculpture in California: The Modern Era* (exhibition catalogue). San Francisco: San Francisco Museum of Modern Art, 1976.
Marshall, Richard, and Suzanne Foley. *Ceramic Sculpture: Six Artists* (exhibition catalogue). New York: Whitney Museum of American Art in association with the University of Washington Press, Seattle and London, 1981.

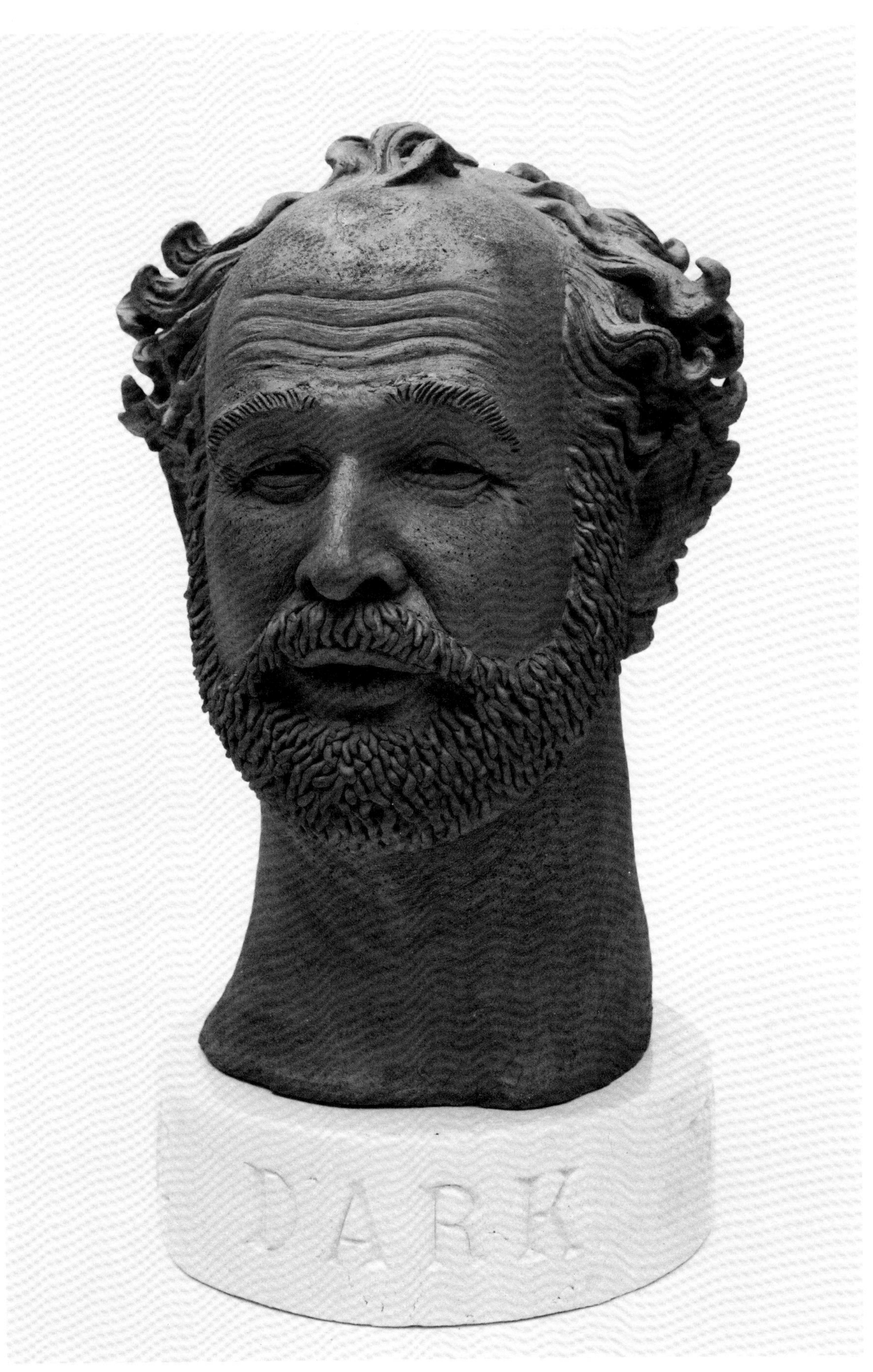

Whistling in the Dark, 1976
Terra-cotta and glazed earthenware, 35¼ x 20 x 20″ (90 x 50.8 x 50.8 cm)
Gift of Frances and Sydney Lewis 77.37

Richard Artschwager

Born in Washington, D.C., 1924
Studied at Cornell University, Ithaca, New York (B.A., 1948)
Lives in New York City and Charlotteville, New York

As in any broken-field painting there are parts which reveal themselves as figure or (better) object-of-attention, and then subside back into and join with the groundwork which provides the scenario for some other object-of-attention. All this is a script for the viewer's eye roving from right to left, up and down, the head pivoting on the spinal column; a script for the "factual" business of seeing as it might be practiced by a coyote or an artillery observer. . . . There is also a scanning from near to far (and back) of some inches or miles, which is generated by one's inherent, on-going intention of physical movement, sometimes to a particular purpose. The viewer brings this capability—or desire—with him. It is a mind trip, and it is invited or mandated by the one or more perspective structures in the painting. This painting has two.

Quoted from statement dated July 15, 1983, Artists' Files, Whitney Museum of American Art, New York.

Selected One-Artist Exhibitions

1965
Leo Castelli Gallery, New York

1968
Galerie Konrad Fischer, Düsseldorf

1969
Galerie Ricke, Cologne

1972
Leo Castelli Gallery, New York

1973
Museum of Contemporary Art, Chicago

1975
Galerie Neuendorf, Hamburg
Daniel Weinberg Gallery, San Francisco

1978
The Clocktower, Institute for Art and Urban Resources, New York
Kunstverein in Hamburg

1979
Albright-Knox Art Gallery, Buffalo, New York (traveled)

1980
Museum of Art, Rhode Island School of Design, Providence

1981
Leo Castelli Gallery, New York

Selected Group Exhibitions

1964
Albright-Knox Art Gallery, Buffalo, New York, "Plastics Show"

1966
The Jewish Museum, New York, "Primary Structures: Younger American and British Sculptors"
Whitney Museum of American Art, New York, "Annual Exhibition 1966: Contemporary Sculpture and Prints"

1968
Kassel, West Germany, "Documenta 4"

1969
Kunsthalle Bern, Switzerland, "When Attitudes Become Form"

1970
The Museum of Modern Art, New York, "Information"
Whitney Museum of American Art, New York, "1970 Annual Exhibition: Contemporary American Sculpture"

1974
Whitney Museum of American Art, New York, "American Pop Art"

1975
Bykert Gallery, New York, "Artschwager, Gordon, Torreano, Zucker"

1976
Fine Arts Center Gallery, University of Massachusetts, Amherst, "Critical Perspectives in American Art" (traveled)

1977
Institute of Contemporary Art, University of Pennsylvania, Philadelphia, "Improbable Furniture"

1978
Albright-Knox Art Gallery, Buffalo, New York, "American Painting of the 1970s" (traveled)

1980
United States Pavilion, 39th Venice Biennale, Italy, "Drawings: The Pluralist Decade" (traveled)

1981
Hayden Gallery, Massachusetts Institute of Technology, Cambridge, "Rooms: Installations by Richard Artschwager, Cynthia Carlson, Richard Haas"

1982
Kassel, West Germany, "Documenta 7"

Selected Bibliography

Alloway, Lawrence. *American Pop Art* (exhibition catalogue). New York: Whitney Museum of American Art, 1974.

Armstrong, Richard, Linda L. Cathcart, and Suzanne Delehanty. *Richard Artschwager's Theme(s)* (exhibition catalogue). Buffalo, New York: Albright-Knox Art Gallery, 1979.

Cathcart, Linda L. *American Painting of the 1970s* (exhibition catalogue). Buffalo, New York: Albright-Knox Art Gallery, 1978.

Davies, Hugh M., ed. *Critical Perspectives in American Art* (exhibition catalogue). Amherst, Massachusetts: Fine Arts Center Gallery, University of Massachusetts, 1976.

Delehanty, Suzanne. *Improbable Furniture* (exhibition catalogue). Philadelphia: Institute of Contemporary Art, University of Pennsylvania, 1977.

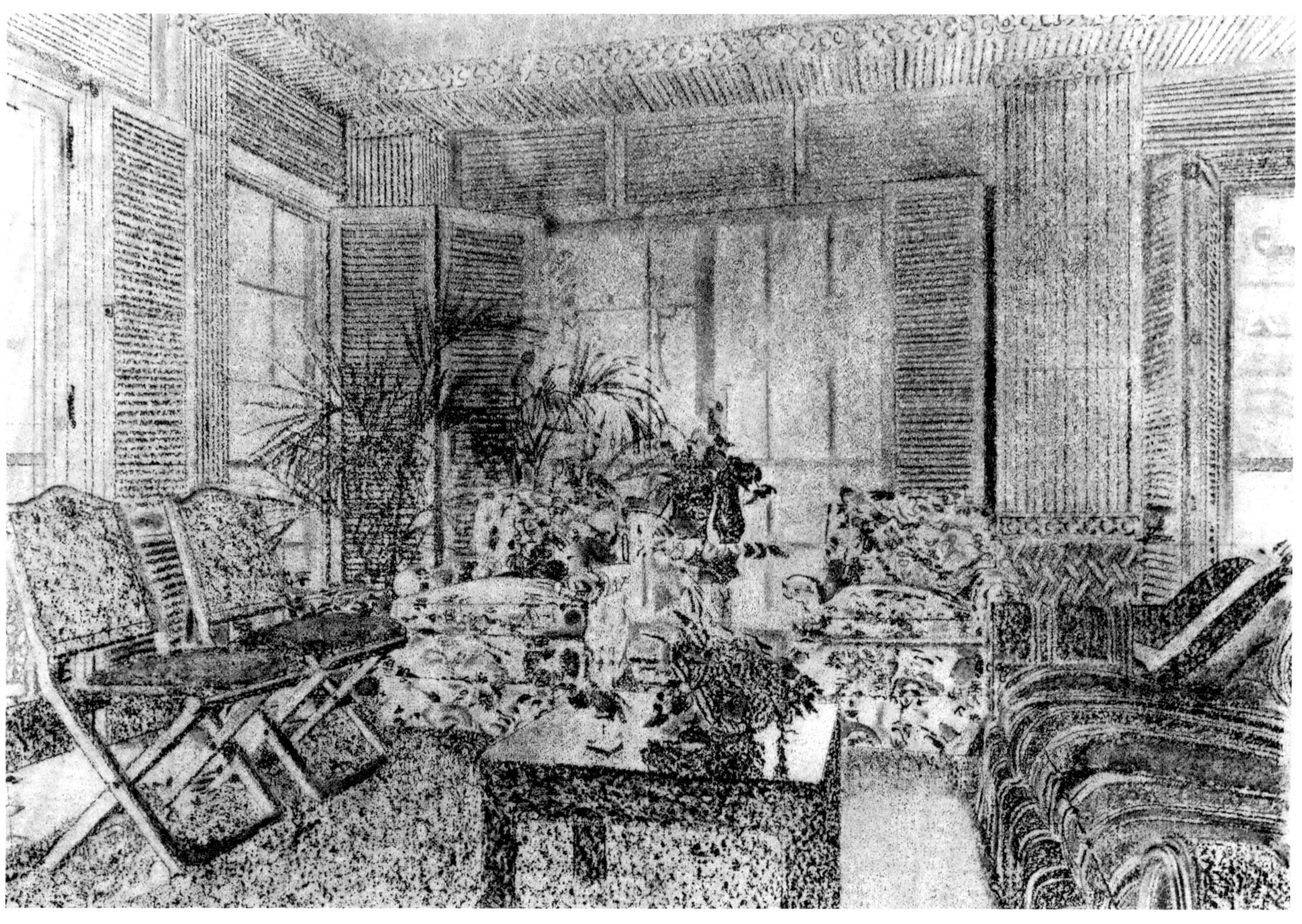

The Bush, 1971
Synthetic polymer on composition board, 48½ x 70½″ (123.2 x 179.1 cm)
Gift of Virginia F. and William R. Salomon
72.13

John Baldessari

Born in National City, California, 1931
Studied at San Diego State College (B.A., 1953; M.F.A., 1957); University of California, Berkeley (1954–55); University of California, Los Angeles (1955); Otis Art Institute, Los Angeles (1957–59)
Lives in Santa Monica, California

"Ashputtle" was done, along with five others, for Documenta 7. I had always wanted to work with Grimm's fairy tales and since the brothers lived in Kassel, I decided that Documenta would be the occasion for doing these works. It is not a literal, linear narrative or retelling of the tale but an attempt to engender the psychological tone of the story. The black and white photos are cropped versions of various movie stills available in Los Angeles. Since I believe movies are mythmaking, I decided to transform the tale from one form to another. It originally was an oral tradition anyway and movie stills may reinvigorate the old anxieties these tales addressed. The color shot is by me and is intended to be a synopsis of the tale . . . . My aim is to say the most with the least means. I am more interested in content than form . . . . Row one: Narcissism, death, flight; row two: Degradation, synopsis shot, worthlessness; row three: Oedipal conflict, struggle with vileness, too much love of father; row four: Rises from ashes, superiority discovered, ends with prize and high esteem . . . . Re the synopsis shot, tar was put on steps to catch her. The blood indicates the stepmother's Procrustean shortening of the other sister's feet to fit the slipper.

Quoted from statement dated May 29, 1983, Artists' Files, Whitney Museum of American Art, New York.

Selected One-Artist Exhibitions

1960
La Jolla Museum of Art, California

1966
La Jolla Museum of Art, California

1970
Eugenia Butler Gallery, New York
Richard Feigen Gallery, New York

1971
Art and Project, Amsterdam
Galerie Konrad Fischer, Düsseldorf

1973
Galerie Konrad Fischer, Düsseldorf
Sonnabend Gallery, New York

1975
Galerie MTL, Brussels
Galerie Sonnabend, Paris
Sonnabend Gallery, New York
Stedelijk Museum, Amsterdam

1978
Artists Space, New York
Portland Center for the Visual Arts, Oregon
Whitney Museum of American Art, New York

1979
InK. (Halle für Internationale Neue Kunst), Zuric

1980
Sonnabend Gallery, New York
Stedelijk Van Abbemuseum, Eindhoven, Netherlands (traveled)

1981
The New Museum, New York (traveled)

Selected Group Exhibitions

1960
Los Angeles County Museum of Art, "Artists of Los Angeles County and Vicinity"

1962
San Francisco Museum of Art, "San Francisco Annual"

1969
Hayward Gallery, London, "Pop Art Redefined"
Whitney Museum of American Art, New York, "1969 Annual Exhibition: Contemporary American Painting"

1970
Galleria Civica d'Arte Moderna, Turin, Italy, "Conceptual Art/Arte Povera/Land Art"
The Museum of Modern Art, New York, "Information"

1972
Kassel, West Germany, "Documenta 5"
Pasadena Museum of Art, California, "Southern California Attitudes 1972"
Whitney Museum of American Art, New York, "1972 Annual Exhibition: Contemporary American Painting"

1974
Long Beach Museum of Art, California, "Southland Video Anthology"

1975
The Museum of Modern Art, New York, "Projects: Video"

1976
The Detroit Institute of Arts, "American Artists: A New Decade"
P.S. 1, Institute for Art and Urban Resources, Long Island City, New York, "Rooms"
San Francisco Museum of Modern Art, "Painting and Sculpture in California: The Modern Era" (traveled)

1977
Museum of Fine Arts, Houston, "Works"
Whitney Museum of American Art, New York, "1977 Biennial Exhibition"

1978
Contemporary Arts Museum, Houston, "American Narrative/Story Art: 1967–1977" (traveled)
Whitney Museum of American Art, New York, "Art About Art" (traveled)

1979
Museum Bochum-Kunstsammlung, Bochum, West Germany, "Words"
Whitney Museum of American Art, New York, "1979 Biennial Exhibition"

1982
Kassel, West Germany, "Documenta 7"

Selected Bibliography

Fuchs, R.H. *John Baldessari* (exhibition catalogue). Eindhoven, Netherlands: Stedelijk Van Abbemuseum, 1980.
Hopkins, Henry T. *Painting and Sculpture in California: The Modern Era* (exhibition catalogue). San Francisco: San Francisco Museum of Modern Art, 1977.
Schimmel, Paul. *American Narrative/Story Art: 1967–1977* (exhibition catalogue). Houston: Contemporary Arts Museum, 1978.
Tucker, Marcia. *John Baldessari* (exhibition catalogue). New York: The New Museum, 1981.

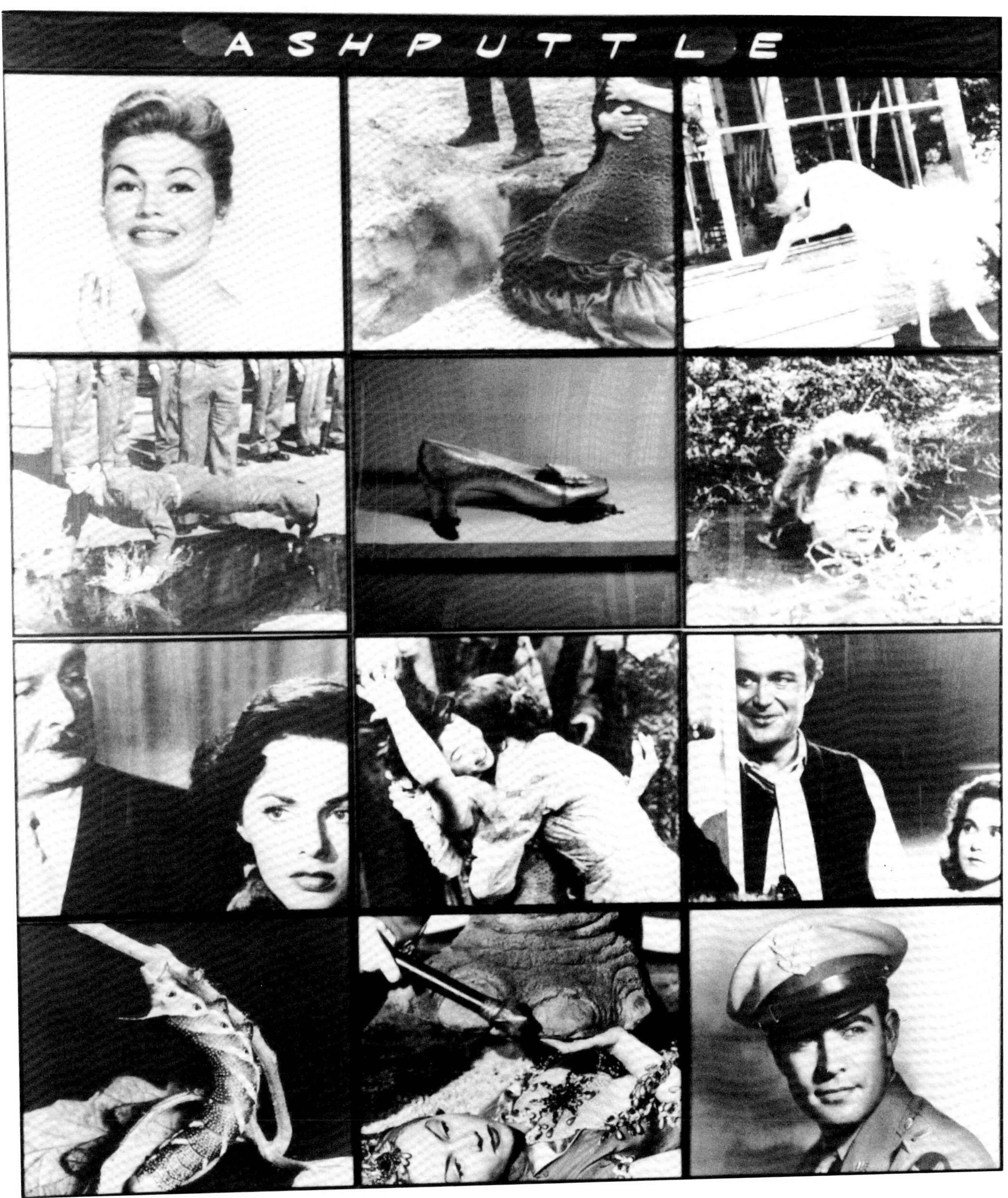

Ashputtle, 1982
Eleven black-and-white photographs, one color photograph, and text panel: overall, 84 x 72″ (213.4 x 182.9 cm)
Purchase, with funds from the Painting and Sculpture Committee 83.8 a–m

Jennifer Bartlett

Born in Long Beach, California, 1941
Studied at Mills College, Oakland, California (B.A., 1963); Yale University, New Haven, Connecticut (B.F.A., 1964; M.F.A., 1965)
Lives in New York

The house is also just a given image that I work with. It is like a throwaway, and its construction is very abstract, just squares that are very stable and that are divisible in an interesting number of ways. My interest is in how it can be done rather than what the imagery is . . . . If a painting is comprised of units, it is possible to think of it as always being divisible or changeable. The gridded steel plates allow me to approach painting in a very methodical manner, where each thought can be seen as if it were a clause. The white spaces between the plates act as punctuation—they function like the space between words and sentences, dividing one unit from another.

Quoted in Richard Marshall, *New Image Painting*, exhibition catalogue (New York: Whitney Museum of American Art, 1978), p. 20.

Selected One-Artist Exhibitions

1963
Mills College, Oakland, California

1970
119 Spring Street Gallery, New York

1972
Reese Paley Gallery, New York

1974
Paula Cooper Gallery, New York

1976
Contemporary Arts Center, Cincinnati
Paula Cooper Gallery, New York

1977
Wadsworth Atheneum, Hartford, Connecticut

1978
Fine Art Gallery, University of California, Irvine
Hansen Fuller Gallery, San Francisco

1979
The Clocktower, Institute for Art and Urban Resources, New York
Margo Leavin Gallery, Los Angeles

1980
Akron Art Institute, Ohio
Albright-Knox Art Gallery, Buffalo, New York
Galerie Mukai, Tokyo

1981
Paula Cooper Gallery, New York
Margo Leavin Gallery, Los Angeles

1982
Paula Cooper Gallery, New York
Joslyn Art Museum, Omaha
Tate Gallery, London

1983
Paula Cooper Gallery, New York

Selected Group Exhibitions

1971
The Museum of Modern Art, New York, "Seven Walls"

1972
Whitney Museum of American Art, New York, "1972 Annual Exhibition: Contemporary American Painting"

1973
Whitney Museum of American Art, New York, "American Drawings: 1963–1973"

1975
The Corcoran Gallery of Art, Washington, D.C., "37th Corcoran Biennial"

1976
Århus Kunstmuseum, Denmark, "The Liberation: Fourteen American Artists"

1977
Kassel, West Germany, "Documenta 6"
New York State Museum, Albany, "New York: The State of Art"
Whitney Museum of American Art, New York, "1977 Biennial Exhibition"

1978
Whitney Museum of American Art, New York, "New Image Painting"

1979
Whitney Museum of American Art, New York, "1979 Biennial Exhibition"

1980
Contemporary Arts Museum, Houston, "Extensions: Jennifer Bartlett, Lynda Benglis, Robert Longo, Judy Pfaff"
United States Pavilion, 39th Venice Biennale, Italy, "Drawings: The Pluralist Decade" (traveled)

Selected Bibliography

Cathcart, Linda L. *Extensions: Jennifer Bartlett, Lynda Benglis, Robert Longo, Judy Pfaff* (exhibition catalogue). Houston: Contemporary Arts Museum, 1980.
Day, Holliday T. *I-80 Series: Jennifer Bartlett* (exhibition catalogue). Omaha: Joslyn Art Museum, 1982.
Kardon, Janet, ed. *Drawings: The Pluralist Decade* (exhibition catalogue). Texts by John Hallmark Neff, Rosalind Krauss, Richard Lorber, Edit deAk, John Perreault, Howard N. Fox, and Nancy Foote. Philadelphia: Institute of Contemporary Art, University of Pennsylvania, 1980.
Kotik, Charlotta. *Jennifer Bartlett: Selected Works* (exhibition catalogue). Buffalo, New York: Albright-Knox Art Gallery, 1980.
Marshall, Richard. *New Image Painting* (exhibition catalogue). New York: Whitney Museum of American Art, 1978.
Russell, John. *Jennifer Bartlett: In the Garden*. New York: Harry N. Abrams, 1982.

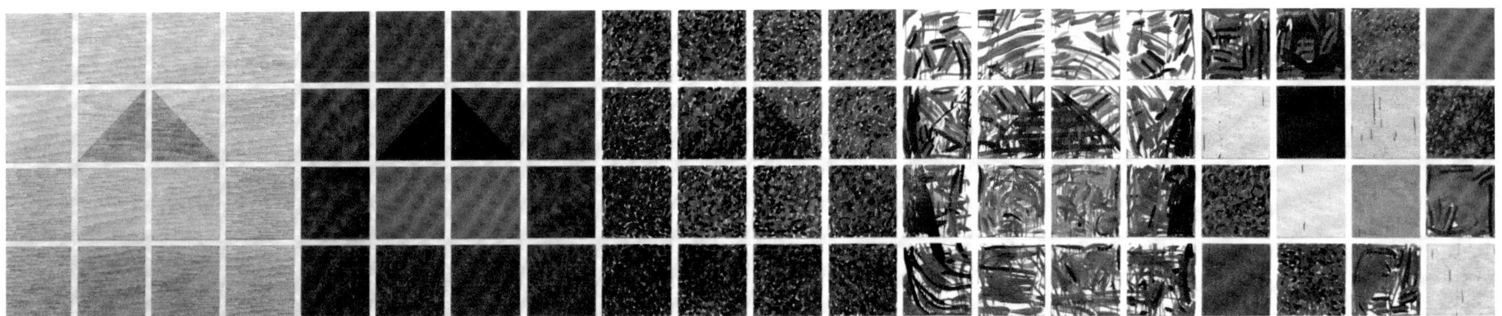

Falcon Avenue, Seaside Walk, Dwight Street, Jarvis Street, Greene Street, 1976
Enamel on steel, baked enamel, and silkscreen grid, 51 x 259″ (129.5 x 657.9 cm)
Gift of the Louis and Bessie Adler Foundation, Inc., Seymour M. Klein, President, and the National Endowment for the Arts 77.22

Lynda Benglis

Born in Lake Charles, Louisiana, 1941
Studied at Newcomb College, New Orleans (B.F.A., 1964)
Lives in New York

What interested me in the . . . knots . . . was the quality that I found in African sculpture. . . . That quality was the repose and the tension inherent in the form. In the cubist planar situation in the African works, it was the way the surface and the form came together. . . . The knots were an organic or modified variation on the whole cubist idea; I found the variations extremely complex, enough to occupy me for five years. . . . I also decided to stress their sculptural aspects by spraying them with different metals. I began spraying them with a final aluminum coat; then they existed in a final tin coat. The copper series . . . were the last series of knots that I did.

Quoted in "Interview: Lynda Benglis," *Ocular*, 4 (Summer 1979), p. 41.

Selected One-Artist Exhibitions

1970
Paula Cooper Gallery, New York

1971
Paula Cooper Gallery, New York
Hayden Gallery, Massachusetts Institute of Technology, Cambridge

1972
Hansen Fuller Gallery, San Francisco

1973
The Clocktower, Institute for Art and Urban Resources, New York
Paula Cooper Gallery, New York

1974
Paula Cooper Gallery, New York

1975
Paula Cooper Gallery, New York
Fine Arts Center Gallery, State University of New York, College at Oneonta
The Kitchen Center for Video, Music and Dance, New York

1976
Paula Cooper Gallery, Los Angeles

1977
Margo Leavin Gallery, Los Angeles

1978
Paula Cooper Gallery, New York

1979
Georgia State University Art Gallery, Atlanta
Texas Gallery, Houston

1980
Paula Cooper Gallery, New York
Portland Center for the Visual Arts, Oregon
University of South Florida, Tampa (traveled)

1981
University of Arizona Museum of Art, Tucson

1982
Paula Cooper Gallery, New York

Selected Group Exhibitions

1969
The Detroit Institute of Arts, "Other Ideas"
Finch College Museum of Art, New York, "Art and Process IV"
Whitney Museum of American Art, New York, "1969 Annual Exhibition: Contemporary American Painting"

1971
Walker Art Center, Minneapolis, "Works for New Spaces"

1972
Walker Art Center, Minneapolis, "Painting: New Options"

1973
Whitney Museum of American Art, New York, "1973 Biennial Exhibition: Contemporary American Art"

1975
Institute of Contemporary Art, University of Pennsylvania, Philadelphia, "Video Art" (traveled)

1977
Museum of Contemporary Art, Chicago, "A View of a Decade"

1978
Stedelijk Museum, Amsterdam, "Made by Sculptors"

1979
The Museum of Modern Art, New York, "Contemporary Sculpture: Selections from the Collection of The Museum of Modern Art"

1980
Contemporary Arts Museum, Houston, "Extensions: Jennifer Bartlett, Lynda Benglis, Robert Longo, Judy Pfaff"
Museum of Contemporary Art, Chicago, "3 Dimensional Painting"
San Diego Museum of Art, "Sculpture in California 1975–1980"
United States Pavilion, 39th Venice Biennale, Italy, "Drawings: The Pluralist Decade" (traveled)

1981
Whitney Museum of American Art, New York, "Developments in Recent Sculpture"
Whitney Museum of American Art, New York, "1981 Biennial Exhibition"

1982
The Art Institute of Chicago, "74th American Exhibition"
The New Museum, New York, "Early Work: Lynda Benglis, Joan Brown, Luis Jimenez, Gary Stephan, Laurence Weiner"

Selected Bibliography

Armstrong, Richard. *Sculpture in California 1975–1980* (exhibition catalogue). San Diego: San Diego Museum of Art, 1980.
Friedman, Martin. *Works for New Spaces* (exhibition catalogue). Minneapolis: Walker Art Center, 1971.
Kertess, Klaus. "Foam Structures," *Art and Artists*, 7 (May 1972), pp. 33–37.
Marshall, Richard. *Developments in Recent Sculpture* (exhibition catalogue). New York: Whitney Museum of American Art, 1981.
Pincus-Witten, Robert. "Lynda Benglis: The Frozen Gesture," *Artforum*, 13 (November 1974), pp. 54–59.
Schjeldahl, Peter. *Lynda Benglis: 1968–1978* (exhibition catalogue). Tampa: University of South Florida, 1980.

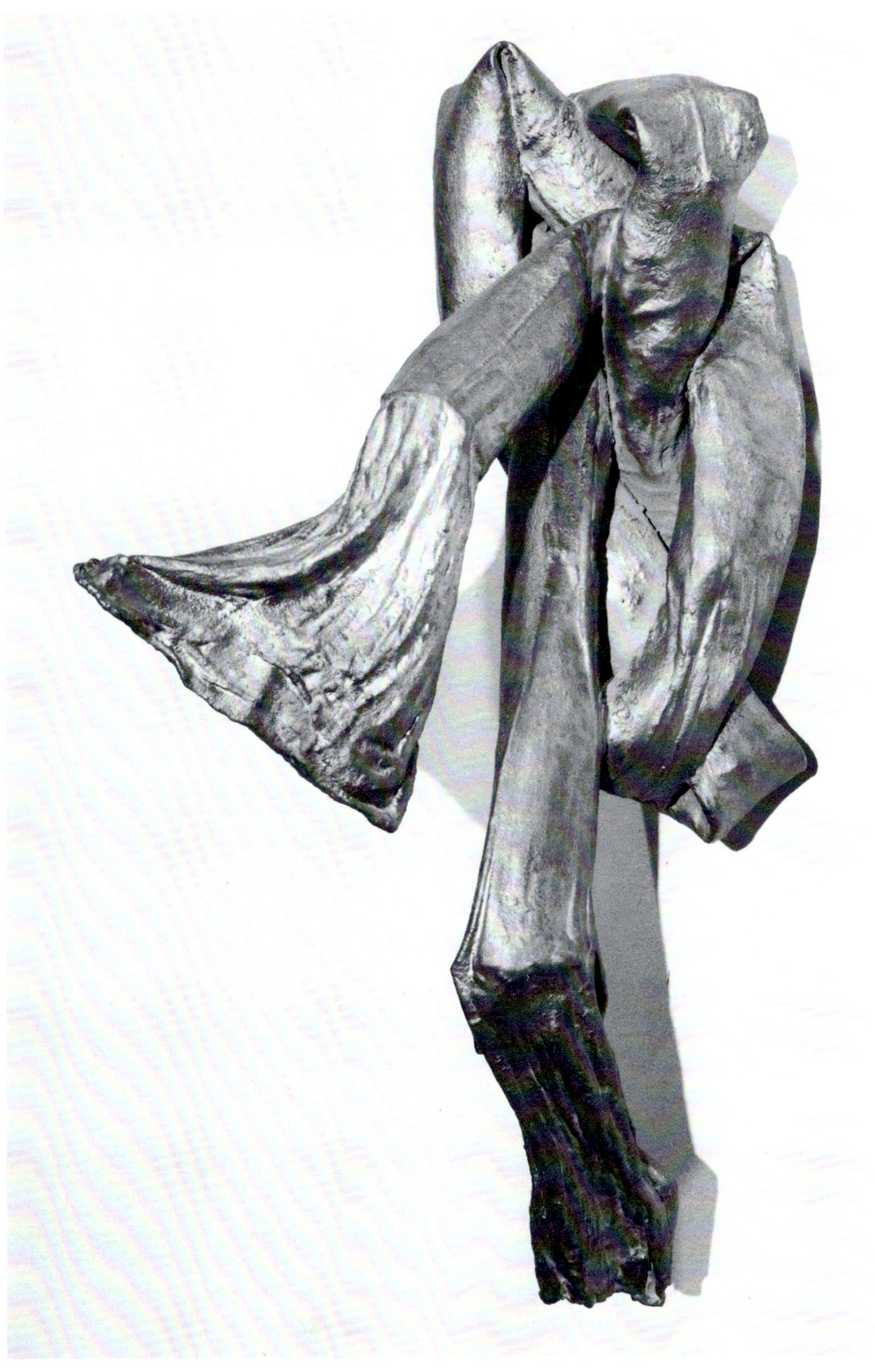

Bravo 2, 1975–76
Copper, steel, tin, and zinc on plaster, cotton bunting, and aluminum screen, 52 x 21 x 30″ (132.1 x 53.3 x 76.2 cm)
Purchase, with funds from the Burroughs Wellcome Purchase Fund, Neysa McMein Purchase Award 81.13

Mel Bochner

Every work of art is consciousness viewed from outside. . . . As I reflect on each sequence of works and watch their wholly unanticipated resolution, modifications to the direction of my thinking occur. This movement is always from the substantive to the relational, but the thoughts themselves are visual. . . . When I did "Ten to 10" I remember it being clear and precise. Then it was a statement on the issue of paradigmatic relationships. Today it appears both austere and sensuous. What is most meaningful to me, now, is not its strength, but its concurrent vulnerability.

Quoted in Jennifer Licht, *Some Recent American Art*, exhibition catalogue (Melbourne, Australia: National Gallery of Victoria, 1973), p. 21.

Born in Pittsburgh, 1940
Studied at Carnegie Institute of Technology, Pittsburgh (B.F.A., 1962); Northwestern University, Evanston, Illinois (1963)
Lives in New York

Selected One-Artist Exhibitions

1966
Visual Arts Gallery, School of Visual Arts, New York

1969
Ace Gallery, Los Angeles
Galerie Konrad Fischer, Düsseldorf
Galerie Heiner Friedrich, Munich

1970
Galleria Sperone, Turin, Italy

1971
The Museum of Modern Art, New York

1972
Galerie Sonnabend, Paris
Sonnabend Gallery, New York

1974
Galleria Schema, Florence
University Art Museum, University of California, Berkeley

1975
Galerie Ricke, Cologne
Sonnabend Gallery, New York

1976
The Baltimore Museum of Art

1978
Galerie Sonnabend, Paris
Sonnabend Gallery, New York
Daniel Weinberg Gallery, San Francisco

1980
Sonnabend Gallery, New York

1981
University Gallery, Meadows School of the Arts, Southern Methodist University, Dallas
Daniel Weinberg Gallery, San Francisco

1982
Sonnabend Gallery, New York

Selected Group Exhibitions

1969
Finch College Museum of Art, New York, "Art and Process IV"
Kunsthalle Bern, Switzerland, "When Attitudes Become Form"
Museum of Contemporary Art, Chicago, "Art by Telephone"

1970
Museo Civico d'Arte Moderna, Turin, Italy, "Conceptual Art/Arte Povera/Land Art"
The Museum of Modern Art, New York, "Information"

1972
Kassel, West Germany, "Documenta 5"

1973
Whitney Museum of American Art, New York, "American Drawings: 1963–1973"

1974
The Art Institute of Chicago, "Idea and Image in Recent Art"
The Art Museum, Princeton University, New Jersey, "Line as Language: Six Artists Draw"

1975
Contemporary Arts Center, Cincinnati, "Mel Bochner, Barry Le Va, Dorothea Rockburne, Richard Tuttle"

1976
The Art Institute of Chicago, "72nd American Exhibition"
The Museum of Modern Art, New York, "Drawing Now"

1977
Museum of Contemporary Art, Chicago, "A View of a Decade"
Whitney Museum of American Art, New York, "1977 Biennial Exhibition"

1978
Philadelphia Museum of Art, "Eight Artists"

1979
Musée National d'Art Moderne, Centre National d'Art et de Culture Georges Pompidou, Paris, "Oeuvres contemporains des collections nationales"
Palazzo Reale, Milan, "Pittura Ambiente"
Whitney Museum of American Art, New York, "1979 Biennial Exhibition"

1980
Hayden Gallery, Massachusetts Institute of Technology, Cambridge, "Mel Bochner/Richard Serra"

1982
The Art Institute of Chicago, "74th American Exhibition"

Selected Bibliography

Dunham, Carroll. *Mel Bochner, Barry Le Va, Dorothea Rockburne, Richard Tuttle* (exhibition catalogue). Cincinnati: Contemporary Arts Center, 1975.
Halbreich, Kathy. *Mel Bochner/Richard Serra* (exhibition catalogue). Cambridge: Hayden Gallery, Massachusetts Institute of Technology, 1980.
Johnson, Ellen. *Modern Art and the Object*. New York: Harper & Row, 1976.
Krauss, Rosalind. *Line as Language: Six Artists Draw* (exhibition catalogue). Princeton, New Jersey: The Art Museum, Princeton University, 1974.
Pincus-Witten, Robert. "Mel Bochner: The Constant as Variable," *Artforum*, 11 (December 1972), pp. 28–34.
Richardson, Brenda. *Mel Bochner: Number and Shape* (exhibition catalogue). Baltimore: The Baltimore Museum of Art, 1976.

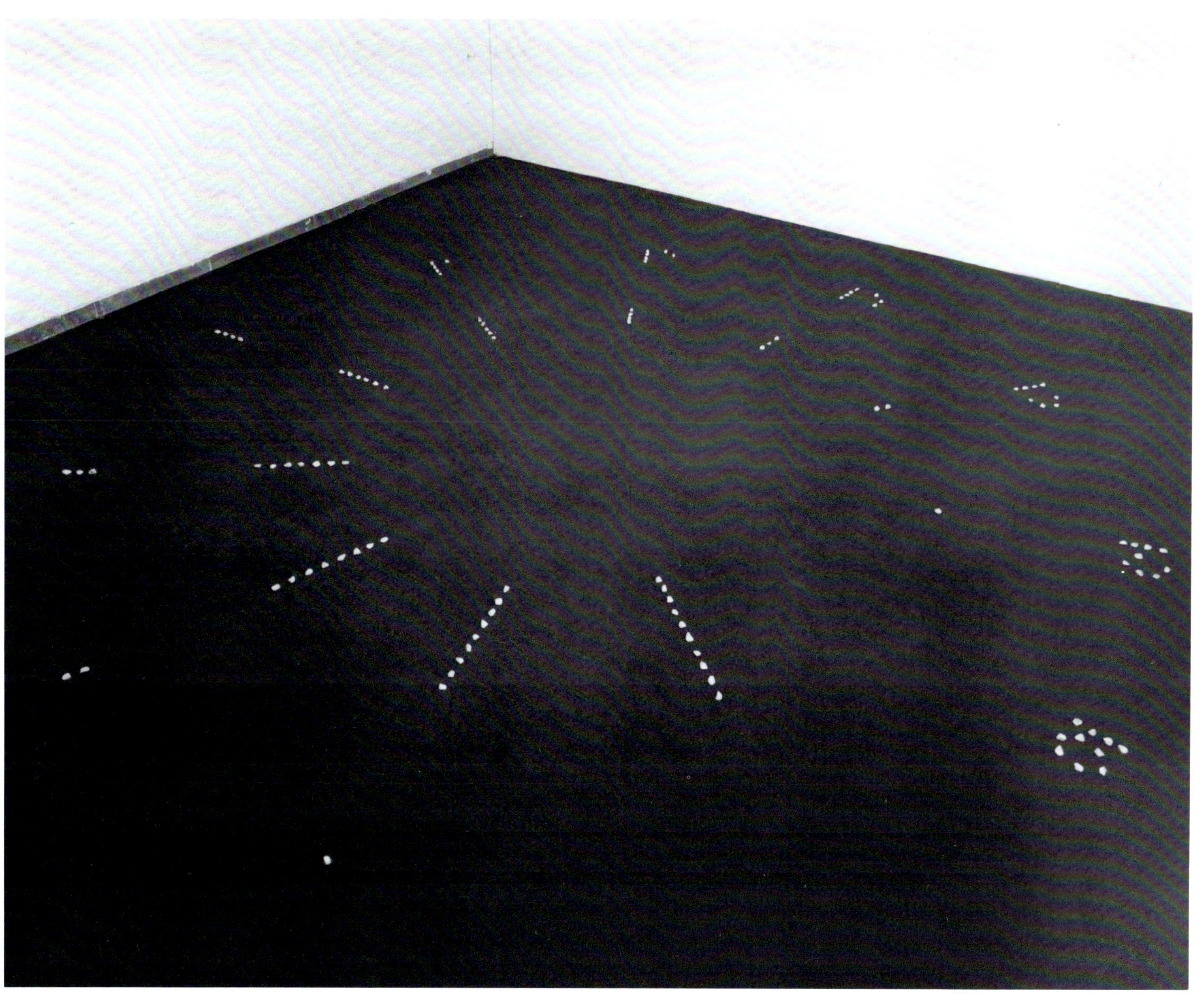

Ten to 10, 1972
Stones, 120″ (304.8 cm) diameter
Gift of the Gilman Foundation, Inc. 77.28

Jonathan Borofsky

I began to write the numbers small on 8½-by-11 inch sheets of paper, using both sides. I thought if I kept this up for a while it might teach me something or give me the answer I was searching for. . . . After counting for a few hours at a time, I often found myself making little scribbles on the page—stick figures, heads attached to trees—but I let them go by. Then one day I looked at one of the past scribbles and thought, I'd like to make a painting of that. . . . Then I took the number I had been on in my counting and put it in the corner of the painting. Something connected there. I had both a recognizable image and a conceptual ordering in time. . . . Looking back on it now I see it as a reaction to Minimalism, like everyone's saying now. But I was really fond of Minimalist work, Andre's especially, and I still like it. My counting represents that side of me. But there was the other side—the more emotional, intuitive side—that was crying to be heard. . . . The head with pointed ears—I think it's me, but I also think it's me as an animal. Me as a dog or goat. It's about hearing, about the sensitivity of animal ears, like radar.

Quoted in Joan Simon, "An Interview with Jonathan Borofsky," *Art in America*, 69 (November 1981), pp. 157–164.

Born in Boston, 1942
Studied at Carnegie-Mellon University, Pittsburgh (B.F.A., 1964); Ecole de Fontainebleau (1964); Yale University, New Haven, Connecticut (M.F.A., 1966)
Lives in Venice, California

Selected One-Artist Exhibitions

1975
Paula Cooper Gallery, New York

1976
Paula Cooper Gallery, New York
Wadsworth Atheneum, Hartford, Connecticut

1977
Fine Art Gallery, University of California, Irvine

1978
Corps de Garde, Groningen, Netherlands
The Museum of Modern Art, New York
University Art Museum, University of California, Berkeley

1979
InK. (Halle für Internationale Neue Kunst), Zurich
Portland Center for the Visual Arts, Oregon

1980
Paula Cooper Gallery, New York
Hayden Gallery, Massachusetts Institute of Technology, Cambridge

1981
Contemporary Arts Museum, Houston
Institute for Contemporary Arts, London
Kunsthalle Basel, Switzerland
Galerie Rudolf Zwirner, Cologne

1982
Paula Cooper Gallery, New York
Museum Boymans-van Beuningen, Rotterdam
Museum van Hedendaagse Kunst, Ghent, Belgium

1983
Kunstmuseum Basel, Switzerland
Paula Cooper Gallery, New York

Selected Group Exhibitions

1969
Paula Cooper Gallery, New York, "No. 7"

1975
Fine Arts Building, New York, "Lives"
Whitney Museum of American Art, New York, Downtown Branch, "Autogeography"

1976
Akademie der Künste, West Berlin, "Soho" (traveled)
International Pavilion, 37th Venice Biennale, Italy, "International Tendencies: 1972–1976"

1979
Neuberger Museum, State University of New York, College at Purchase, "Ten Artists/Artists Space"
Renaissance Society, University of Chicago, "Visionary Images"
Whitney Museum of American Art, New York, "1979 Biennial Exhibition"

1980
United States Pavilion, 39th Venice Biennale, Italy, "Drawings: The Pluralist Decade" (traveled)

1981
Akron Art Museum, Ohio, "The Image in American Painting and Sculpture: 1950–1980"
Los Angeles County Museum of Art, "Art in Los Angeles—The Museum as Site: Sixteen Projects"
Musée National d'Art Moderne, Centre National d'Art et de Culture Georges Pompidou, Paris, "Murs"
Whitney Museum of American Art, New York, "1981 Biennial Exhibition"

1982
Kassel, West Germany, "Documenta 7"
Martin-Gropius-Bau, West Berlin, "Zeitgeist"
The Museum of Modern Art, New York, "New Work on Paper 2: Five Artists"
Walker Art Center, Minneapolis, "Eight Artists: The Anxious Edge"
Whitney Museum of American Art, New York, "Focus on the Figure: Twenty Years"

1983
Whitney Museum of American Art, New York, "1983 Biennial Exhibition"

Selected Bibliography

Barron, Stephanie. *Art in Los Angeles—The Museum as Site: Sixteen Projects* (exhibition catalogue). Los Angeles: Los Angeles County Museum of Art, 1981.
Lippard, Lucy. "Jonathan Borofsky at 2,096,974," *Artforum*, 13 (November 1974), pp. 63–64.
Rose, Bernice. *New Work on Paper 2: Five Artists* (exhibition catalogue). New York: The Museum of Modern Art, 1982.
Rosenthal, Mark. "From Primary Structures to Primary Imagery," *Arts*, 53 (October 1978), pp. 106–107.
Simon, Joan. "An Interview with Jonathan Borofsky," *Art in America*, 69 (November 1981), pp. 156–167.
———. *Jonathan Borofsky: Dreams 1973–1981* (exhibition catalogue). London: Institute of Contemporary Arts, and Basel: Kunsthalle Basel, 1981.

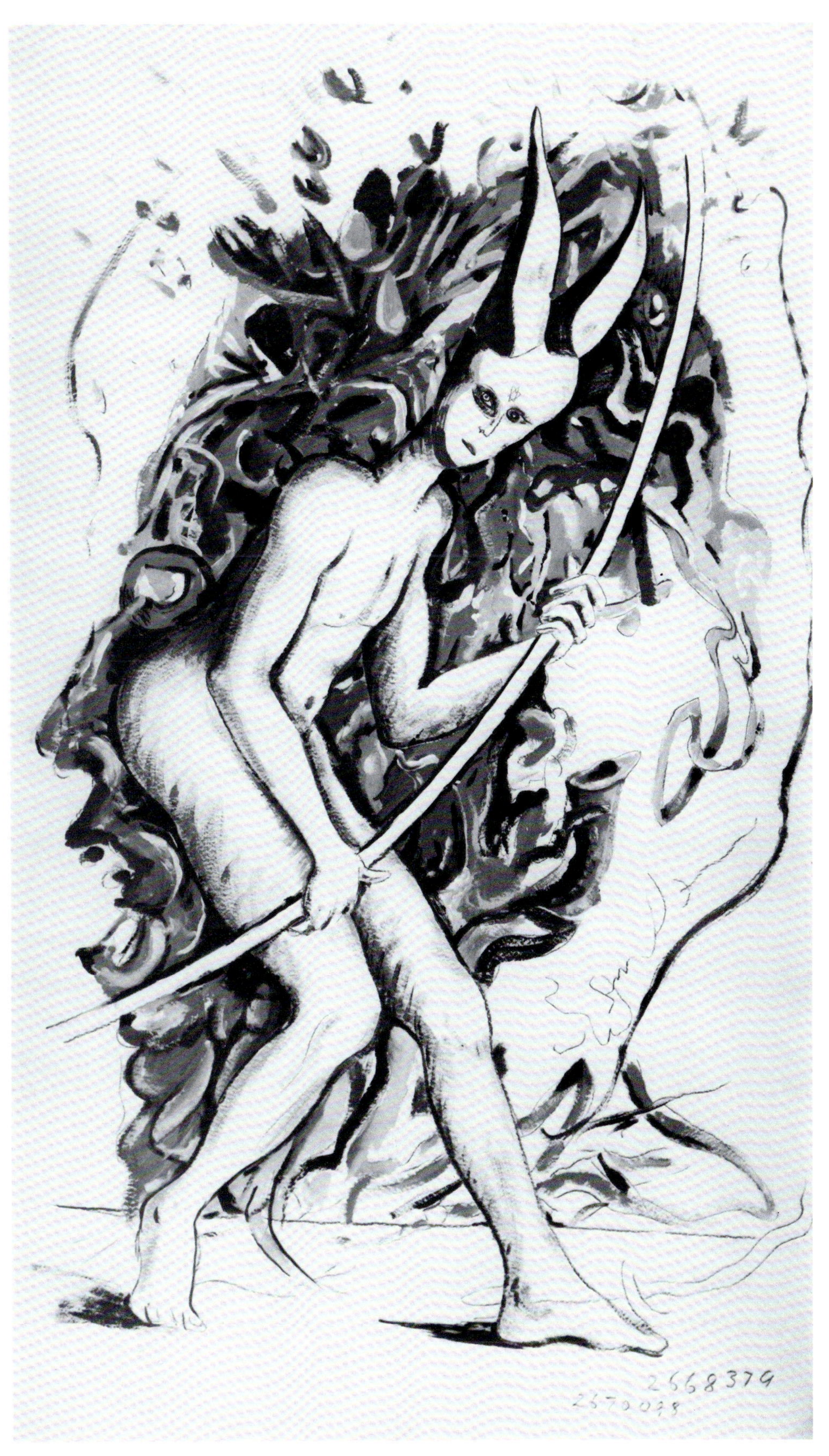

Self-Portrait at 2668379 and 2670098, 1979–80
Acrylic and charcoal on paper, 84¾ x 48″ (215.3 x 122 cm)
Purchase, with funds from Joel and Anne Ehrenkranz 82.3

Roger Brown

There has to be complexity in a painting, but to make things instantly readable is very important. . . . Reducing a certain form so that you can repeat it over and over again, and then continually adding new forms and getting more complex as you go along is what I am trying to do. . . . I light things from the back, emphasize their shape, so they're more two-dimensional. Even my figures are often silhouettes rather than full bodies. . . . If there was a specific thing that made me more interested in two-dimensional patterns, it was contemporary architecture—you know, like the patterns in glass curtain walls of Miesian buildings. These are patterns that reflect or, in fact, are part of the building's structure. That's the way I wanted it to work in my paintings.

Quoted in Russell Bowman, "An Interview with Roger Brown," *Art in America*, 66 (January/February 1978), pp. 107–108.

Born in Hamilton, Alabama, 1941
Studied at the School of The Art Institute of Chicago (B.F.A., 1968; M.F.A., 1970)
Lives in Chicago

Selected One-Artist Exhibitions

1971
Phyllis Kind Gallery, Chicago

1973
Phyllis Kind Gallery, Chicago

1974
Galerie Darthea Speyer, Paris

1975
Phyllis Kind Gallery, Chicago

1976
Phyllis Kind Gallery, Chicago

1977
Phyllis Kind Gallery, Chicago
Phyllis Kind Gallery, New York

1979
Phyllis Kind Gallery, Chicago
Phyllis Kind Gallery, New York

1980
The Saint Louis Art Museum (traveled)
Montgomery Museum of Fine Arts, Alabama (traveled)

Selected Group Exhibitions

1968
Hyde Park Art Center, Chicago, "The False Image"

1969
The Art Institute of Chicago, "72nd Exhibition by Artists of Chicago and Vicinity"

1972
Museum of Contemporary Art, Chicago, "Chicago Imagist Art"

1973
Whitney Museum of American Art, New York, "Extraordinary Realities"
Whitney Museum of American Art, New York, "1973 Biennial Exhibition: Contemporary American Art"

1974
The Art Institute of Chicago, "72nd American Exhibition"
National Collection of Fine Arts, Smithsonian Institution, Washington, D.C., "Made in Chicago"

1977
Institute of Contemporary Art, University of Pennsylvania, Philadelphia, "Improbable Furniture"
Museum of Contemporary Art, Chicago, "A View of a Decade"

1978
Albright-Knox Art Gallery, Buffalo, New York, "American Painting of the 1970s" (traveled)

1979
Whitney Museum of American Art, New York, "Decade in Review: Selections from the Seventies"
Whitney Museum of American Art, New York, "1979 Biennial Exhibition"

1980
P.S. 1, Institute for Art and Urban Resources, Long Island City, New York, "Image into Pattern: Paintings by Roger Brown, Robert Gordy and John Tweddle"
Whitney Museum of American Art, New York, "The Figurative Tradition and the Whitney Museum of American Art: Paintings and Sculpture from the Permanent Collection"

Selected Bibliography

Adrian, Dennis, and Whitney Halstead. *Made in Chicago* (exhibition catalogue). Washington, D.C.: Smithsonian Institution Press, 1974.
Cathcart, Linda L. *American Painting of the 1970s* (exhibition catalogue). Buffalo, New York: Albright-Knox Art Gallery, 1978.
Hills, Patricia, and Roberta K. Tarbell. *The Figurative Tradition and the Whitney Museum of American Art: Paintings and Sculpture from the Permanent Collection* (exhibition catalogue). New York: Whitney Museum of American Art in association with University of Delaware Press, Newark, 1980.
Kahan, Mitchell Douglas. *American Painting of the Sixties and Seventies—The Real—The Ideal—The Fantastic: Selections from the Whitney Museum of American Art* (exhibition catalogue). Montgomery, Alabama: Montgomery Museum of Fine Arts, 1980.
Klopfenstein, Philip A. *Roger Brown* (exhibition catalogue). Montgomery, Alabama: Montgomery Museum of Fine Arts, 1980.
Wallace, Brenda. *Image into Pattern: Paintings by Roger Brown, Robert Gordy and John Tweddle* (exhibition catalogue). New York: Institute for Art and Urban Resources, 1980.

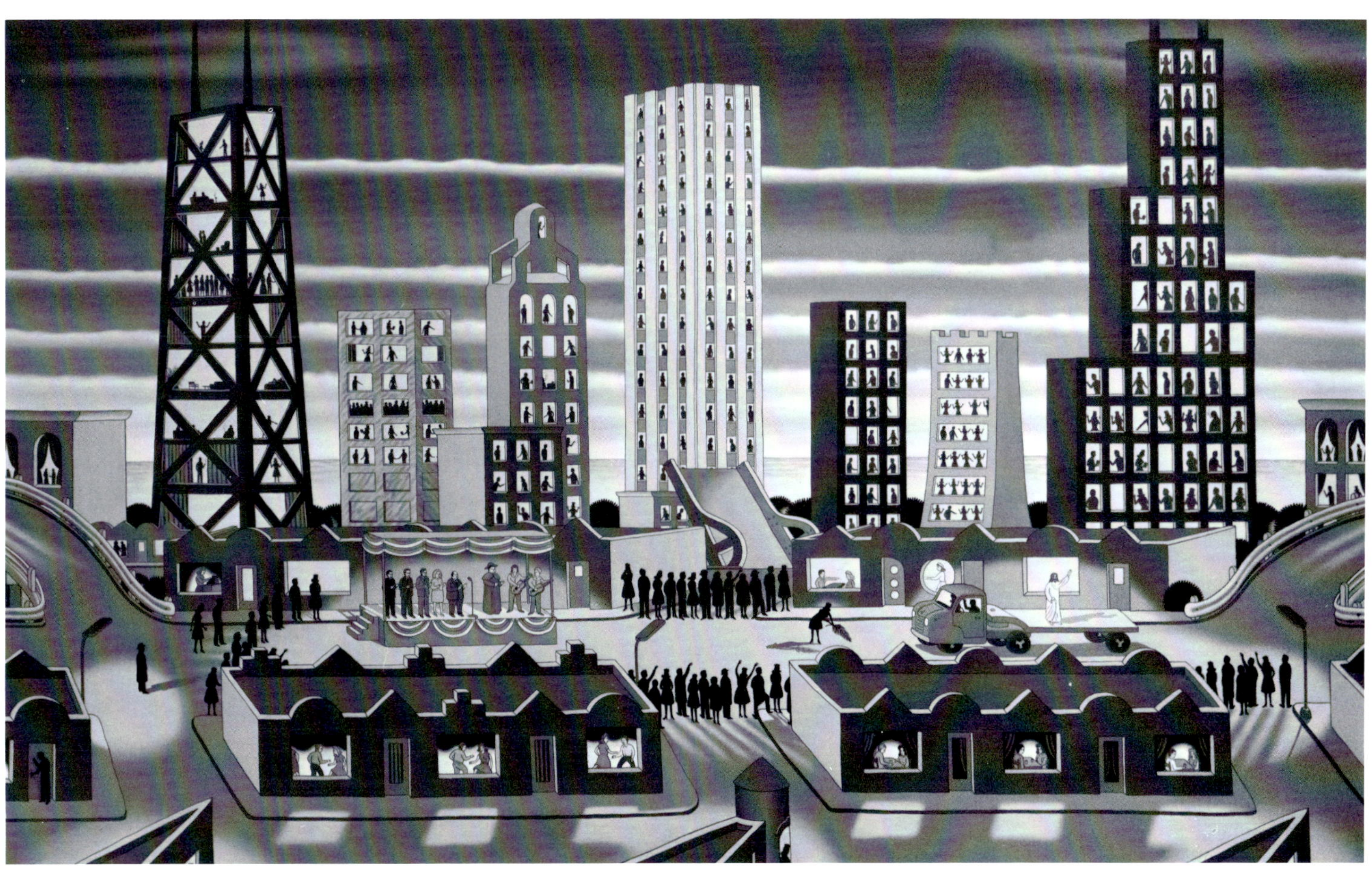

The Entry of Christ into Chicago in 1976, 1976
Oil on canvas, 72 x 120″ (182.9 x 304.8 cm)
Gift of Mr. and Mrs. Joel S. Ehrenkranz (by exchange), Mr. and Mrs. Edwin A. Bergman, and the National Endowment for the Arts 77.56

Vija Celmins

Born in Riga, Latvia, 1939
Studied at John Herron Art Institute, Indianapolis (B.F.A., 1962); University of California, Los Angeles (M.F.A., 1965)
Lives in Los Angeles and New York

This work is one of many with the use of an ocean image—the first of these (1968–71) focused mainly on the surface and its tight relationship to the image. In 1972–73 the outside dimensions of the work became more elongated—an extreme which called attention to the outside shape while still dealing with surface and image. The work in question here has been elongated by the use of seven repetitive images which grow in value from light to medium dark. Another work of the same dimensions was done at this time which graded down to an even darker value. Thus I have been trying to work with two-dimensional divisions to give these drawings some movement and structure. My main concerns have been to balance and integrate properties of surface, shape with image, in a conscious way.

Quoted from statement dated May 28, 1974, Artists' Files, Whitney Museum of American Art, New York.

Selected One-Artist Exhibitions

1966
David Stuart Galleries, Los Angeles

1969
Riko Mizuno Gallery, Los Angeles

1973
Riko Mizuno Gallery, Los Angeles
Whitney Museum of American Art, New York

1975
Broxton Gallery, Los Angeles
Felicity Samuel Gallery, London

1980
Newport Harbor Art Museum, Newport Beach, California (traveled)

1983
David McKee Gallery, New York

Selected Group Exhibitions

1966
California State College, Hayward, "Four Painters"

1969
Fort Worth Art Museum, "Contemporary American Drawing"

1970
Whitney Museum of American Art, New York, "1970 Annual Exhibition: Contemporary American Sculpture"

1971
La Jolla Museum of Contemporary Art, California, "Continuing Surrealism"
Los Angeles County Museum of Art, "24 Young Los Angeles Artists"

1972
The Museum of Modern Art, New York, "California Prints"
Pasadena Museum of Modern Art, California, "Prints from the Permanent Collection"

1973
Los Angeles Municipal Art Gallery, "Separate Realities"
Whitney Museum of American Art, New York, "American Drawings: 1963–1973"

1974
The Art Institute of Chicago, "71st American Exhibition"

1976
The American Federation of Arts, New York, "American Master Drawings and Watercolors" (traveled)
The Detroit Institute of Arts, "American Artists: A New Decade" (traveled)
San Francisco Museum of Modern Art, "Painting and Sculpture in California: The Modern Era" (traveled)

1977
The Frederick S. Wight Art Gallery, University of California, Los Angeles, "The Early Sixties at UCLA"
Whitney Museum of American Art, New York, "1977 Biennial Exhibition"

1979
Whitney Museum of American Art, New York, "The Decade in Review: Selection of the 1970s"

1981
Hirschl & Adler Galleries, New York, "The Contemporary American Landscape"

Selected Bibliography

Hopkins, Henry T. *Painting and Sculpture in California: The Modern Era* (exhibition catalogue). San Francisco: San Francisco Museum of Modern Art, 1977.

Larsen, Susan C. *Vija Celmins: A Survey Exhibition* (exhibition catalogue). Newport Beach, California: Newport Harbor Art Museum, 1980.

Plagens, Peter. *Sunshine Muse: Contemporary Art on the West Coast.* New York: Praeger Publishers, 1974.

Solomon, Elke M. *American Drawings: 1963–1973* (exhibition catalogue). New York: Whitney Museum of American Art, 1973.

———. *Vija Celmins Drawings* (exhibition catalogue). New York: Whitney Museum of American Art, 1973.

Stebbins, Theodore E., Jr. *American Master Drawings and Watercolors.* New York: Harper & Row, in association with The Drawing Society, Inc., 1976.

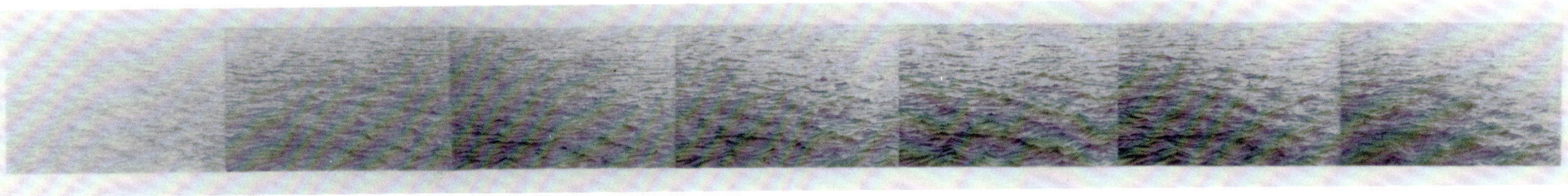

Ocean, 1972–73
Graphite on acrylic sprayed paper, 12⅝ x 99⅛″
(32.1 x 251.8 cm)
Gift of Mr. and Mrs. Joshua A. Gollin 73.71

Ocean, 1972–73 (detail)

Chuck Close

Born in Monroe, Washington, 1940
Studied at the University of Washington, Seattle (B.A., 1962); Yale University, New Haven, Connecticut (B.F.A., 1963; M.F.A., 1964)
Lives in New York

I am definitely interested in trying to nail down the camera's vision, that frozen moment in time. . . . I've kept the image constant and manipulated the process of developing that image. Some works are done in continuous tone, black and white on canvas; sometimes it's building a color painting with three superimposed color layers; the next piece might be done with thousands of colors with pastels, my fingerprints, rubber stamp, whatever. I try to keep myself interested or engaged, altering my experience. . . . When one stands in front of a small work done with thumbprints, there occurs a different experience than when one confronts one of the large black and white paintings. . . . I'm trying to build experiences for the viewer. . . . I wanted the thrust to come from the way all the incremental bits stack to build something powerful and aggressive.

Quoted in Douglass De Loach, "Up Close: An Interview with Chuck Close," *Art Papers*, 6 (March/April 1982), pp. 2–3.

Selected One-Artist Exhibitions

1967
Fine Arts Center Gallery, University of Massachusetts, Amherst

1970
Bykert Gallery, New York

1971
Los Angeles County Museum of Art

1972
Museum of Contemporary Art, Chicago

1973
Akron Art Institute, Ohio
Bykert Gallery, New York
The Museum of Modern Art, New York

1975
Art Museum of South Texas, Corpus Christi
Bykert Gallery, New York
Portland Center for the Visual Arts, Oregon
San Francisco Museum of Modern Art

1976
The Baltimore Museum of Art
Contemporary Arts Center, Cincinnati

1977
Pace Gallery, New York
Wadsworth Atheneum, Hartford, Connecticut

1979
Kunstraum, Munich
Pace Gallery, New York

1980
Walker Art Center, Minneapolis (traveled)

Selected Group Exhibitions

1969
Whitney Museum of American Art, New York, "1969 Annual Exhibition: Contemporary American Painting"

1970
Allen Memorial Art Museum, Oberlin College, Ohio, "Three Young Americans"
Whitney Museum of American Art, New York, "22 Realists"

1972
Kassel, West Germany, "Documenta 5"
Whitney Museum of American Art, New York, "1972 Annual Exhibition: Contemporary American Painting"

1973
Musée d'Art Moderne de la Ville de Paris, "Art Conceptuel et Hyperréaliste"
Whitney Museum of American Art, New York, "American Drawings: 1963–1973"

1976
American Federation of Arts, New York, "American Master Drawings and Watercolors" (traveled)
The Museum of Modern Art, New York, "Drawing Now"

1977
Kassel, West Germany, "Documenta 6"
Musée Nationale d'Art Moderne, Centre National d'Art et de Culture Georges Pompidou, Paris, "Paris–New York"
Museum of Contemporary Art, Chicago, "A View of a Decade"
Whitney Museum of American Art, New York, "1977 Biennial Exhibition"

1978
Albright-Knox Art Gallery, Buffalo, New York, "American Painting of the 1970s" (traveled)

1979
Whitney Museum of American Art, New York, "1979 Biennial Exhibition"

1980
The Museum of Modern Art, New York, "Printed Art: A View of Two Decades"

Selected Bibliography

Adrian, Dennis. *Chuck Close* (exhibition catalogue). Chicago: Museum of Contemporary Art, 1972.
Cathcart, Linda L. *American Painting of the 1970s* (exhibition catalogue). Buffalo, New York: Albright-Knox Art Gallery, 1978.
Lyons, Lisa, and Martin Friedman. *Close Portraits* (exhibition catalogue). Minneapolis: Walker Art Center, 1980.
Monte, James K. *22 Realists* (exhibition catalogue). New York: Whitney Museum of American Art, 1970.
Scott, Gail R. *Chuck Close: Recent Work* (exhibition catalogue). Los Angeles: Los Angeles County Museum of Art, 1971.

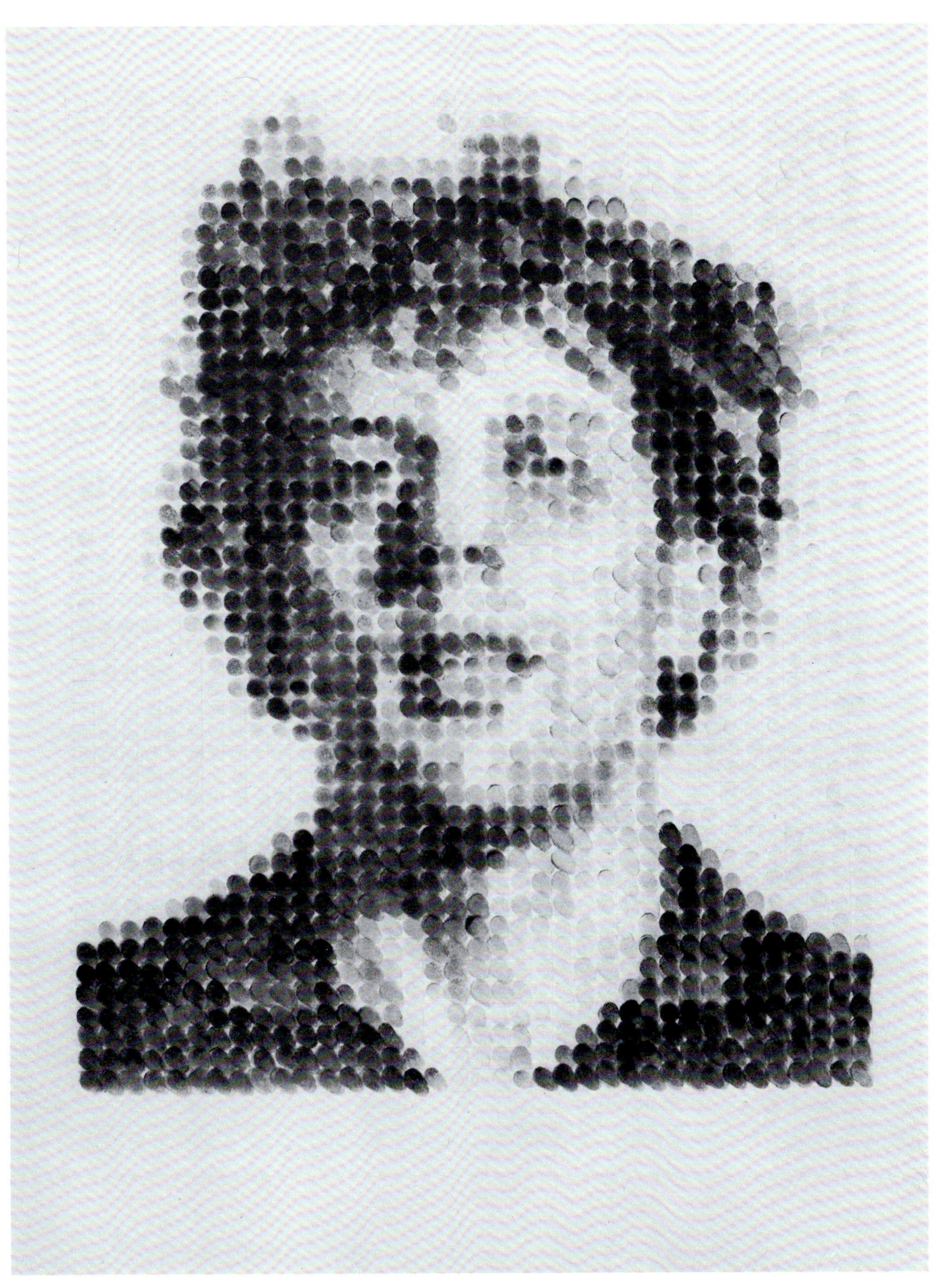

Phil/Fingerprint II, 1978
Stamp-pad ink and pencil on paper, 29¾ x 22¼″
(75.6 x 56.5 cm)
Anonymous gift 78.55

Robert Cottingham

Born in Brooklyn, New York, 1935
Studied at Pratt Institute, Brooklyn, New York (B.F.A., 1963)
Lives in Newtown, Connecticut

As an artist, I use the configurations of a sign as the basis for constructing a painting. They are my "excuse" to make a painting. The end result for me is a composite of line, form, and color that also happens to depict a sign. If the final work can be read on both levels—as a formal painting, taut and succinct, and at the same time as a depiction of a sign—I feel the work approaches success.

Quoted in Jane Cottingham, "Techniques of Three Photo Realist Painters," *American Artist*, 44 (February 1980), p. 62.

Selected One-Artist Exhibitions

1968
Molly Barnes Gallery, Los Angeles

1970
Molly Barnes Gallery, Los Angeles

1971
O.K. Harris Gallery, New York

1974
O.K. Harris Gallery, New York

1975
Galerie de Gestlo, Hamburg

1976
John Berggruen Gallery, San Francisco
O.K. Harris Gallery, New York

1977
Landfall Press Gallery, Chicago

1979
Aldrich Museum of Contemporary Art, Ridgefield, Connecticut

1981
Fendrick Gallery, Washington, D.C.

Selected Group Exhibitions

1969
Long Beach Museum of Art, California, "7th Annual Southern California Exhibition"

1970
Institute of Contemporary Art, University of Pennsylvania, Philadelphia, "The Highway"

1971
Museum of Contemporary Art, Chicago, "Radical Realism"

1972
Kassel, West Germany, "Documenta 5"
New York Cultural Center, "Realism Now"
Art Gallery, University of California, Santa Barbara, "L.A. 14 Painters"

1973
Arts Council of Great Britain, "Image: Reality and Super-Reality"
Los Angeles Municipal Art Gallery, "Separate Realities"

1974
Centre National d'Art Contemporain, Paris, "Hyperréalistes Américains–Réalistes Européens"

1975
Renwick Gallery of the National Collection of Fine Arts, Smithsonian Institution, Washington, D.C., "Signs of Life: Symbols in the City"
Yale University Art Gallery, New Haven, Connecticut, "Richard Brown Baker Collects!"

1976
National Collection of Fine Arts, Smithsonian Institution, Washington, D.C., "America As Art"

1978
Whitney Museum of American Art, New York, "Art About Art" (traveled)

1981
Haus der Kunst, Munich, "Amerikanische Malerei: 1930–1980"
Pennsylvania Academy of the Fine Arts, Philadelphia, "Contemporary American Realism Since 1960"

Selected Bibliography

Battcock, Gregory, ed. *Super Realism: A Critical Anthology*. New York: E.P. Dutton and Company, 1975.
Goodyear, Frank H., Jr. *Contemporary American Realism Since 1960* (exhibition catalogue). Philadelphia: Pennsylvania Academy of the Fine Arts, 1981.
Kultermann, Udo. *New Realism*. Greenwich, Connecticut: New York Graphic Society, 1972.
Lipman, Jean, and Richard Marshall. *Art About Art* (exhibition catalogue). New York: Whitney Museum of American Art, 1978.

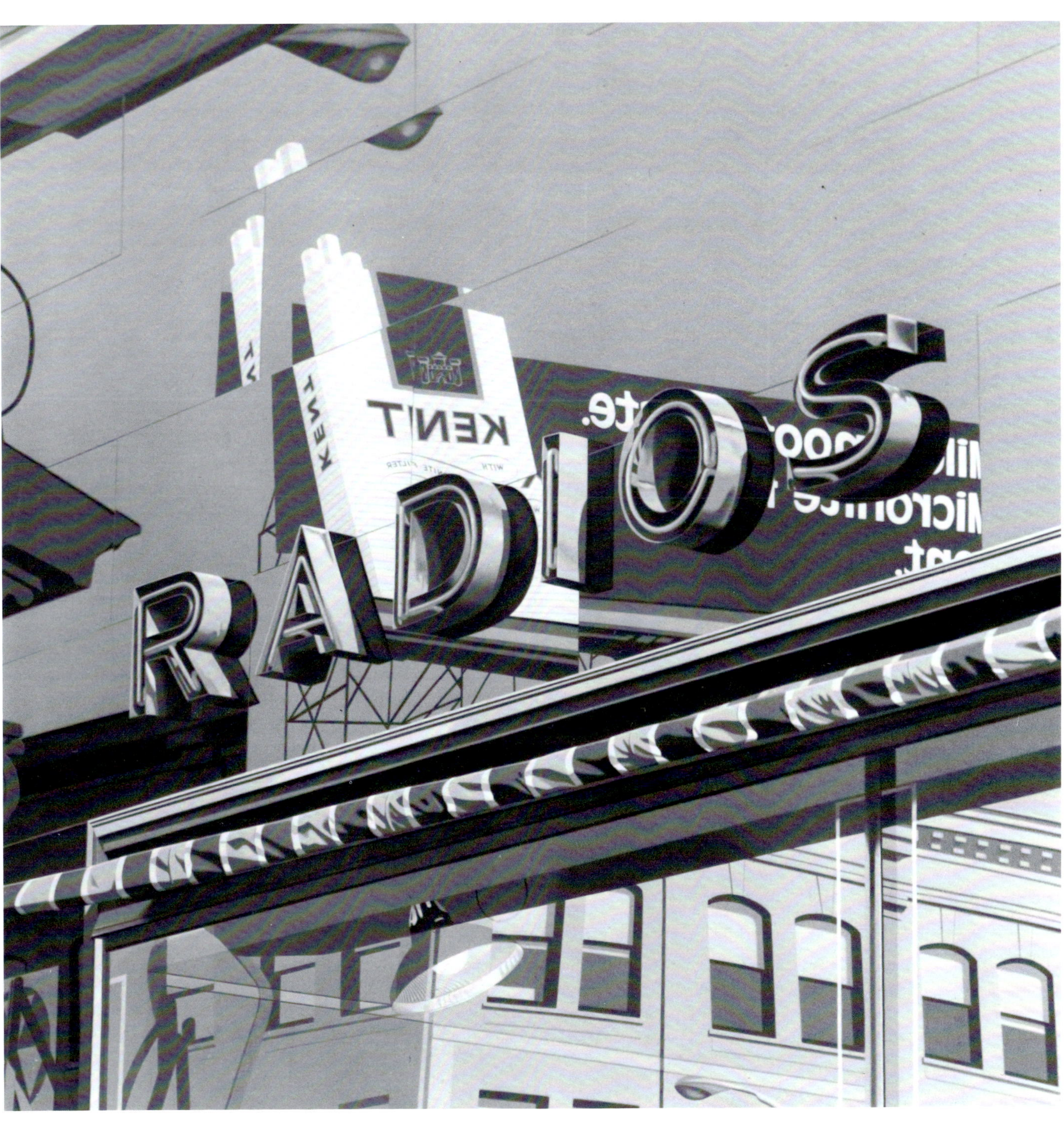

Radios, 1977
Oil on canvas, 78 x 78″ (198.1 x 198.1 cm)
Gift of Frances and Sydney Lewis 77.36

John Duff

Born in Lafayette, Indiana, 1943
Studied at the San Francisco Art Institute (B.F.A., 1967)
Lives in New York

"Two-Part Column" exhibits both a unitary and a binary presence; stating both equally, resolving itself into neither. The piece is felt to be both; a feeling that is ambiguous, or if driven to resolution must remain sequential. Sequential but unresolved, still not opting for one reading or the other. The work juxtaposes seeing and knowing; when it is seen to be one it is known to be two and when it is seen to be two it is known to be one, the knowledge of one modifying the perception of the other. . . . If this (or any) work is deemed to be successful, then some such construction must be in effect; that construction is traceable and knowable and while this elucidation of the functional basis of the work (and the insistence on learning it) may be the pleasure of the viewer it is the obligation of the artist.

Quoted from statement dated April 14, 1983, Artists' Files, Whitney Museum of American Art, New York.

Selected One-Artist Exhibitions

1970
David Whitney Gallery, New York

1971
Galerie Ricke, Cologne
David Whitney Gallery, New York

1972
Irving Blum Gallery, Los Angeles
John Bernard Myers Gallery, New York

1973
John Bernard Myers Gallery, New York

1974
Daniel Weinberg Gallery, San Francisco

1975
Daniel Weinberg Gallery, San Francisco
Willard Gallery, New York

1976
Willard Gallery, New York

1977
Daniel Weinberg Gallery, San Francisco

1978
Willard Gallery, New York

1979
Art Gallery, California State University, Sonoma

1980
Daniel Weinberg Gallery, San Francisco

1981
Margo Leavin Gallery, Los Angeles

Selected Group Exhibitions

1969
Whitney Museum of American Art, New York, "Anti-Illusion: Procedures/Materials"

1970
Whitney Museum of American Art, New York, "1970 Annual Exhibition: Contemporary American Sculpture"

1973
Whitney Museum of American Art, New York, "1973 Biennial Exhibition: Contemporary American Art"

1977
The Solomon R. Guggenheim Museum, New York, "Nine Artists: The Theodoron Awards"

1978
Whitney Museum of American Art, New York, "American Art: 1950 to the Present"

1979
The Museum of Modern Art, New York, "Contemporary Sculpture: Selections from the Collection of The Museum of Modern Art"
Whitney Museum of American Art, New York, "The Decade in Review: Selections from the 1970s"

1980
Norton Gallery and School of Art, West Palm Beach, Florida, "Material Matters: Seven Young Contemporary Artists" (traveled)

1981
Whitney Museum of American Art, New York, "Developments in Recent Sculpture"

1982
Fuller Goldeen Gallery, San Francisco, "Casting: A Survey of Cast Metal Sculpture in the 80s"

Selected Bibliography

Eisenhart, Willy. "John Duff," *Arts Magazine*, 51 (March 1977), p. 10.
Marshall, Richard. *Developments in Recent Sculpture* (exhibition catalogue). New York: Whitney Museum of American Art, 1981.
McDonald, Robert. *John Duff Sculpture Retrospective, 1967–1979* (exhibition catalogue). Sonoma: California State University, 1979.
Monte, James, and Marcia Tucker. *Anti-Illusion: Procedures/Materials* (exhibition catalogue). New York: Whitney Museum of American Art, 1969.
Shearer, Linda. *Nine Artists: The Theodoron Awards* (exhibition catalogue). New York: The Solomon R. Guggenheim Museum, 1977.

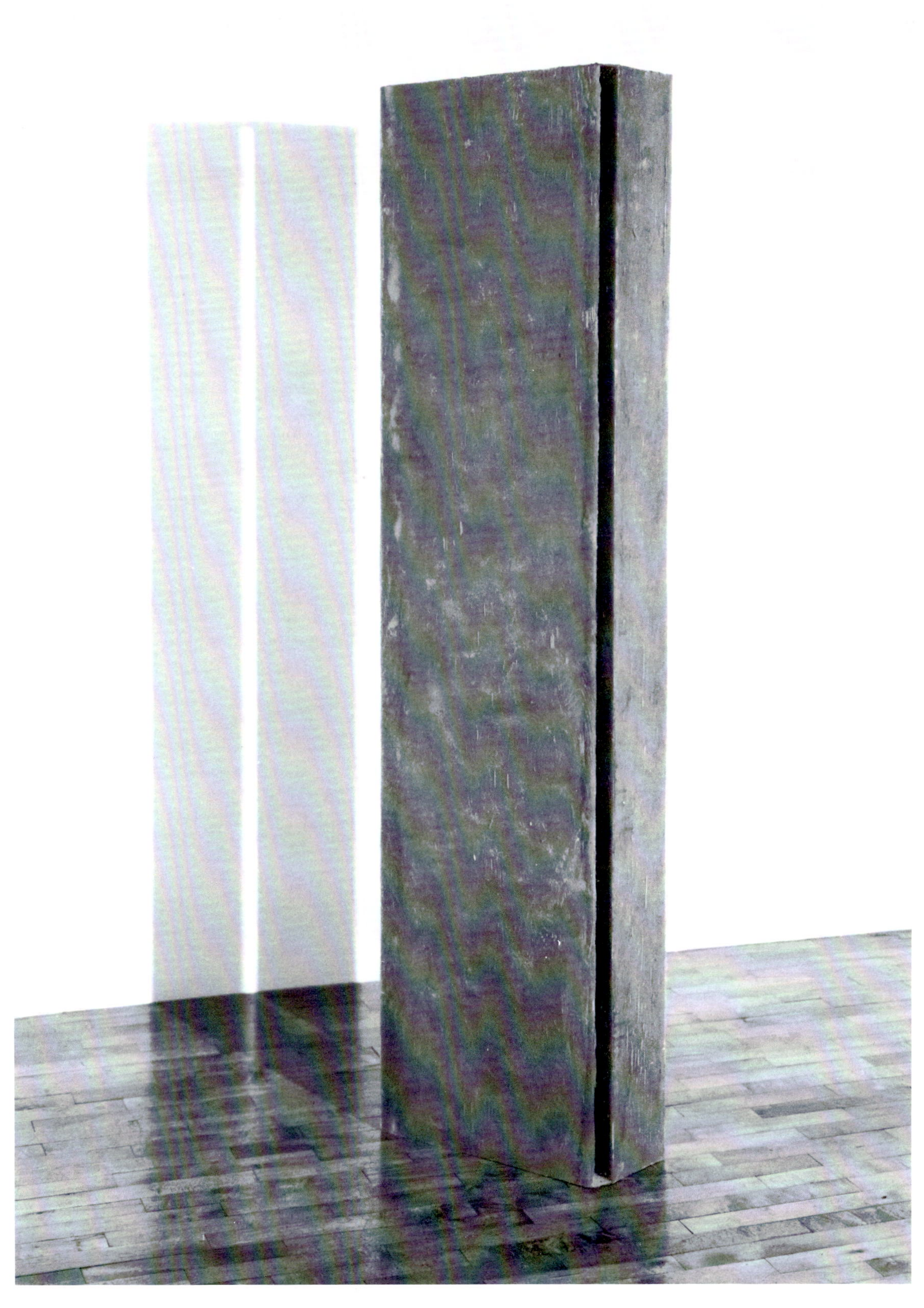

Two Part Column, 1973
Painted fiberglass, 70½ x 7¼ x 17½″ (179.1 x 18.4 x 44.5 cm)
Gift of Barbara Rose 81.40

Richard Estes

Born in Kewanee, Illinois, 1936
Studied at the School of The Art Institute of Chicago (1952–56)
Lives in New York

I'm not trying to reproduce the photograph. I'm trying to use the photograph to do the painting. . . . The great thing about the photograph is that you can stop things—this is one instant. You certainly couldn't do that if you went out there and set yourself up in front of it. . . . When I look at things, some are out of focus. But I don't like to have some things out of focus and others in focus because it makes very specific what you are supposed to look at, and I try to avoid saying that. I want you to look at it all. Everything is in focus. . . . There's a lot of things in painting that you have more control over than you have in a photograph. You can't just ask the people to go away so you can take a picture, or move this car over there. In a painting you can make this line a little stronger, change the depth, things like that.

Quoted in Linda Chase and Ted McBurnett, "The Photo-Realists: 12 Interviews," *Art in America*, 60 (November/December 1972), pp. 79–80.

Selected One-Artist Exhibitions

1968
The Hudson River Museum, Yonkers, New York
Allan Stone Gallery, New York

1969
Allan Stone Gallery, New York

1972
Allan Stone Gallery, New York

1974
Museum of Contemporary Art, Chicago

1978
Museum of Fine Arts, Boston (traveled)

1983
Allan Stone Gallery, New York

Selected Group Exhibitions

1968
Vassar College Art Gallery, Poughkeepsie, New York, "Realism Now"

1969
The Denver Art Museum, "American Report on the 60s"
Milwaukee Art Center, "Directions 2: Aspects of a New Realism"

1970
Whitney Museum of American Art, New York, "22 Realists"

1971
The Corcoran Gallery of Art, Washington, D.C., "32nd Biennial Exhibition of Contemporary American Painting"
Museum of Contemporary Art, Chicago, "Radical Realism"

1972
Kassel, West Germany, "Documenta 5"
Whitney Museum of American Art, New York, "1972 Annual Exhibition: Contemporary American Painting"

1974
Wadsworth Atheneum, Hartford, Connecticut, "New Photo Realism: Paintings and Sculpture in the 1970s"
Worcester Art Museum, Massachusetts, "Three Realists: Close, Estes, Raffael"

1975
Museum of Fine Arts, Boston, "Trends in Contemporary American Realist Painting"

1976
The American Federation of Arts, New York, "American Master Drawings and Watercolors" (traveled)

1977
Whitney Museum of American Art, New York, "1977 Biennial Exhibition"

Selected Bibliography

Arthur, John. *Richard Estes: The Urban Landscape* (exhibition catalogue). Boston: Museum of Fine Arts, 1978.
Battcock, Gregory, ed. *Super Realism: A Critical Anthology*. New York: E.P. Dutton and Company, 1975.
Kultermann, Udo. *New Realism*. Greenwich, Connecticut: New York Graphic Society, 1972.
Monte, James K. *22 Realists* (exhibition catalogue). New York: Whitney Museum of American Art, 1970.

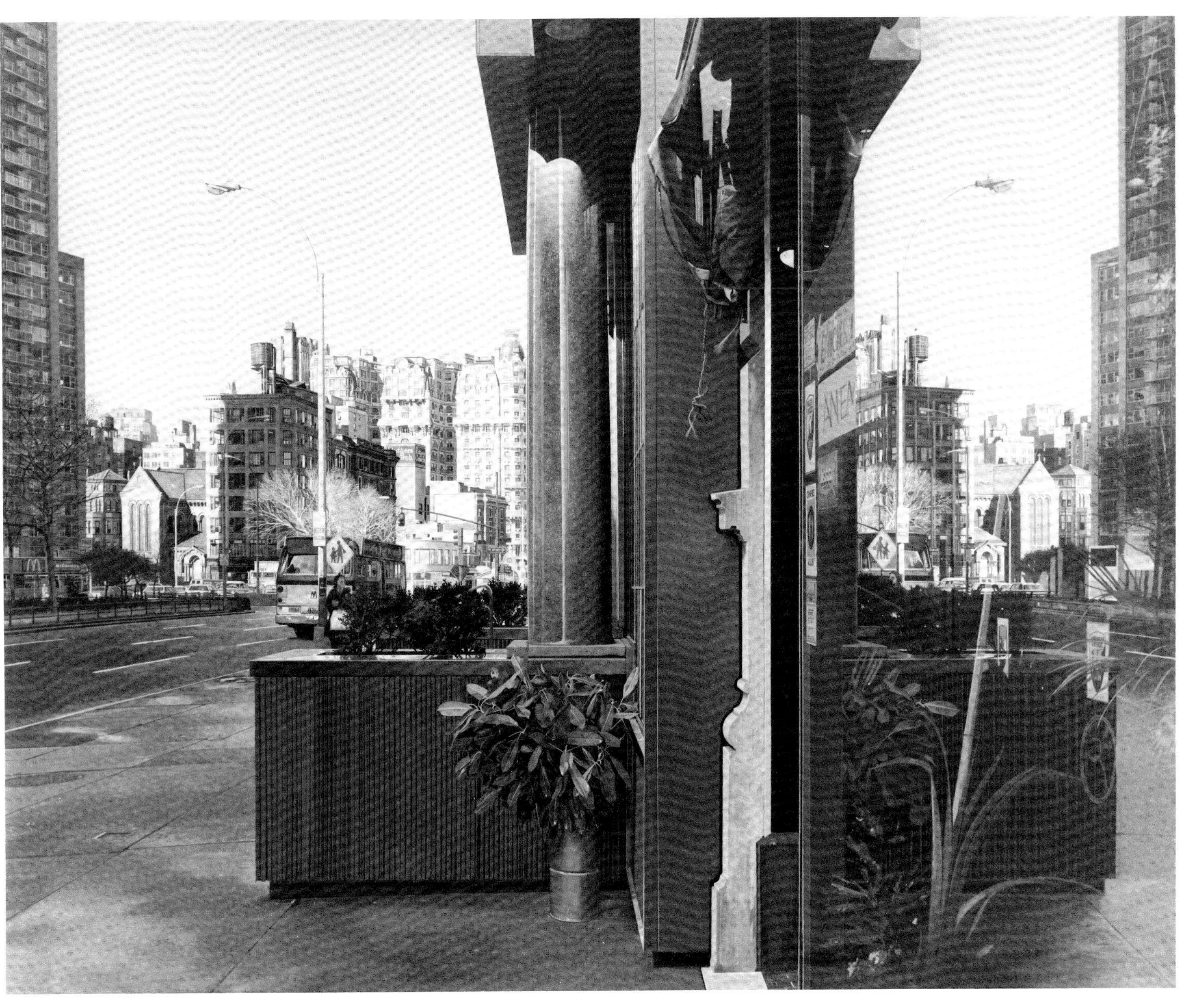

Ansonia, 1977
Oil on canvas, 48 x 60″ (121.9 x 152.4 cm)
Gift of Frances and Sydney Lewis 77.33

Eric Fischl

I think what's going on in painting now is coming out of national identities. People have withdrawn into their own histories to try to find meanings. . . . One thing I love about people like Dove and O'Keeffe and Hartley is that there is this kind of dumbness to their work, a directness. . . . Dove's are so literal and nudgy. But I respond to that. I understand it. I find that those qualities are in my own work, that there is an awkwardness to the forms or to the narrative moment.

Expressionism has been important to me, though, especially the paintings of Max Beckmann. . . . And there was Beckmann's "Departure," a work of art whose meanings were all inside it. Its references weren't art references. They were cultural, so I could hook up certain parts of the image to political violence or historical moments or religious values—all those things that belong to the general culture. . . . It's important for a painter to have the formal means to deal with his vision of the world, but it also helps if that vision is an interesting one.

Quoted in Carter Ratcliff, "Expressionism Today: An Artists' Symposium," *Art in America*, 70 (December 1982), pp. 60–61.

Born in New York, 1948
Studied at California Institute of the Arts, Valencia (B.F.A., 1972)
Lives in New York

Selected One-Artist Exhibitions

1975
Dalhousie University Art Gallery, Halifax, Nova Scotia, Canada

1976
Galerie B, Montreal

1978
Galerie B, Montreal

1980
Davis Art Gallery, University of Akron, Ohio
Edward Thorp Gallery, New York

1981
Sable Castelli Gallery, Toronto
Edward Thorp Gallery, New York

1982
Sable Castelli Gallery, Toronto
Edward Thorp Gallery, New York
University of Colorado Art Galleries, Boulder

1983
Larry Gagosian Gallery, Los Angeles

Selected Group Exhibitions

1976
Vancouver Art Gallery, British Columbia, Canada, "17 Artists: A Protean View"

1978
Kunsthalle Basel, Switzerland, "Neun Kanadisches Künstlers"

1979
P.S.1, Institute for Art and Urban Resources, Long Island City, New York, "The Big Drawing Show"

1981
California Institute of the Arts, Valencia, "Alumni Exhibition"
Nigel Greenwood Gallery, London, "Real Life Magazine Presents"
Museum of Art, Rhode Island School of Design, Providence, "New York: Visiting Artists"
Robeson Center Gallery, Rutgers University, Newark, New Jersey, "The Reality of Perception"

1982
Sidney Janis Gallery, New York, "The American Expressionist Image from Pollock to Today"
Milwaukee Art Museum, "New Figuration in America"
P.S.1, Institute for Art and Urban Resources, Long Island City, New York, "8 Critical Perspectives"
Whitney Museum of American Art, New York, "Focus on the Figure: Twenty Years"

1983
Whitney Museum of American Art, New York, "1983 Biennial Exhibition"

Selected Bibliography

Bowman, Russell. *New Figuration in America* (exhibition catalogue). Milwaukee: Milwaukee Art Museum, 1982.
Kelley, Patrick. "Eric Fischl: Paintings and Drawings," *Dialogue*, September-October 1980, pp. 46–48.
Pincus-Witten, Robert. "Entries: Snatch and Snatching," *Arts Magazine*, 56 (September 1981), pp. 88–91.
Yau, John. "How We Live: The Paintings of Robert Birmelin, Eric Fischl, and Ed Paschke," *Artforum*, 21 (April 1983), pp. 60–67.

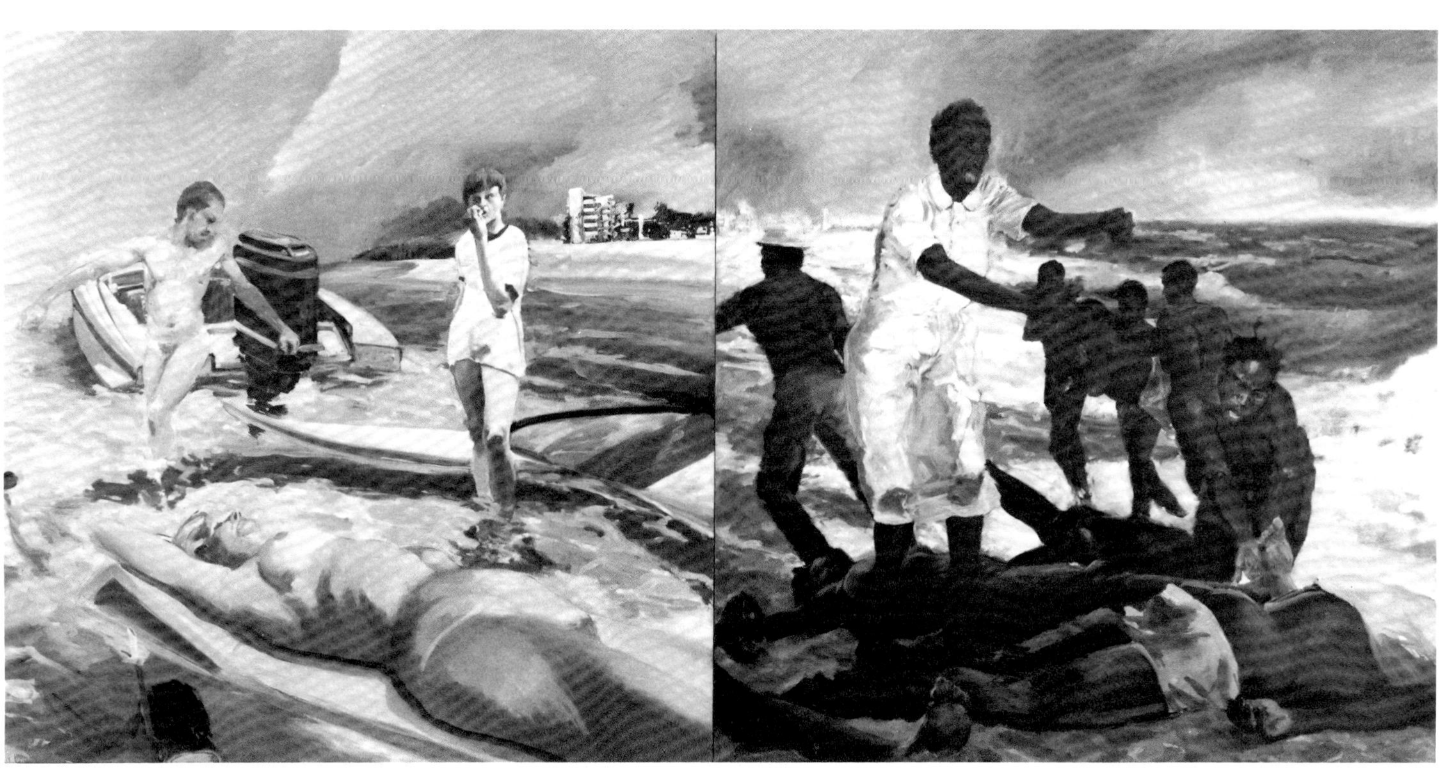

A Visit To
A Visit From
The Island, 1983
Oil on canvas: each of two panels, 84 x 84″ (213.4 x 213.4 cm); overall, 84 x 168″ (213.4 x 426.7 cm)
Purchase, with funds from the Louis and Bessie Adler Foundation, Inc., Seymour M. Klein, President 83.17 a-b

Dan Flavin

Born in New York, 1933

Studied at The New School for Social Research, New York (1956); Columbia University, New York (1957–59)

Lives in Garrison, New York

I came to these conclusions about what I had found in fluorescent light, and about what might be done with it plastically: Now the entire spatial container and its parts—wall, floor, ceiling—could support this strip of light but would not restrict its act of light except to enfold it. Regard the light and you are fascinated—inhibited from grasping its limits at each end. While the tube itself has an actual length of eight feet, its shadow, cast by the supporting pan, has none but an illusion dissolving at its ends. This waning shadow cannot really be measured without resisting its visual effect and breaking the poetry. Realizing this, I knew that the actual space of a room could be broken down and played with by planting illusions of real light (electric light) at crucial junctures in the room's composition.

Quoted in Dan Flavin, "'. . . in daylight or cool white': an autobiographical sketch," *Artforum*, 4 (December 1965), p. 24.

Selected One-Artist Exhibitions

1961
Judson Gallery, New York

1964
Green Gallery, New York

1966
Museum of Contemporary Art, Chicago
Galerie Rudolf Zwirner, Cologne

1968
Dwan Gallery, New York
Galerie Heiner Friedrich, Munich

1969
Irving Blum Gallery, Los Angeles
Galerie Konrad Fischer, Düsseldorf
National Gallery of Canada, Ottawa
The Jewish Museum, New York
Los Angeles County Museum of Art

1971
John Weber Gallery, New York

1975
Fort Worth Art Museum, Texas

1976
Portland Center for the Visual Arts, Oregon

1977
The Art Institute of Chicago
Contemporary Arts Center, Cincinnati

1978
University Art Museum, University of California, Berkeley

1979
The Hudson River Museum, Yonkers, New York (traveled)
National Gallery of Canada, Ottawa

1981
Leo Castelli Gallery, New York

1982
The Solomon R. Guggenheim Museum, New York

Selected Group Exhibitions

1960
Martha Jackson Gallery, New York, "New Forms—New Media I"

1965
Green Gallery, New York, "Flavin/Judd/Morris/Williams"

1966
The Jewish Museum, New York, "Primary Structures: Younger American and British Sculptors"

1967
Los Angeles County Museum of Art, "American Sculpture of the Sixties"

1968
Kassel, West Germany, "Documenta 4"

1969
The Metropolitan Museum of Art, New York, "New York Painting and Sculpture: 1940–1970"

1970
The Museum of Modern Art, New York, "Spaces"
Whitney Museum of American Art, New York, "1970 Annual Exhibition: Contemporary American Sculpture"

1971
Walker Art Center, Minneapolis, "Works for New Spaces"

1972
The Art Institute of Chicago, "Seventieth American Exhibition"

1975
National Collection of Fine Arts, Smithsonian Institution, Washington, D.C., "Sculpture: American Directions 1945–1975"

1976
The Museum of Modern Art, New York, "Drawing Now"
Whitney Museum of American Art, New York, "200 Years of American Sculpture"

1977
Renaissance Society, University of Chicago, "Ideas in Sculpture 1965–1977"

1979
Institute of Contemporary Art, Boston, "The Reductive Object: A Survey of the Minimalist Aesthetic in the 1960s"
The Museum of Modern Art, New York, "Contemporary Sculpture: Selections from the Collection of The Museum of Modern Art"
Whitney Museum of American Art, New York, "The Decade in Review: Selections from the 1970s"

Selected Bibliography

Belloli, Jay, and Emily S. Rauh. *Dan Flavin: Drawings, Diagrams and Prints 1972–1975* (exhibition catalogue). Fort Worth: Fort Worth Art Museum, 1977.
Flavin, Dan. *Drawn Along the Shores 1959–1976* (exhibition catalogue). Yonkers, New York: The Hudson River Museum, 1979.
Geldzahler, Henry. *New York Painting and Sculpture: 1940–1970* (exhibition catalogue). New York: The Metropolitan Museum of Art, 1969.
Smith, Brydon. *Dan Flavin Fluorescent Light Etc.* (exhibition catalogue). Ottawa: National Gallery of Canada, 1969.

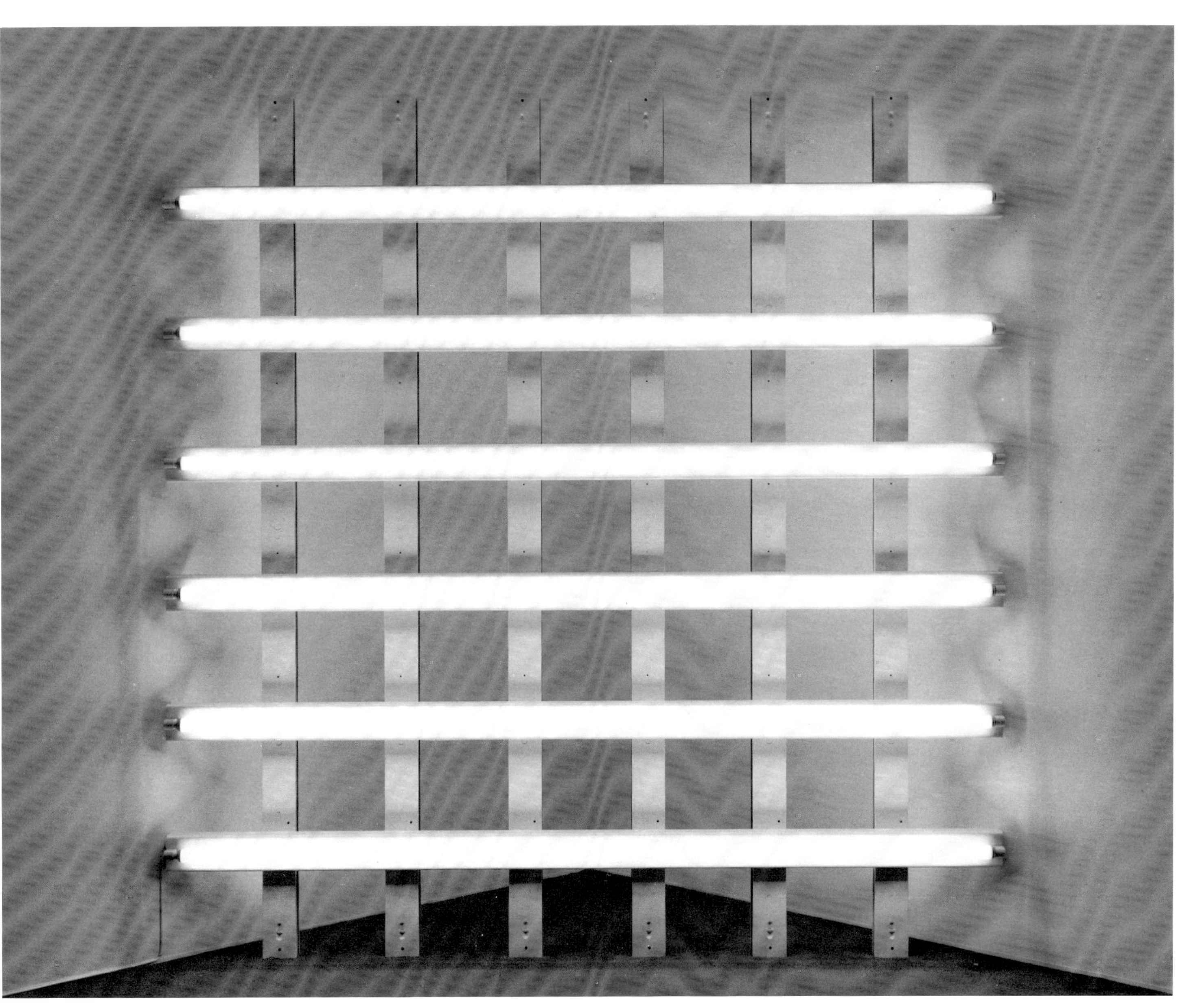

Untitled (for Robert, with fond regards), 1977
Pink, yellow, and red fluorescent light, 96 x 96″ (243.8 x 243.8 cm) across corner
Gift of the Howard and Jean Lipman Foundation, Inc. (by exchange), Peter M. Brant (by exchange), and the Louis and Bessie Adler Foundation, Inc., Seymour M. Klein, President 78.57

Jedd Garet

Born in Los Angeles, 1955
Studied at Rhode Island School of Design, Providence (1974–76); School of Visual Arts, New York (1976–77)
Lives in New York

One thing I try to avoid, even though I have a pop sensibility, is making value judgements in terms of taste. Everything is acceptable. Even though there is an underlying pop ideal, there are no specific references to modern culture, at least in terms of consumerism. . . . They look contemporary but the specifics just aren't there. Both history and the future are transformed into another, quite unique appearance without utilizing any icons of 1980. I want them to represent right now without being specific. . . . I look at almost everything. Influences come out of art history, especially clichés of art history. Instead of specific artists, movements are more important to me. I think abstractly about rococo or about classicism or about cubism. I don't try to think about a specific painting. When I think about art I blur the whole thing into a kind of general image.

Quoted in Philip Smith, "Jedd Garet and the Atomic Age," *Arts Magazine*, 55 (June 1981), pp. 159–160.

Selected One-Artist Exhibitions

1979
Robert Miller Gallery, New York
Felicity Samuel Gallery, London

1980
Galerie Bruno Bischofberger, Zurich

1981
Larry Gagosian Gallery, Los Angeles
Hallwalls Gallery, Buffalo, New York
Robert Miller Gallery, New York

1982
John Berggruen Gallery, San Francisco

1983
Robert Miller Gallery, New York

Selected Group Exhibitions

1980
Hans Strelow Gallery, Düsseldorf, "Young Americans of the Eighties"
International Pavilion, 39th Venice Biennale, Italy, "Art in the Seventies: Open '80"
Whitney Museum of American Art, New York, Downtown Branch, "Wall Reliefs"

1981
P.S. 1, Institute for Art and Urban Resources, Long Island City, New York, "New York/New Wave"
Margo Leavin Gallery, Los Angeles, "Changing Visions"
The Squibb Art Gallery, Princeton, New Jersey, "Aspects of Post-Modernism: Decorative and Narrative Art"
Whitney Museum of American Art, New York, "1981 Biennial Exhibition"
Whitney Museum of American Art, Fairfield County, Connecticut, "American Landscape: Recent Developments"

1982
Contemporary Arts Center, Cincinnati, "Dynamix" (traveled)
Milwaukee Art Museum, "New Figuration in America"
University Art Museum, University of California, Santa Barbara, "Contemporary Figuration"
Whitney Museum of American Art, New York, "Focus on the Figure: Twenty Years"
The New Museum, New York, "Extended Sensibilities"

1983
Robert Miller Gallery, New York, "Surreal"

Selected Bibliography

Cameron, Daniel J. *Extended Sensibilities* (exhibition catalogue). New York: The New Museum, 1982.
Hunter, Sam. *Aspects of Post-Modernism: Decorative and Narrative Art* (exhibition catalogue). Princeton, New Jersey: The Squibb Art Gallery, 1981.
1981 Biennial Exhibition (exhibition catalogue). Foreword by Tom Armstrong. Preface by John G. Hanhardt, Barbara Haskell, Richard Marshall, and Patterson Sims. New York: Whitney Museum of American Art, 1981.
Plous, Phyllis, and Michael Klein. *Contemporary Figuration* (exhibition catalogue). Santa Barbara, California: University Art Museum, 1982.
Smith, Philip. "Jedd Garet and the Atomic Age," *Arts Magazine*, 55 (June 1981), pp. 158–160.

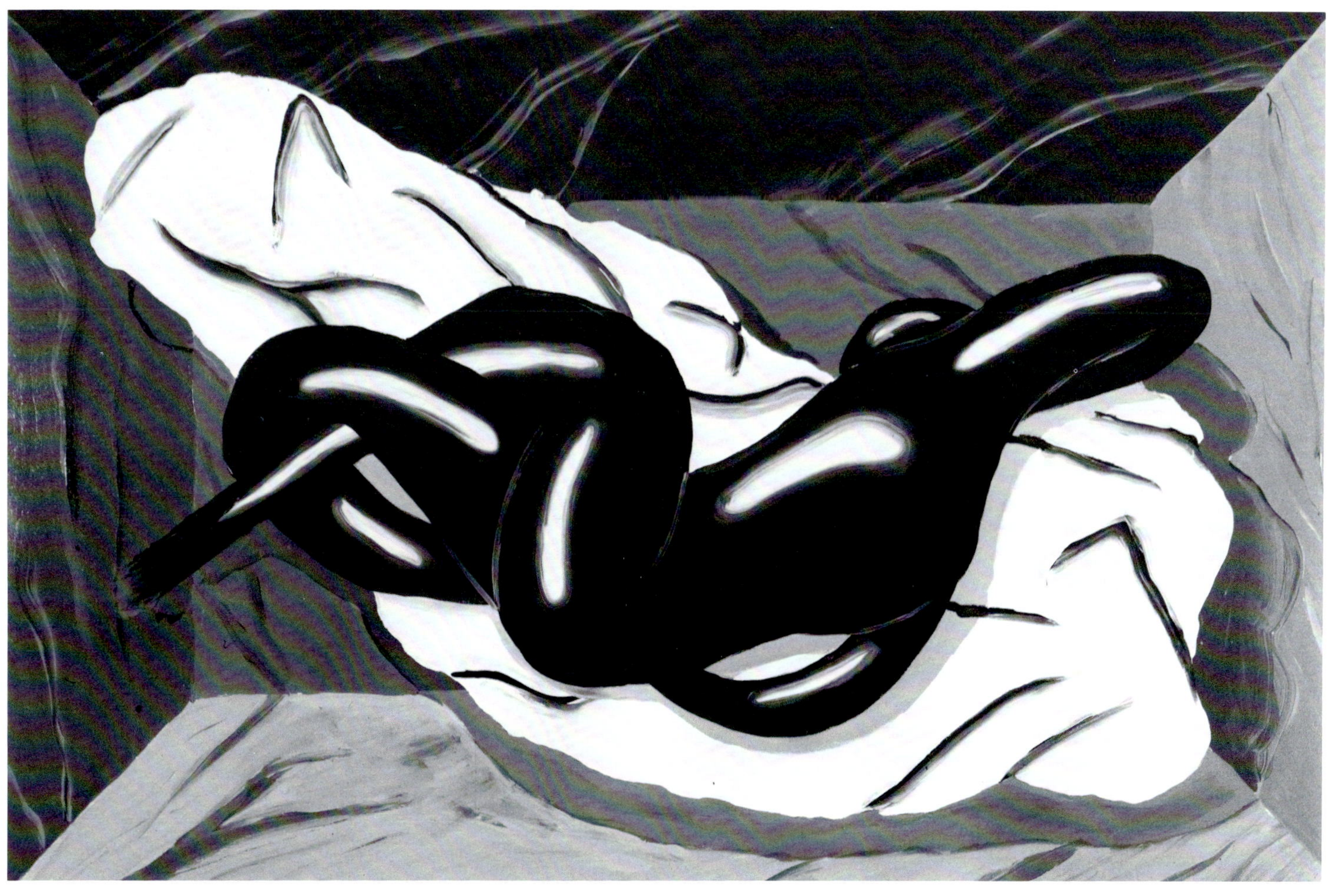

Precarious Notoriety, 1982
Acrylic on canvas, 70 x 110″ (177.8 x 279.4 cm)
Gift of Fred Mueller 83.15

Robert Graham

Born in Mexico City, 1938
Studied at San Jose State College, California (1961–63); San Francisco Art Institute (1963–64)
Lives in Venice, California

By themselves, they have no size. . . . Putting the horse next to her scaled her to it. And together, they have a size to each other; that makes it very important. The relationship is very exact. . . . I developed a passion for the horse, the way the muscles and volumes adjoined each other, the way they fit. But I wasn't interested in the cliché idea of girls and their horses. I think of it as a double portrait. . . . By the time I finished, she was very specific, just as all my statues are. . . . The only way I can make them is as effigies of a particular person, and this horse is a very particular animal. I didn't make a thoroughbred, but a specific horse.

Quoted in Grace Glueck, "Art People," *New York Times*, January 22, 1982, p. C22.

Selected One-Artist Exhibitions

1966
Nicholas Wilder Gallery, Los Angeles

1968
Kornblee Gallery, New York
Galerie Neuendorf, Hamburg

1969
Kornblee Gallery, New York
Nicholas Wilder Gallery, Los Angeles

1970
Galerie René Block, West Berlin
Whitechapel Art Gallery, London

1971
Kunstverein in Hamburg
Sonnabend Gallery, New York

1972
Dallas Museum of Fine Arts

1974
Galerie Rudolf Zwirner, Cologne
Gimpel & Hanover Gallery, Zurich

1975
Felicity Samuel Gallery, London
Texas Gallery, Houston
Nicholas Wilder Gallery, Los Angeles

1976
Gimpel Fils Gallery, London

1977
Robert Miller Gallery, New York
Nicholas Wilder Gallery, Los Angeles

1978
Los Angeles County Museum of Art
Robert Miller Gallery, New York

1979
Robert Miller Gallery, New York
Galerie Neuendorf, Hamburg

1981
Los Angeles County Museum of Art
Dorothy Rosenthal Gallery, Chicago
Visual Arts Gallery, School of Visual Arts, New York
Walker Art Center, Minneapolis (traveled)

1982
Robert Miller Gallery, New York

Selected Group Exhibitions

1966
Whitney Museum of American Art, New York, "Annual Exhibition 1966: Contemporary Sculpture and Prints"

1969
Whitney Museum of American Art, New York, "1968 Annual Exhibition: Contemporary American Sculpture"

1972
Kunstverein in Hamburg, "West Coast USA"

1976
San Francisco Museum of Modern Art, "Painting and Sculpture in California: The Modern Era" (traveled)

1979
Whitney Museum of American Art, New York, "1979 Biennial Exhibition"

1981
Los Angeles County Museum of Art, "Art in Los Angeles—The Museum as Site: Sixteen Projects"
Pennsylvania Academy of the Fine Arts, Philadelphia, "Contemporary American Realism Since 1960" (traveled)

1982
San Francisco Museum of Modern Art, "20 American Artists: Sculpture 1982"

Selected Bibliography

Barron, Stephanie. *Art in Los Angeles—The Museum as Site: Sixteen Projects* (exhibition catalogue). Los Angeles: Los Angeles County Museum of Art, 1981.

Beal, Graham W.J. *Robert Graham: Statues* (exhibition catalogue). Minneapolis: Walker Art Center, 1981.

Glazebrook, Mark. *Robert Graham* (exhibition catalogue). London: Whitechapel Art Gallery, 1970.

Goodyear, Frank H., Jr. *Contemporary American Realism Since 1960* (exhibition catalogue). Philadelphia: Pennsylvania Academy of the Fine Arts, 1981.

Hopkins, Henry T. *Painting and Sculpture in California: The Modern Era* (exhibition catalogue). San Francisco: San Francisco Museum of Modern Art, 1977.

Murdock, Robert. *Robert Graham* (exhibition catalogue). Dallas Museum of Fine Arts, 1972.

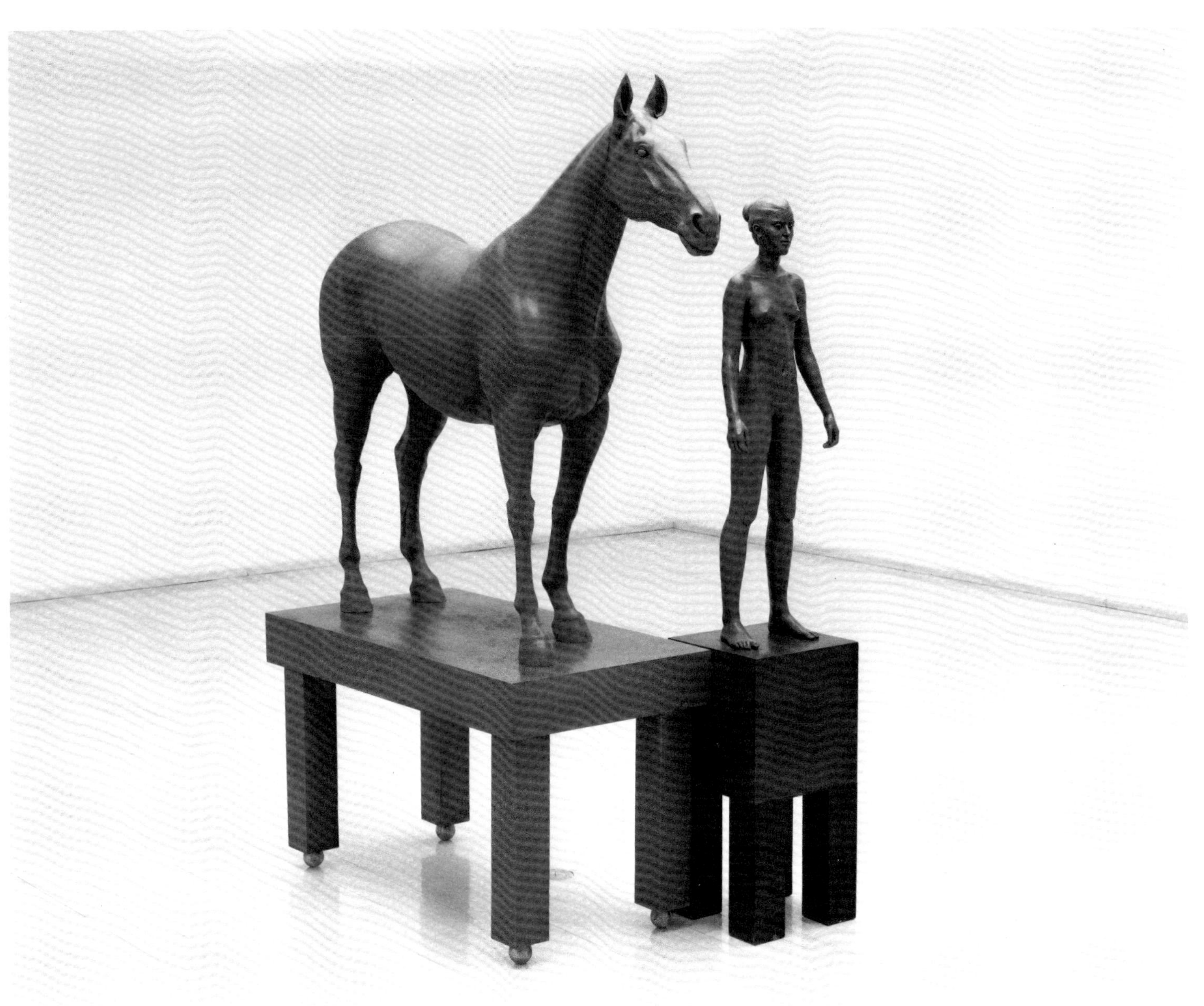

Stephanie and Spy, 1980–81
Bronze, two-part piece: Stephanie, 61 ½ x 12 x 12″ (156.2 x 30.5 x 30.5 cm); Spy, 70 ¾ x 54 x 21″ (179.7 x 137.2 x 53.3 cm)
Promised gift of Roy and Carol Doumani
P.2a-b.83

Philip Guston

I use the complete range of everything I've ever learned in painting: To be tight, to be loose, to be conscious, to be not conscious. Sometimes I make sketches of paintings, plan it out and change little in the doing of it. At others I start with nothing on my mind. Everything is possible, everything except dogma, of any kind. . . . The worst thing in the world is to make judgements. What I always try to do is to eliminate, as much as possible, the time span between thinking and doing. The ideal is to think and to do at the same second, the same split second. . . . You see, I look at my paintings, speculate about them. They baffle me, too. That's all I'm painting for.

Quoted in Norbert Lynton, *Philip Guston: Paintings 1969–80*, exhibition catalogue (London: Whitechapel Art Gallery, 1982), pp. 55–56.

Born in Montreal, 1913
Studied at Otis Art Institute, Los Angeles (1930)
Died in Woodstock, New York, 1980

Selected One-Artist Exhibitions

1945
Midtown Galleries, New York

1951
Peridot Gallery, New York

1953
Egan Gallery, New York

1956
Sidney Janis Gallery, New York

1959
Museu de Arte Moderna, São Paulo, Brazil

1962
The Solomon R. Guggenheim Museum, New York (traveled)

1966
Rose Art Museum, Brandeis University, Waltham, Massachusetts

1970
Marlborough Gallery, New York

1973
The Metropolitan Museum of Art, New York

1976
David McKee Gallery, New York

1978
Allan Frumkin Gallery, Chicago
David McKee Gallery, New York

1979
David McKee Gallery, New York

1980
San Francisco Museum of Modern Art (traveled)

1981
The Phillips Collection, Washington, D.C. (traveled)

1982
Whitechapel Art Gallery, London (traveled)

Selected Group Exhibitions

1938
Los Angeles County Museum, "Fourteenth Annual Exhibition of Painters and Sculptors"

1939
M.H. de Young Memorial Museum, San Francisco, "Frontiers of American Art: Works Progress Administration Federal Art Project"

1940
Whitney Museum of American Art, New York, "Annual Exhibition of Contemporary American Art"

1942
The Art Institute of Chicago, "The Fifty-third Annual Exhibition of American Paintings and Sculpture"

1943
The Corcoran Gallery of Art, Washington, D.C., "The Eighteenth Biennial Exhibition of Contemporary American Oil Paintings"

1947
Carnegie Institute of Technology, Pittsburgh, "Painting in the United States, 1947"

1951
The Museum of Modern Art, New York, "Abstract Painting and Sculpture in America"
Whitney Museum of American Art, New York, "Annual Exhibition of Contemporary American Sculpture, Watercolors and Drawings"

1956
The Museum of Modern Art, New York, "12 Americans"

1958
Whitney Museum of American Art, New York, "Nature in Abstraction: The Relation of Abstract Painting and Sculpture to Nature in Twentieth-Century American Art"

1961
The Solomon R. Guggenheim Museum, New York, "American Abstract Expressionists and Imagists"

1963
Whitney Museum of American Art, New York, "Annual Exhibition 1963: Contemporary American Painting"

1966
Whitney Museum of American Art, New York, "Art of the United States: 1670–1966"

1969
The Metropolitan Museum of Art, New York, "New York Painting and Sculpture: 1940–1970"

1973
National Gallery of Art, Washington, D.C., "American Art at Mid-Century"

1978
Albright-Knox Art Gallery, Buffalo, New York, "American Painting of the 1970s" (traveled)

1979
Whitney Museum of American Art, New York, "1979 Biennial Exhibition"

1981
Haus der Kunst, Munich, "Amerikanische Malerei: 1930–1980"
Royal Academy of Arts, London, "A New Spirit in Painting"

Selected Bibliography

Arnason, H. H. *Philip Guston* (exhibition catalogue). New York: The Solomon R. Guggenheim Museum, 1962.
Feld, Ross. *Philip Guston* (exhibition catalogue). San Francisco: The San Francisco Museum of Modern Art, 1980.
Feldman, Morton. *Philip Guston: The Last Works* (exhibition catalogue). Washington, D.C.: The Phillips Collection, 1981.
Lynton, Norbert. *Philip Guston: Paintings 1969–1980* (exhibition catalogue). London: Whitechapel Art Gallery, 1982.
Seitz, William. *Philip Guston: A Selective Retrospective Exhibition: 1945–1965* (exhibition catalogue). Waltham, Massachusetts: Rose Art Museum, Brandeis University, 1966.

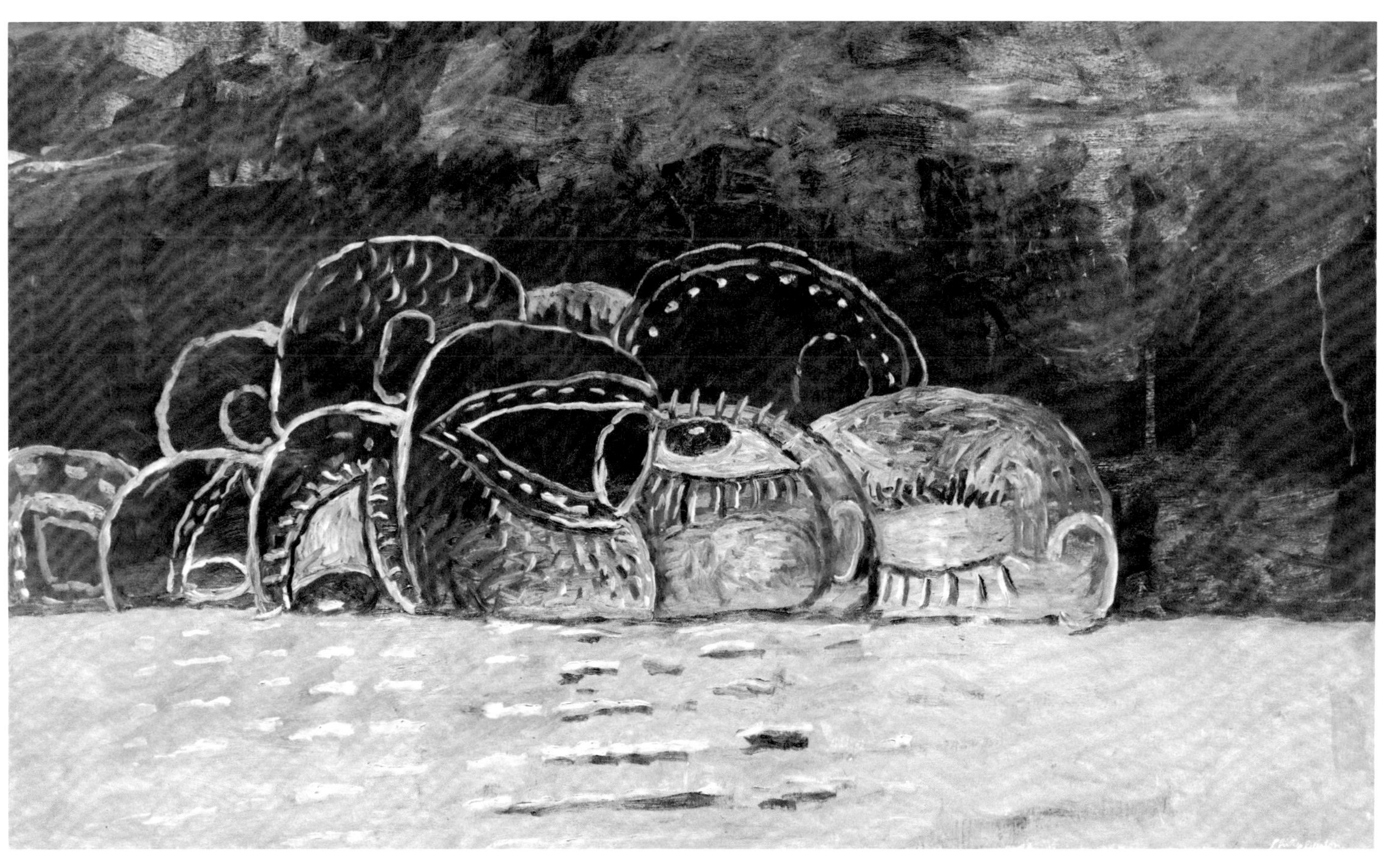

Cabal, 1977
Oil on canvas, 68 x 116″ (172.7 x 294.6 cm)
50th Anniversary Gift of Mr. and Mrs. Raymond J. Learsy 81.38

Al Held

Born in New York, 1928
Studied at the Art Students League of New York (1948–49); Académie de la Grande Chaumière, Paris (1950)
Lives in New York City and Boiceville, New York

I never make a drawing for a painting. I use the drawings to think out a lot of the problems. . . . There's no strategy or plan. The imagery grows and grows. . . . There are some basic geometric configurations, but I don't know the scale of them, I don't know their relationships, I don't know their sequence, I don't know their number, I don't know anything about them except those are the things that exist. It's an alphabet that I then juggle around.

Quoted in Paul Cummings, "Interview: Al Held Talks with Paul Cummings," *Drawing* (July–August 1980), pp. 34–37.

Selected One-Artist Exhibitions

1952
Gallery Eight, Paris

1959
Poindexter Gallery, New York

1962
Poindexter Gallery, New York

1965
Andre Emmerich Gallery, New York

1966
Stedelijk Museum, Amsterdam

1968
The Corcoran Gallery of Art, Washington, D.C.
San Francisco Museum of Art

1970
Andre Emmerich Gallery, New York

1973
Andre Emmerich Gallery, New York

1974
Whitney Museum of American Art, New York

1975
Andre Emmerich Gallery, New York
Jared Sable Gallery, Toronto, Canada

1977
Galerie Roger d'Amecourt, Paris
Galerie Andre Emmerich, Zurich

1978
Institute of Contemporary Art, Boston

1979
Andre Emmerich Gallery, New York

1980
Robert Miller Gallery, New York

1982
Andre Emmerich Gallery, New York
Robert Miller Gallery, New York
Juda Rowan Gallery, London

Selected Group Exhibitions

1958
Spoleto, Italy, "Festival of Two Worlds"

1962
Whitney Museum of American Art, New York, "Geometric Abstraction in America"
Los Angeles County Museum of Art, "Post Painterly Abstraction" (traveled)

1964
Whitney Museum of American Art, New York, "Annual Exhibition 1964: Contemporary American Sculpture"

1965
Whitney Museum of American Art, New York, "1965 Annual Exhibition: Contemporary American Painting"

1966
The Solomon R. Guggenheim Museum, New York, "Systematic Paintings"

1967
Whitney Museum of American Art, New York, "1967 Annual Exhibition of Contemporary Painting"

1968
Kassel, West Germany, "Documenta 4"

1972
Whitney Museum of American Art, New York, "1972 Annual Exhibition: Contemporary American Painting"

1973
Whitney Museum of American Art, New York, "1973 Biennial Exhibition: Contemporary American Art"

1975
The Corcoran Gallery of Art, Washington, D.C., "34th Biennial of Contemporary American Painting"

1976
Whitney Museum of American Art, New York, Downtown Branch, "Surface, Edge and Color"

1977
Museum of Contemporary Art, Chicago, "A View of a Decade"
New York State Museum, Albany, "New York: The State of Art"

1980
The Brooklyn Museum, New York, "American Drawing in Black and White: 1970–80"

1981
Haus der Kunst, Munich, "Amerikanische Malerei: 1930–1980"

1982
Washburn Gallery, New York, "American Artists Abroad 1900–1950"

Selected Bibliography

Forge, Andrew. *Al Held: New Paintings* (exhibition catalogue). New York: Andre Emmerich Gallery, 1977.
Green, Eleanor. *Al Held* (exhibition catalogue). San Francisco: San Francisco Museum of Art, 1968.
Sandler, Irving. *Al Held 1959–1961* (exhibition catalogue). New York: Robert Miller Gallery, 1980.
———. *Al Held: Paintings from the Years 1954–1959* (exhibition catalogue). New York: Robert Miller Gallery, 1982.
Tucker, Marcia. *Al Held* (exhibition catalogue). New York: Whitney Museum of American Art, 1974.

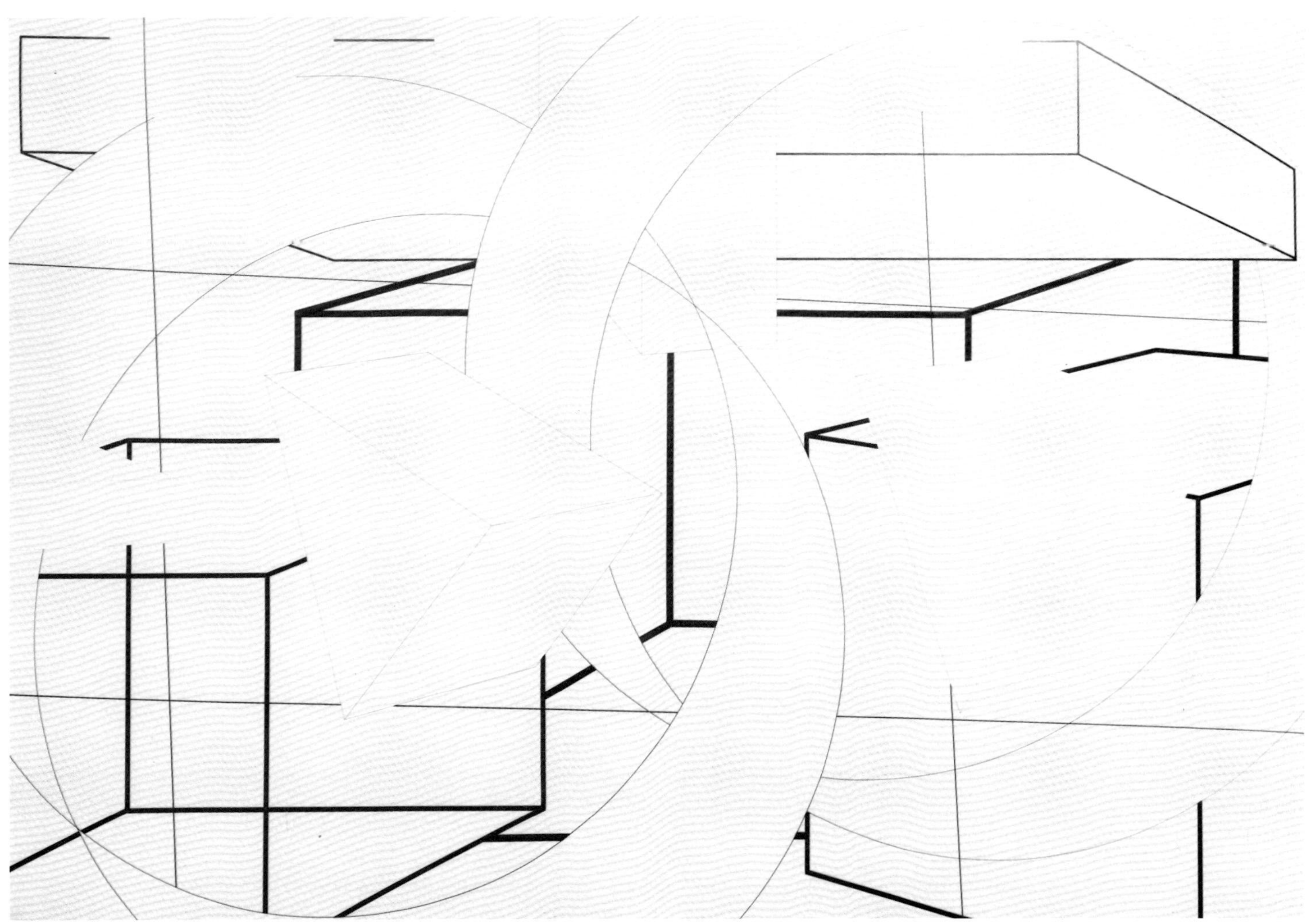

South Southwest, 1973
Synthetic polymer on canvas, 96 x 144″ (243.8 x 365.8 cm)
Purchase 73.65

Bryan Hunt

Born in Terre Haute, Indiana, 1947
Studied at the University of South Florida, Tampa (1966–68); Otis Art Institute, Los Angeles (B.F.A., 1971); Whitney Museum of American Art Independent Study Program, New York (1972)
Lives in New York

Minimal sculpture was really a foundation for me. I like the idea of having a simplified shape, one that can be understood easily, and yet suggests geometric or even mathematical properties. . . . A waterfall is, on the one hand, just a quantity of falling water, but it becomes interesting to me when I abstract and recreate in sculptural terms my conceptual knowledge of it. . . . I don't think I'm as much interested in manipulating the idea of what a waterfall is, as much as broadening the idea of sculpture, or creating my own statement out of the sculpture. I do a lot of looking for images or situations, but I look also for interrelating ideas that can lead to a new piece. . . . I'm not trying to get at the essence of waterfall. I don't think that's sculpturally possible. I'm only interested in a dynamic and a form and the way they connect. I'm always thinking in terms of threads and connections.

Quoted in Linda Shearer, *Young American Artists: 1978 Exxon National Exhibition*, exhibition catalogue (New York: The Solomon R. Guggenheim Museum, 1978), pp. 32–35.

Selected One-Artist Exhibitions

1974
The Clocktower, Institute for Art and Urban Resources, New York
Jack Glenn Gallery, Corona del Mar, California

1976
Daniel Weinberg Gallery, San Francisco

1977
Blum/Helman Gallery, New York

1978
Blum/Helman Gallery, New York
Greenberg Gallery, St. Louis
Daniel Weinberg Gallery, San Francisco

1979
Blum/Helman Gallery, New York
Galerie Bruno Bischofberger, Zurich
Bernard Jacobson Gallery, London

1980
Margo Leavin Gallery, Los Angeles

1981
Akron Art Museum, Ohio
Galerie Hans Strelow, Düsseldorf

1983
Blum/Helman Gallery, New York

Selected Group Exhibitions

1976
Portland Center for the Visual Arts, Oregon, "Via Los Angeles"

1978
The Solomon R. Guggenheim Museum, New York, "Young American Artists"
Stedelijk Museum, Amsterdam, "Made by Sculptors"
Vassar College Art Gallery, Poughkeepsie, New York, "Hunt, Jenney, Lane, Shapiro, Rothenberg"

1979
The Museum of Modern Art, New York, "Contemporary Sculpture: Selections from the Collection of The Museum of Modern Art"
Renaissance Society, University of Chicago, "Visionary Images"
Whitney Museum of American Art, New York, "1979 Biennial Exhibition"

1980
San Francisco Museum of Modern Art, "Twenty American Artists"
University Gallery, University of Massachusetts, Amherst, "Sculpture on the Wall—Relief Sculpture of the 70s"

1981
Akron Art Museum, Ohio, "The Image in American Painting and Sculpture: 1950–1980"
Whitney Museum of American Art, New York, "1981 Biennial Exhibition"

1982
The Art Institute of Chicago, "74th American Exhibition"

Selected Bibliography

Hopkins, Henry T. *Twenty American Artists* (exhibition catalogue). San Francisco: San Francisco Museum of Modern Art, 1980.

The Image in American Painting and Sculpture: 1950–1980 (exhibition catalogue). Preface by Michael Danoff. Introduction by Carolyn Kinder Carr. Akron, Ohio: Akron Art Museum, 1981.

McShine, Kynaston. *Contemporary Sculpture: Selections from the Collection of The Museum of Modern Art* (exhibition catalogue). New York: The Museum of Modern Art, 1979.

Morrin, Peter, ed. *Hunt, Jenney, Lane, Rothenberg, Shapiro* (exhibition catalogue). Poughkeepsie, New York: Vassar College Art Gallery, 1978.

1981 Biennial Exhibition (exhibition catalogue). Foreword by Tom Armstrong. Preface by John G. Hanhardt, Barbara Haskell, Richard Marshall, and Patterson Sims. New York: Whitney Museum of American Art, 1981.

Rorimer, Anne. *74th American Exhibition* (exhibition catalogue). Chicago: The Art Institute of Chicago, 1982.

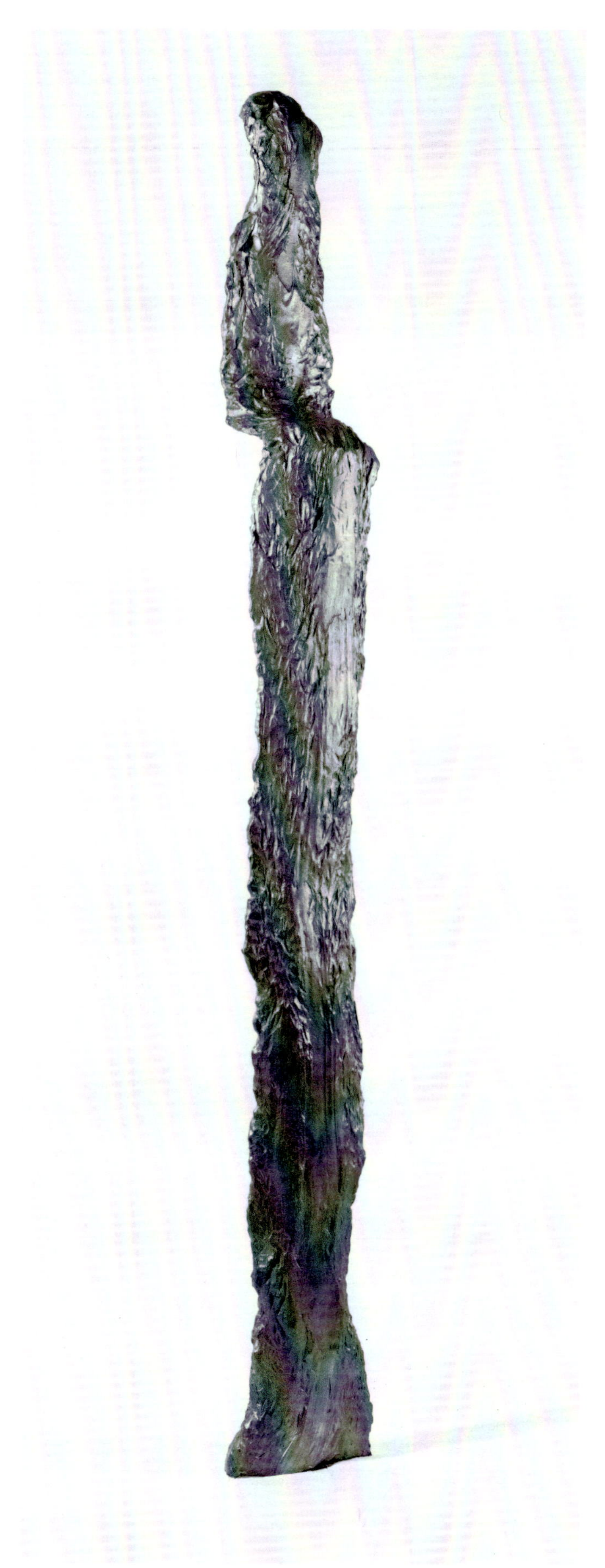

Step Falls, 1978
Bronze, 114 x 12 x 12″ (289.6 x 30.5 x 30.5 cm)
Gift of Edward R. Downe, Jr. 78.68

Neil Jenney

I realized that I could not avoid idealizing each painting. There is actually no distinction between abstraction and realism. All realism must resolve abstract complications because you are involved with space and balance and harmony. Realism is a higher art form because it is more precise—it not only solves all abstract concerns, but it involves precise philosophical interpretation. . . . Realism is illusionism and all illusionistic painting requires frames. At first, I did not realize the crucial factor that frames can play in the illusion. The frame is the foreground and it simply enhances the illusion—it makes the illusion more functional. I designed and built the frames to suit the paintings—I realized that the frames would enhance the illusion and be a perfect place to put the title.

Quoted in Richard Marshall, *New Image Painting*, exhibition catalogue (New York: Whitney Museum of American Art, 1978), p. 44.

Born in Torrington, Connecticut, 1945
Studied at Massachusetts College of Art, Boston (1964–65)
Lives in New York

Selected One-Artist Exhibitions

1968
Galerie Rudolf Zwirner, Cologne

1970
Richard Bellamy/Noah Goldowsky Gallery, New York
David Whitney Gallery, New York

1973
98 Greene Street Loft, New York

1974
Blum/Helman Gallery, New York

1975
Wadsworth Atheneum, Hartford, Connecticut

1981
University Art Museum, University of California, Berkeley (traveled)

Selected Group Exhibitions

1969
Andrew Dickson White Museum, Cornell University, Ithaca, New York, "Earth Art"
Kunsthalle Bern, Switzerland, "When Attitudes Become Form"
Whitney Museum of American Art, New York, "Anti-Illusion: Procedures/Materials"

1972
Kassel, West Germany, "Documenta 5"

1973
Whitney Museum of American Art, New York, "1973 Biennial Exhibition: Contemporary American Art"

1974
Art Museum of South Texas, Corpus Christi, "Eight Artists" (traveled)

1977
New York State Museum, Albany, "New York: The State of Art"
P.S. 1, Institute for Art and Urban Resources, Long Island City, New York, "A Painting Show"

1978
Albright-Knox Art Gallery, Buffalo, New York, "American Painting of the 1970s" (traveled)
The New Museum, New York, "Bad Painting"
Vassar College Art Gallery, Poughkeepsie, New York, "Hunt, Jenney, Lane, Rothenberg, Shapiro"
Whitney Museum of American Art, New York, "New Image Painting"

1980
International Pavilion, 39th Venice Biennale, Italy, "Art in the Seventies: Open '80"

1981
Whitney Museum of American Art, New York, "1981 Biennial Exhibition"

Selected Bibliography

Cathcart, Linda L. *American Painting of the 1970s* (exhibition catalogue). Buffalo, New York: Albright-Knox Art Gallery, 1978.
Marshall, Richard. *New Image Painting* (exhibition catalogue). New York: Whitney Museum of American Art, 1978.
Rosenthal, Mark. *Neil Jenney: Painting and Sculpture 1967–1980* (exhibition catalogue). Berkeley: University Art Museum, University of California, 1981.
Tucker, Marcia. *Bad Painting* (exhibition catalogue). New York: The New Museum, 1978.
Tucker, Marcia, and James Monte. *Anti-Illusion: Procedures/Materials* (exhibition catalogue). New York: Whitney Museum of American Art, 1969.

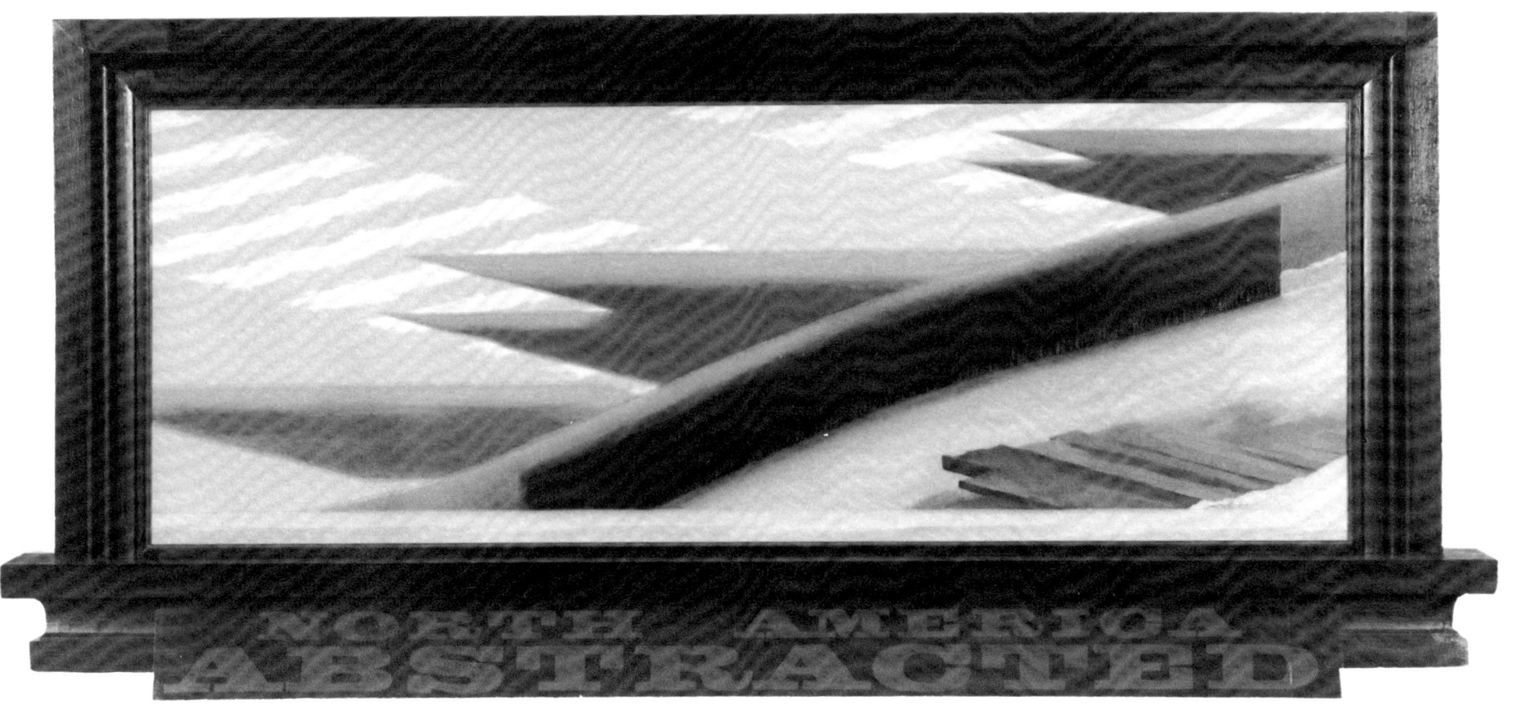

North America Abstracted, 1978–80
Oil on wood, 38 x 85¼ x 5¼″ (96.5 x 216.5 x 13.3 cm)
Purchase, with funds from the Burroughs Wellcome Purchase Fund, the Wilfred P. and Rose Cohen Purchase Fund, and the Painting and Sculpture Committee 83.19

Bill Jensen

Born in Minneapolis, 1945
Studied at the University of Minnesota, Minneapolis (B.F.A., 1968; M.F.A., 1970)
Lives in New York

My paintings are not really abstract. I never heard of Pollock or de Kooning talking about their paintings as being purely abstract, completely devoid of any glimpses, of signs, of things they imagined they saw, things they really saw, things they felt. I see too many things. I walk down the street. I see an airplane or a shoe. I saw things when I was a little kid. They all come back when I'm working. . . . I like paintings that are very serene. . . . Sometimes I have to push them further. I know that when I go further, something else is going to happen. That awesomeness begins. I start searching for the awesome quality in the painting. It can become very frightening, very threatening.

Quoted in Hayden Herrera, "Expressionism Today: An Artists' Symposium," *Art in America*, 70 (December 1982), p. 73.

Selected One-Artist Exhibitions

1973
Fischbach Gallery, New York

1974
The Gallery of July and August, Woodstock, New York

1975
Fischbach Gallery, New York

1980
Washburn Gallery, New York

1981
Washburn Gallery, New York

1982
Washburn Gallery, New York

Selected Group Exhibitions

1976
Lowe Art Gallery, Syracuse University, New York, "Contemporary Painting"
P.S. 1, Institute for Art and Urban Resources, Long Island City, New York, "Rooms"

1978
The New Museum, New York, "Double Take"

1979
Grey Art Gallery and Study Center, New York University, "American Painting: The Eighties"

1980
Neuberger Museum, State University of New York, College at Purchase, "Seven Artists"

1981
University Art Museum, University of California, Santa Barbara, "Contemporary Drawings: In Search of an Image"
Whitney Museum of American Art, New York, "1981 Biennial Exhibition"

Selected Bibliography

Heiss, Alanna, ed. *Rooms* (exhibition catalogue). New York: Institute for Art and Urban Resources, 1977.

1981 Biennial Exhibition (exhibition catalogue). Foreword by Tom Armstrong. Preface by John G. Hanhardt, Barbara Haskell, Richard Marshall, and Patterson Sims. New York: Whitney Museum of American Art, 1981.

Plous, Phyllis. *Contemporary Drawings: In Search of an Image* (exhibition catalogue). Santa Barbara, California: University Art Museum, University of California, 1981.

Rose, Barbara. *American Painting: The Eighties* (exhibition catalogue). New York: Vista Press, 1979.

Smith, Roberta. "Bill Jensen's Abstractions," *Art in America*, 68 (November), pp. 109–113.

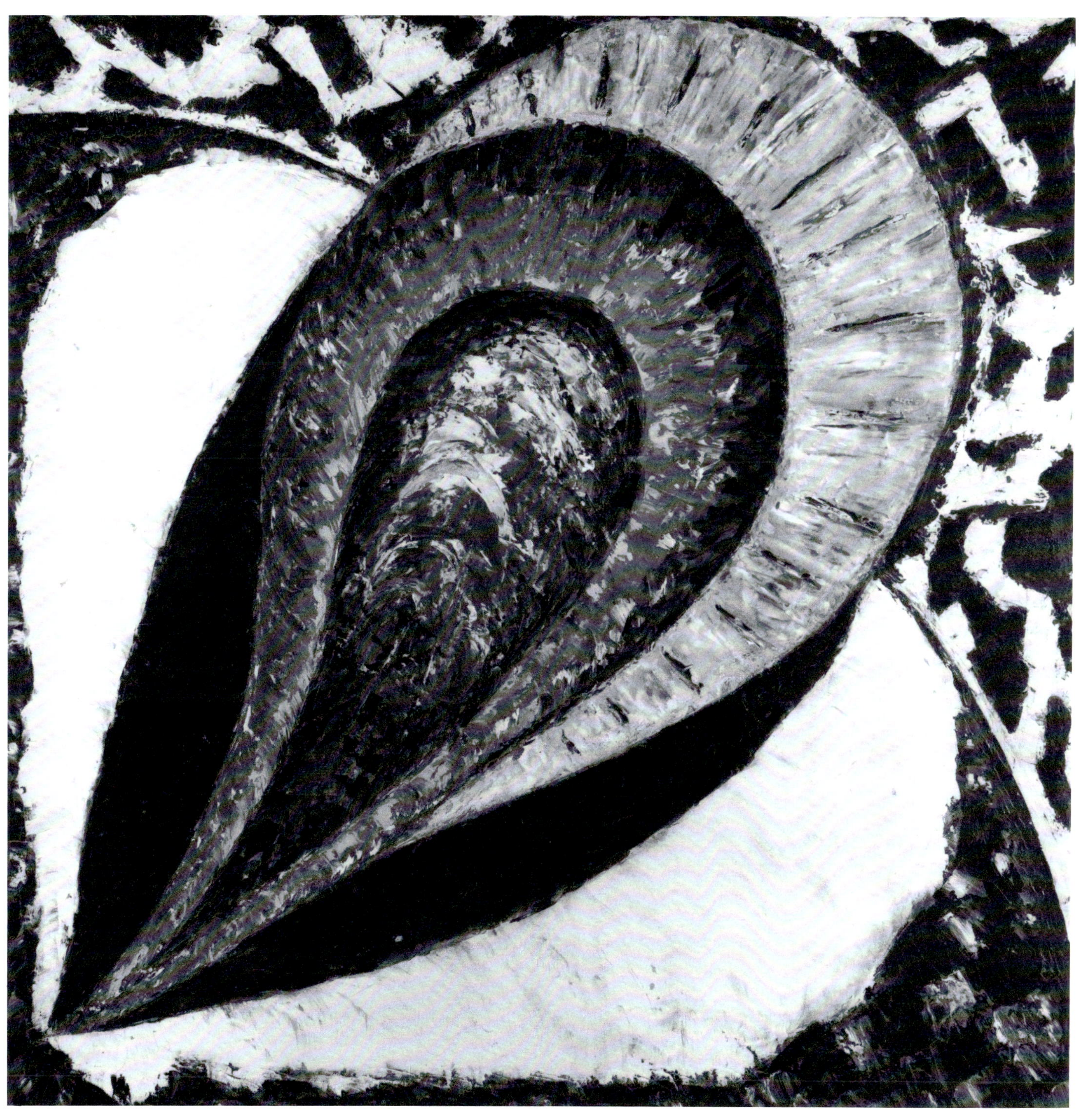

The Meadow, 1980–81
Oil on linen, 22 x 22″ (55.9 x 55.9 cm)
Purchase, with funds from the Wilfred P. and Rose Cohen Purchase Fund 81.36

Alex Katz

Born in Brooklyn, New York, 1927
Studied at the Cooper Union Art School, New York (1946–49); Skowhegan School of Painting and Sculpture, Maine (1949–50)
Lives in New York

Generally, I do people I know, and people I find interesting enough to want to spend a couple of hours with. . . . I have a weakness for painting beautiful people. I enjoy painting beautiful people of all kinds. It's a sensual thing—it has something to do with the person, but it's not necessarily falling in love with your sitter. . . . When you're involved in portrait painting, it's an optical thing, an optical form. And the form is the end, almost—it's a real challenge to paint in that form. Any digression from the form—like painting from a photograph—would be to me an intellectual compromise of that form. The portrait form is where the challenge is.

Quoted in Gerrit Henry, "The Artist and the Face: A Modern American Sampling," *Art in America*, 63 (February 1975), p. 37.

Selected One-Artist Exhibitions

1954
Roko Gallery, New York

1959
Tanager Gallery, New York

1960
Stable Gallery, New York

1964
Fischbach Gallery, New York

1966
David Stuart Gallery, Los Angeles

1967
Fischbach Gallery, New York

1969
Phyllis Kind Gallery, Chicago

1971
Utah Museum of Fine Arts, University of Utah, Salt Lake City (traveled)

1973
Marlborough Gallery, New York

1974
Whitney Museum of American Art, New York (traveled)

1975
Marlborough Fine Art Gallery, London

1976
Marlborough Gallery, New York

1977
Fresno Arts Center, California (traveled)

1978
Marlborough Gallery, New York
Rose Art Museum, Brandeis University, Waltham, Massachusetts

1979
Brooke Alexander Gallery, New York

1980
The Queens Museum, Flushing, New York

1981
Robert Miller Gallery, New York
Portland Center for the Visual Arts, Oregon

1982
Marlborough Gallery, New York

Selected Group Exhibitions

1955
Stable Gallery, New York, "New York Artists Annual"

1960
Whitney Museum of American Art, New York, "Young Americans 1960" (traveled)

1964
The Museum of Modern Art, New York, "Landscapes by Eight Americans" (traveled)
Wadsworth Atheneum, Hartford, Connecticut, "Contemporary Realism in Figure and Landscape"

1965
The Museum of Modern Art, New York, "American Collage" (traveled)

1967
Whitney Museum of American Art, New York, "Annual Exhibition of Contemporary Painting"

1969
Milwaukee Art Center, "Aspects of a New Realism" (traveled)

1970
The Art Museum, Princeton University, New Jersey, "American Art Since 1960"

1971
The Corcoran Gallery of Art, Washington, D.C., "Thirty-Second Biennial Exhibition of Contemporary American Painting"

1972
Whitney Museum of American Art, New York, "1972 Annual Exhibition: Contemporary American Painting"

1973
Seattle Art Museum, "American Art: Third Quarter Century"

1975
Museum of Fine Arts, St. Petersburg, Florida, "Figure as Form: American Painting 1930–1975" (traveled)

1977
New York State Museum, Albany, "New York: The State of Art"

1979
The Museum of Modern Art, New York, "Printed Art: A View of Two Decades"
Whitney Museum of American Art, New York, "1979 Biennial Exhibition"

1981
Pennsylvania Academy of the Fine Arts, Philadelphia, "Contemporary American Realism Since 1960" (traveled)

1982
Whitney Museum of American Art, New York, "Focus on the Figure: Twenty Years"

Selected Bibliography

Alex Katz: Drawings, 1944–1981 (exhibition catalogue). New York: Marlborough Gallery, 1982.
Alex Katz: Recent Paintings (exhibition catalogue). New York: Marlborough Gallery, 1978.
Sandler, Irving. *Alex Katz*. New York: Harry N. Abrams, Inc., 1979.
———. *Alex Katz, 1957–1959* (exhibition catalogue). New York: Robert Miller Gallery, 1981.
Sandler, Irving, and Bill Berkson, eds. *Alex Katz*. New York: Frederick A. Praeger, 1971.
Solomon, Elke M., and Richard S. Field. *Alex Katz: Prints* (exhibition catalogue). New York: Whitney Museum of American Art, 1974.

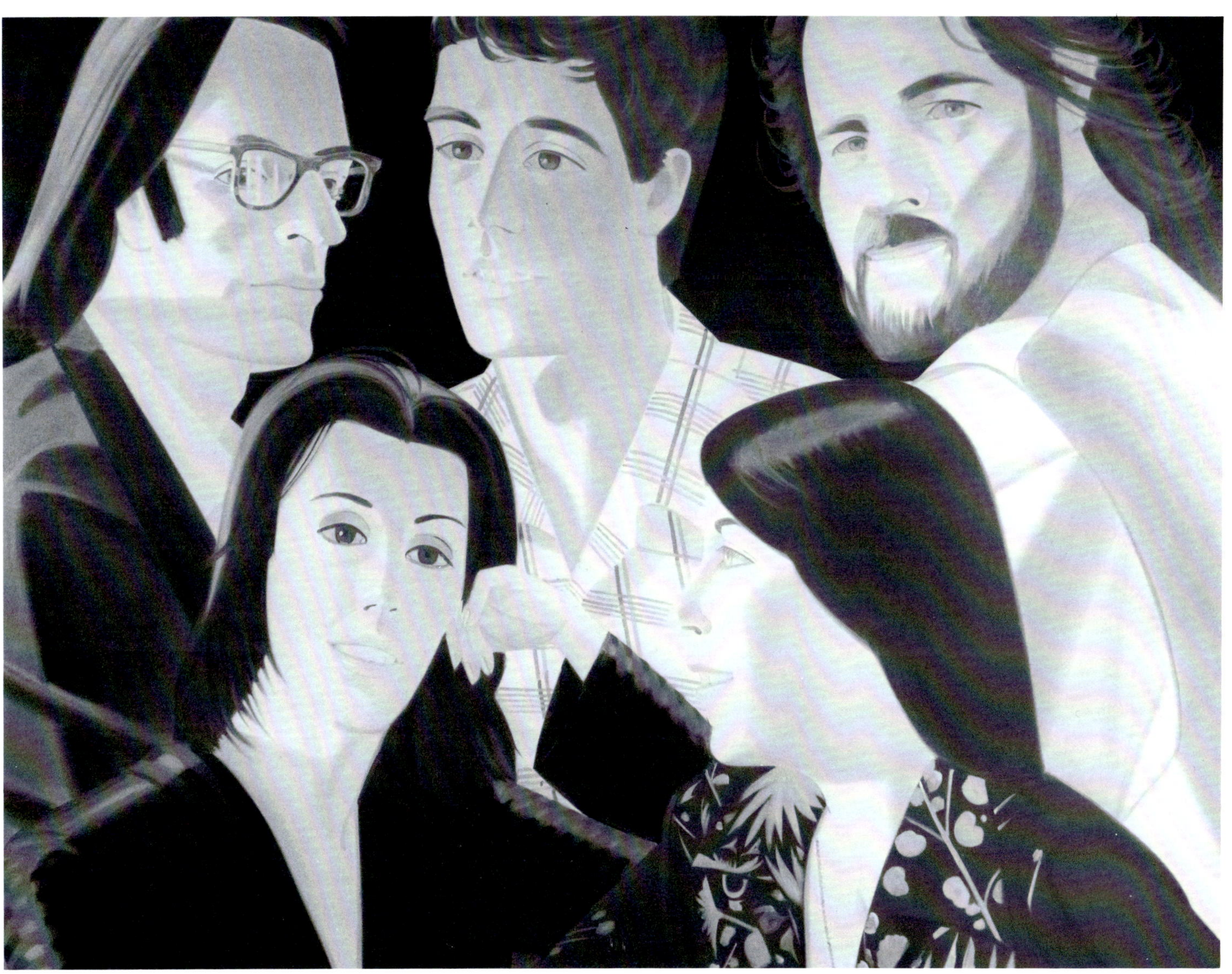

Place, 1977
Oil on canvas, 108 x 144″ (274.3 x 365.8 cm)
Gift of Frances and Sydney Lewis 78.23

Steve Keister

My work deals with the range of formal considerations: light, color, structure, texture, etc. I think of them as being inside-out paintings. . . . In this case the outer shape suggested an animalistic impulse which led to the zebra skin idea. . . . I used most of one complete hide. I took advantage of the natural symmetry of the animal, while disregarding the natural position of the parts in relation to each other. For example, the mane from the zebra's neck is relocated to the rear underside of the sculpture.

Quoted from statement dated November 21, 1981, Artists' Files, Whitney Museum of American Art, New York.

Born in Lancaster, Pennsylvania, 1949
Studied at Tyler School of Art, Temple University, Philadelphia (B.F.A., 1970; M.F.A., 1972)
Lives in New York

Selected One-Artist Exhibitions

1977
Nancy Lurie Gallery, Chicago

1978
Pam Adler Gallery, New York

1979
Nancy Lurie Gallery, Chicago

1980
Joslyn Art Museum, Omaha
Museum of Contemporary Art, Chicago
Texas Gallery, Houston

1981
Blum/Helman Gallery, New York

1982
Larry Gagosian Gallery, Los Angeles
Blum/Helman Gallery, New York

Selected Group Exhibitions

1978
The New Museum, New York, "New Work/New York"
P.S. 1, Institute for Art and Urban Resources, Long Island City, New York, "Special Projects"

1979
Albright-Knox Art Gallery, Buffalo, New York, "Eight Sculptors"
Barbara Gladstone Gallery, New York, "Canal Street"

1980
Texas Gallery, Houston, "N.Y. Teowz"

1981
William Paterson College, Wayne, New Jersey, "Color on Structure"
Whitney Museum of American Art, New York, "1981 Biennial Exhibition"

1982
Contemporary Arts Center, Cincinnati, "Dynamix" (traveled)
Hayden Gallery, Massachusetts Institute of Technology, Cambridge, "Constructed Color"
Whitney Museum of American Art, New York, "Selected Painting and Sculpture Acquired Since 1978"

Selected Bibliography

Halbreich, Kathy. *Constructed Color* (exhibition catalogue). Cambridge, Massachusetts: Massachusetts Institute of Technology Committee on the Visual Arts, 1982.
Schultz, Douglas G. *Eight Sculptors* (exhibition catalogue). Buffalo, New York: Albright-Knox Art Gallery, 1979.
Schwartzman, Allan, and Susan Logan. *New Work/New York* (exhibition catalogue). New York: The New Museum, 1978.
Stearns, Robert. *Dynamix* (exhibition catalogue). Cincinnati: Contemporary Arts Center, 1982.

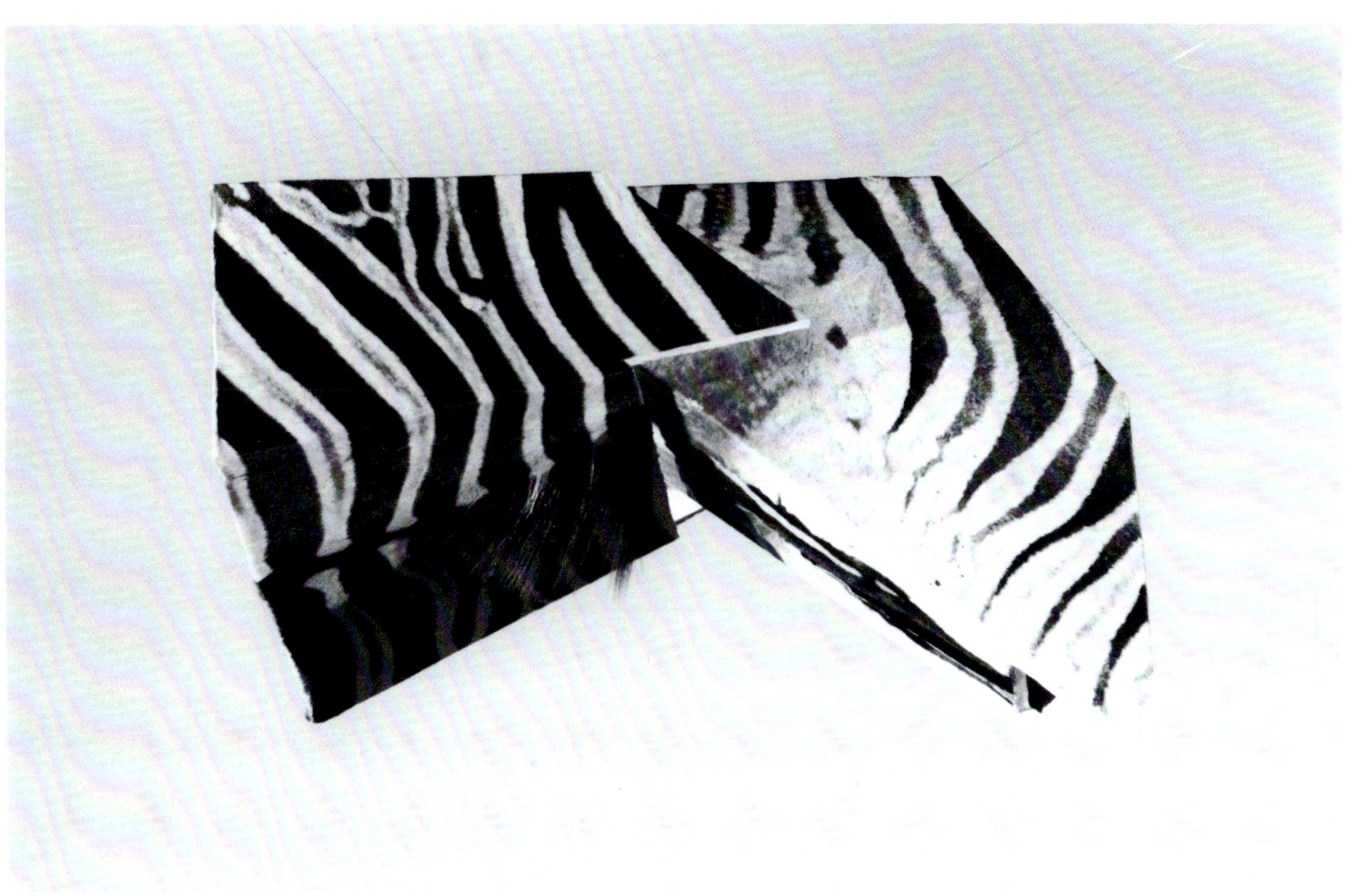

U.S.O. #68, 1981
Zebra skin and acrylic on wood, 24 x 22 x 33″
(61 x 56 x 84 cm)
Purchase, with funds from the Louis and Bessie
Adler Foundation, Inc., Seymour M. Klein,
President 81.14

Robert Kushner

Born in Pasadena, California, 1949
Studied at the University of California, San Diego (B.A., 1970)
Lives in New York

Expansiveness, flatness and all-overness is the domain of decoration. These factors define any purely decorative art. There really is no more—no statement, no meaning, no space. But what a varied realm in which to sojourn. . . . When using imagery, I want either to use decorative clichés (i.e. flowers, putti, birds) or to choose images that nearly fall out of the traditional decorative contexts (chic men and ladies, kissing, cubist faces, landscape). . . . Somewhere the issue of taste enters. I seem consistently interested in a thing's being slightly unacceptable, yet seductive, compositionally interesting. . . . When using faces or bodies I try to find ways to break up the forms into flat color areas. The body gave me a whole new range of shapes with which to work. No matter how you draw a face, some sort of expression emerges—especially if you draw very fast. . . . I want the eye to move all over the surface. No one part is a central focus. I want to engage and entertain the viewer.

Quoted in Robert Kushner, "Things I think about my work," *Flash Art*, 103 (Summer 1981), p. 40.

Selected One-Artist Exhibitions

1976
Holly Solomon Gallery, New York

1977
Philadelphia College of Art
Holly Solomon Gallery, New York

1978
Mayor Gallery, London

1979
Holly Solomon Gallery, New York
Galerie Daniel Templon, Paris

1980
Dart Gallery, Chicago

1981
Asher/Faure Gallery, Los Angeles
Galerie Bruno Bischofberger, Zurich
Akira Ikeda Gallery, Nagoya, Japan
Holly Solomon Gallery, New York

1982
American Graffiti Gallery, Amsterdam
Marconi Gallery, Milan
Holly Solomon Gallery, New York
Galerie Rudolf Zwirner, Cologne

Selected Group Exhibitions

1975
Whitney Museum of American Art, New York, "1975 Biennial Exhibition"

1977
The Museum of the American Foundation for the Arts, Miami, Florida, "Patterning and Decoration"
P.S. 1, Institute for Art and Urban Resources, Long Island City, New York, "Pattern Painting"

1978
Contemporary Arts Center, Cincinnati, "Arabesque"

1979
Albright-Knox Art Gallery, Buffalo, New York, "Patterns"
Institute of Contemporary Art, University of Pennsylvania, Philadelphia, "The Decorative Impulse" (traveled)
Los Angeles Institute of Contemporary Art, "Clothing Constructions"

1980
Contemporary Arts Center, Cincinnati, "From Performances: Costumes and Other Works"
Mannheimer Kunstverein, Mannheim, West Germany, "Dekor" (traveled)
Neue Galerie, Sammlung Ludwig, Aachen, West Germany, "Les Nouveaux Fauves—Die Neuen Wilden"
United States Pavilion, 39th Venice Biennale, Italy, "Drawings: The Pluralist Decade" (traveled)

1981
The New Museum, New York, "Alternatives in Retrospect: An Historical Overview, 1969–1975"
The Squibb Gallery, Princeton, New Jersey, "Aspects of Post-Modernism: Decorative and Narrative Art"
Whitney Museum of American Art, New York, "1981 Biennial Exhibition"

1982
Madison Art Center, Wisconsin, "New American Graphics"
Whitney Museum of American Art, New York, "Focus on the Figure: Twenty Years"

Selected Bibliography

Armstrong, Richard. *Dreams and Visions* (exhibition catalogue). New York: Holly Solomon Gallery, 1981.
Kardon, Janet. *The Decorative Impulse* (exhibition catalogue). Philadelphia: Institute of Contemporary Art, University of Pennsylvania, 1979.
Kardon, Janet, ed. *Drawings: The Pluralist Decade* (exhibition catalogue). Texts by John Hallmark Neff, Rosalind Krauss, Richard Lorber, Edit deAk, John Perreault, Howard N. Fox, and Nancy Foote. Philadelphia: Institute of Contemporary Art, University of Pennsylvania, 1980.
Meyer, Ruth K. *Arabesque* (exhibition catalogue). Cincinnati: Contemporary Arts Center, 1978.
1981 Biennial Exhibition (exhibition catalogue). Foreword by Tom Armstrong. Preface by John G. Hanhardt, Barbara Haskell, Richard Marshall, and Patterson Sims. New York: Whitney Museum of American Art, 1981.
Schlemmer, Raman. *Dekor* (exhibition catalogue). Oxford, England: Museum of Modern Art, 1980.

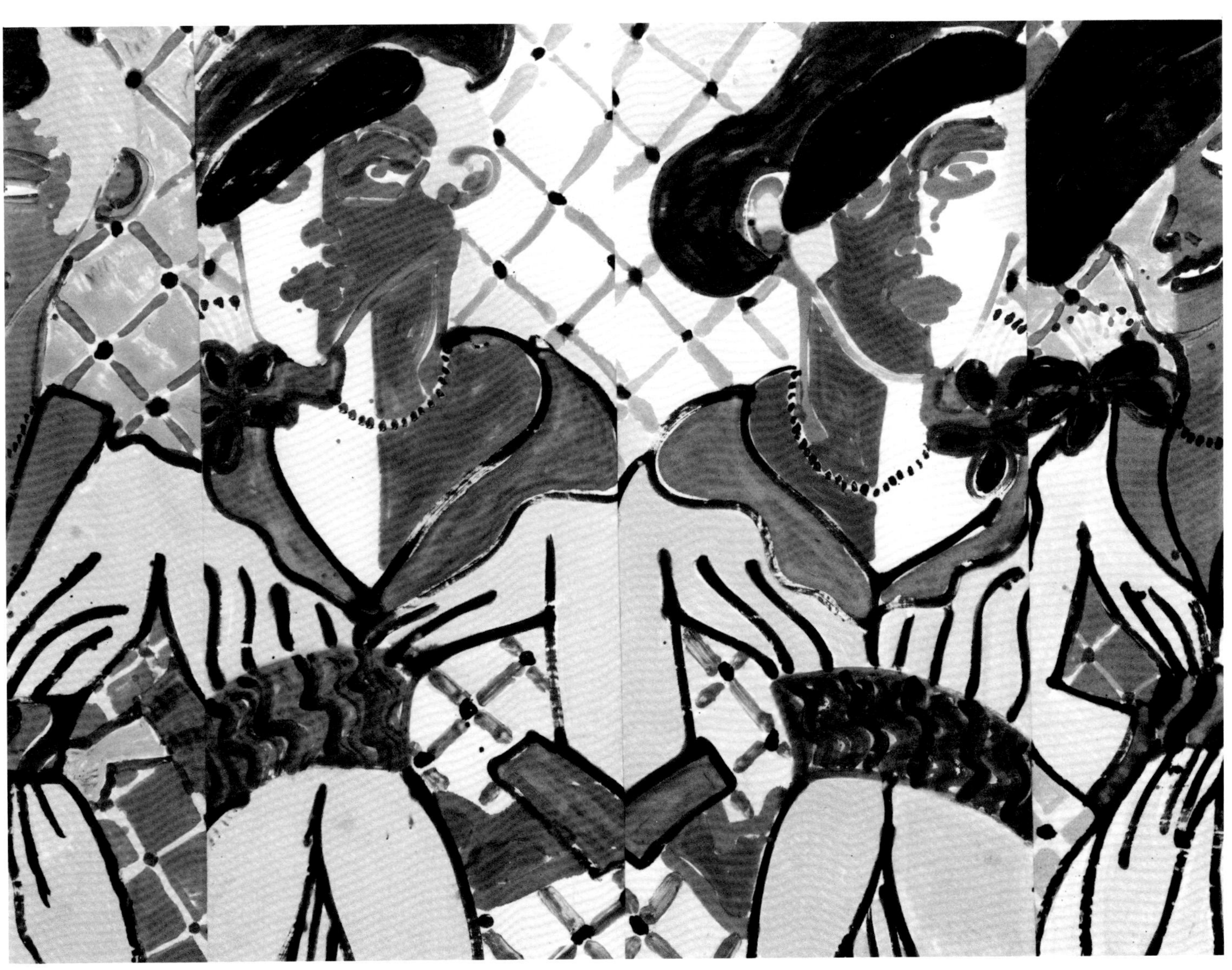

French Tart, 1978
Acrylic on cotton, 96 x 127⅜″ (243.8 x 323.6 cm)
Gift of Holly and Horace Solomon 83.16

Lois Lane

Born in Philadelphia, 1948
Studied at Philadelphia College of Art (B.F.A., 1969); Yale University Summer School of Art and Music, Norfolk, Connecticut (M.F.A., 1971)
Lives in New York

When I am working on a painting or drawing, I feel most satisfied when I can look at the work and sense that the image is isolated, that it leaves me with some sense of isolation, that it is not entirely clear to me, and that this will be shared experience. . . . The canvases are usually split. In the earlier white paintings, this split was forms running vertically up the center. The split then developed into two plant forms, one on either side of the canvas, deflected by the closeness in color value, furthered by one's inability to focus on both forms at once. The split then became the clothesline. At first I used a central image with things hanging on the line or perched on top. Later came the clothesline with forms attached to the far left and far right—a double split.

Quoted in Richard Marshall, *New Image Painting*, exhibition catalogue (New York: Whitney Museum of American Art, 1978), p. 44.

Selected One-Artist Exhibitions

1974
Artists Space, New York

1977
Willard Gallery, New York

1979
Willard Gallery, New York

1980
Akron Art Museum, Ohio
Greenberg Gallery, St. Louis
Willard Gallery, New York

1982
Nigel Greenwood Gallery, London
Pennsylvania Academy of the Fine Arts, Philadelphia

1983
Willard Gallery, New York

Selected Group Exhibitions

1977
P.S. 1, Institute for Art and Urban Resources, Long Island City, New York, "A Painting Show"

1978
Vassar College Art Gallery, Poughkeepsie, New York, "Hunt, Jenney, Lane, Rothenberg, Shapiro"
Whitney Museum of American Art, New York, "New Image Painting"

1979
Grey Art Gallery and Study Center, New York University, "American Painting: The Eighties"
Neuberger Museum, State University of New York, College at Purchase, "Ten Artists/Artists Space"
Whitney Museum of American Art, New York, "1979 Biennial Exhibition"

1980
Hallwalls Gallery, Buffalo, New York, "Emblems and Paint"
Indianapolis Museum of Art, "Painting and Sculpture Today 1980"

1981
Akron Art Museum, Ohio, "The Image in American Painting and Sculpture: 1950–1980"
Institute of Contemporary Art of the Virginia Museum, "A New Bestiary: Animal Imagery in Contemporary Art"

Selected Bibliography

Carr, Carolyn Kinder. *The Image in American Painting and Sculpture: 1950–1980* (exhibition catalogue). Akron, Ohio: Akron Art Museum, 1981.
Marshall, Richard. *New Image Painting* (exhibition catalogue). New York: Whitney Museum of American Art, 1978.
Morrin, Peter, ed. *Hunt, Jenney, Lane, Rothenberg, Shapiro* (exhibition catalogue). Poughkeepsie, New York: Vassar College Art Gallery, 1978.
Rose, Barbara. *American Painting: The Eighties* (exhibition catalogue). New York: Vista Press, 1979.
Sandler, Irving, and Helene Winer. *Ten Artists/Artists Space* (exhibition catalogue). Purchase, New York: Neuberger Museum, State University of New York, 1979.

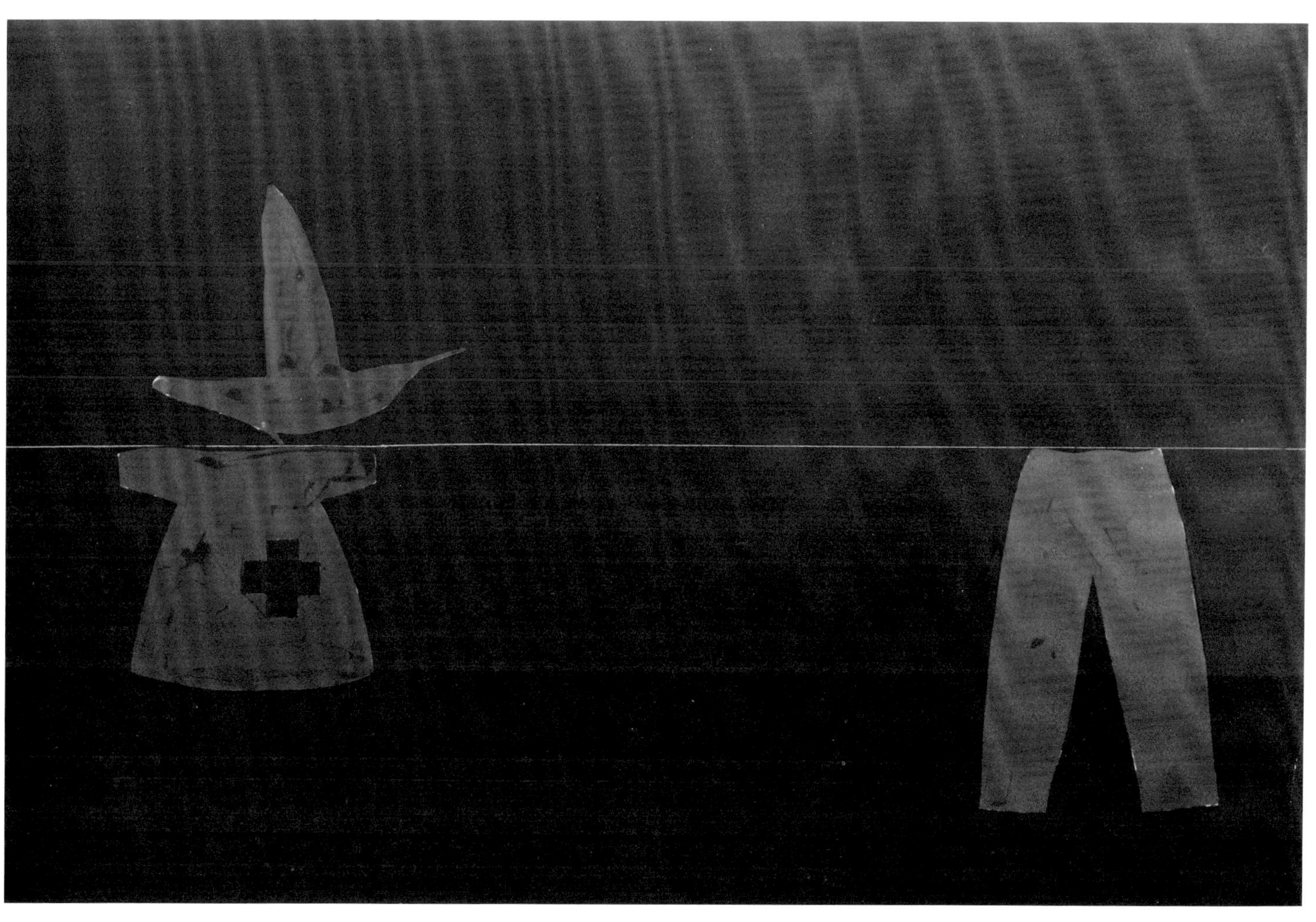

Untitled, 1978
Oil on canvas, 75 x 120″ (190.5 x 304.8 cm)
Gift of Mr. and Mrs. Rudolph B. Schulhof 79.3

Barry Le Va

Like the sculpture, drawings become activated upon mental and visual interaction between an observer and the work. Since only limited information is presented, a deciphering process similar to what occurs within the sculpture is necessary. Since traces of a logical procedure are obscured and cannot be reconstructed in a step by step manner, information which is visually absent can only be gathered by attempting to form logical connections between locations of one set of elements and another set. The eye slides back and forth across the surface, focusing on specific regions, making connections between elements which are not related to each other in the logical procedure of the drawing. . . . The constant adjustment of assumptions about underlying procedure eventually calls perceptual judgment into question, often causing misreadings. At certain points while deciphering, the observer seems to be on the verge of grasping underlying logic, only to find it slipping away.

Quoted in Ragland Watkins, *Bochner, Le Va, Rockburne, Tuttle*, exhibition catalogue (Cincinnati: Contemporary Arts Center, 1975), p. 24.

Born in Long Beach, California, 1941
Studied at Otis Art Institute, Los Angeles (M.F.A., 1967)
Lives in New York

Selected One-Artist Exhibitions

1969
The Minneapolis Institute of Arts

1970
Galerie Ricke, Cologne

1971
Nigel Greenwood Gallery, London

1972
Bykert Gallery, New York
Galerie Ricke, Cologne

1973
Bykert Gallery, New York
Galerie Rudolf Zwirner, Cologne

1974
Bykert Gallery, New York
Texas Gallery, Houston
Galleria Toselli, Milan

1975
Musée d'Art Contemporain, Montreal
Daniel Weinberg Gallery, San Francisco

1976
Claire Copley Gallery, Los Angeles
Galerie Sonnabend, Paris
Sonnabend Gallery, New York

1977
Wright State University, Dayton, Ohio

1978
Sonnabend Gallery, New York

1979
The New Museum, New York
Sonnabend Gallery, New York

1980
Los Angeles Institute of Contemporary Art

1981
Sonnabend Gallery, New York

1982
P.S. 1, Institute for Art and Urban Resources, Long Island City, New York
Daniel Weinberg Gallery, San Francisco

Selected Group Exhibitions

1969
San Francisco Art Institute, "Conception—Perception"
Whitney Museum of American Art, New York, "Anti-Illusion: Procedures/Materials"

1970
Allen Memorial Art Museum, Oberlin College, Ohio, "Art in the Mind"
The Museum of Modern Art, New York, "Information"

1972
Kassel, West Germany, "Documenta 5"

1973
Whitney Museum of American Art, New York, "American Drawings: 1963–1973"

1974
The Art Institute of Chicago, "71st American Exhibition"

1975
The Baltimore Museum of Art, "Fourteen Artists"
Contemporary Arts Center, Cincinnati, "Bochner, Le Va, Rockburne, Tuttle"

1976
Whitney Museum of American Art, New York, "200 Years of American Sculpture"

1977
Renaissance Society, University of Chicago, "Installations"
Whitney Museum of American Art, New York, "1977 Biennial Exhibition"

1979
Aldrich Museum of Contemporary Art, Ridgefield, Connecticut, "Traditions in Minimalism"

1980
United States Pavilion, 39th Venice Biennale, Italy, "Drawings: The Pluralist Decade" (traveled)

1981
Louisiana Museum, Humlebaek, Denmark, "Drawing Distinctions: Tendencies in American Drawings of the Seventies" (traveled)

1982
Kassel, West Germany, "Documenta 7"
Whitney Museum of American Art, New York, "Abstract Drawings, 1911–1981"

Selected Bibliography

Bear, Liza, and Willoughby Sharp. "Discussions with Barry Le Va," *Avalanche*, 3 (Fall 1971), pp. 62–75.

Bochner, Le Va, Rockburne, Tuttle (exhibition catalogue). Essays by Carroll Dunham, Naomi Spector, Dorothy Alexander, and Barry Le Va. Cincinnati: Contemporary Arts Center, 1975.

McShine, Kynaston L., ed. *Information* (exhibition catalogue). New York: The Museum of Modern Art, 1970.

Tucker, Marcia. *Barry Le Va: Four Consecutive Installations and Drawings 1967–1978* (exhibition catalogue). New York: The New Museum, 1979.

Tucker, Marcia, and James Monte. *Anti-Illusion: Procedures/Materials* (exhibition catalogue). New York: Whitney Museum of American Art, 1969.

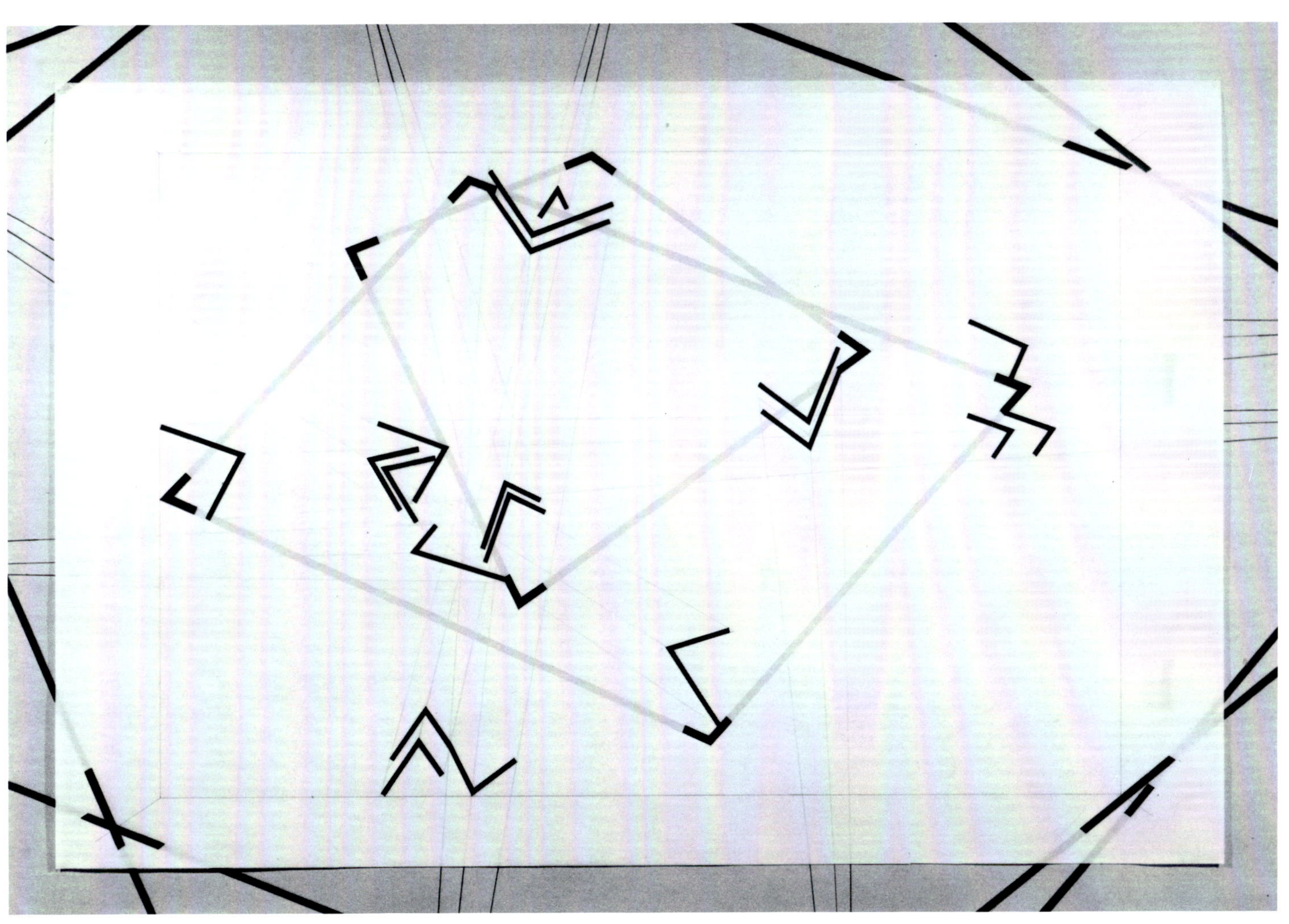

Installation Study for Any Rectangular Space: Accumulated Vision: Boundaries Designated (Configurations Indicated), 1977
Ink and pencil on construction paper and tracing paper, 42 x 62½″ (106.7 x 158.8 cm)
The List Purchase Fund 77.71

Sol LeWitt

Born in Hartford, Connecticut, 1928
Studied at Syracuse University, New York (B.F.A., 1949)
Lives in New York

I wanted to do a work of art that was as two-dimensional as possible. It seems more natural to work directly on walls than to make a construction, to work on that, and then put construction on the wall. The physical properties of the wall: height, length, color, material, and architectural conditions and intrusions, are a necessary part of the wall drawings. Different kinds of walls make for different kinds of drawings. Imperfections on the wall surface are occasionally apparent after the drawing is completed. These should be considered a part of the wall drawing. . . . The wall drawing is a permanent installation, until destroyed. Once something is done, it cannot be undone.

Quoted in Sol LeWitt, "Wall Drawings," in Gregory Battcock, "Documentation in Conceptual Art," *Arts Magazine*, 44 (April 1970), p. 45.

Selected One-Artist Exhibitions

1965
Daniels Gallery, New York

1966
Dwan Gallery, New York

1968
Galerie Konrad Fischer, Düsseldorf

1969
Museum Haus Lange, Krefeld, West Germany

1970
Art & Project, Amsterdam
Pasadena Art Museum, California

1971
John Weber Gallery, New York

1972
Hayden Gallery, Massachusetts Institute of Technology, Cambridge

1973
Museum of Modern Art, Oxford, England
Portland Center for the Visual Arts, Oregon

1974
New York Cultural Center, New York
Stedelijk Museum, Amsterdam
John Weber Gallery, New York

1975
Kunsthalle Basel, Switzerland

1977
University Gallery, University of Massachusetts, Amherst

1978
The Museum of Modern Art, New York (traveled)

1979
Galerie Konrad Fischer, Düsseldorf
InK. (Halle für Internationale Neue Kunst), Zurich
Margo Leavin Gallery, Los Angeles

1980
Texas Gallery, Houston
John Weber Gallery, New York

1981
Yvon Lambert Gallery, Paris
Wadsworth Atheneum, Hartford, Connecticut

Selected Group Exhibitions

1966
Finch College Museum of Art, New York, "Art in Process"
The Jewish Museum, New York, "Primary Structures: Younger American and British Sculptors"

1967
Los Angeles County Museum of Art, "American Sculpture of the Sixties"

1968
The Museum of Modern Art, New York, "Art of the Real" (traveled)

1969
Kunsthalle Bern, Switzerland, "When Attitudes Become Form" (traveled)

1970
The Museum of Modern Art, New York, "Information"

1972
Institute of Contemporary Art, University of Pennsylvania, Philadelphia, "Grids"

1974
The Art Museum, Princeton University, New Jersey, "Line as Language: Six Artists Draw"

1976
The Museum of Modern Art, New York, "American Art Since 1945: From the Collection of The Museum of Modern Art" (traveled)
Whitney Museum of American Art, New York, "200 Years of American Sculpture"

1977
The Brooklyn Museum, New York, "Prints in Series"
Kassel, West Germany, "Documenta 6"

1979
Aldrich Museum of Contemporary Art, Ridgefield, Connecticut, "The Minimal Tradition"
The Art Institute of Chicago, "73rd American Exhibition"
Whitney Museum of American Art, New York, "1979 Biennial Exhibition"

1982
The Art Institute of Chicago, "74th American Exhibition"
Kassel, West Germany, "Documenta 7"

Selected Bibliography

Krauss, Rosalind. *Line as Language: Six Artists Draw* (exhibition catalogue). Princeton, New Jersey: The Art Museum, Princeton University, 1974.
LeWitt, Sol. *Incomplete Open Cubes* (exhibition catalogue). New York: John Weber Gallery, 1974.
Lippard, Lucy R. *Grids* (exhibition catalogue). Philadelphia: Institute of Contemporary Art, University of Pennsylvania, 1972.
McShine, Kynaston. *Primary Structures: Younger American and British Sculptors* (exhibition catalogue). New York: The Jewish Museum, 1966.
Rose, Bernice. *Drawing Now* (exhibition catalogue). New York: The Museum of Modern Art, 1976.
Rose, Bernice. *Sol LeWitt* (exhibition catalogue). New York: The Museum of Modern Art, 1978.
200 Years of American Sculpture (exhibition catalogue). Essays by Tom Armstrong, Wayne Craven, Norman Feder, Barbara Haskell, Rosalind Krauss, Daniel Robbins, and Marcia Tucker. New York: Whitney Museum of American Art, 1976.
Wember, Paul. *Sol LeWitt: Sculptures and Wall Drawings* (exhibition catalogue). Krefeld, West Germany: Museum Haus Lange, 1969.

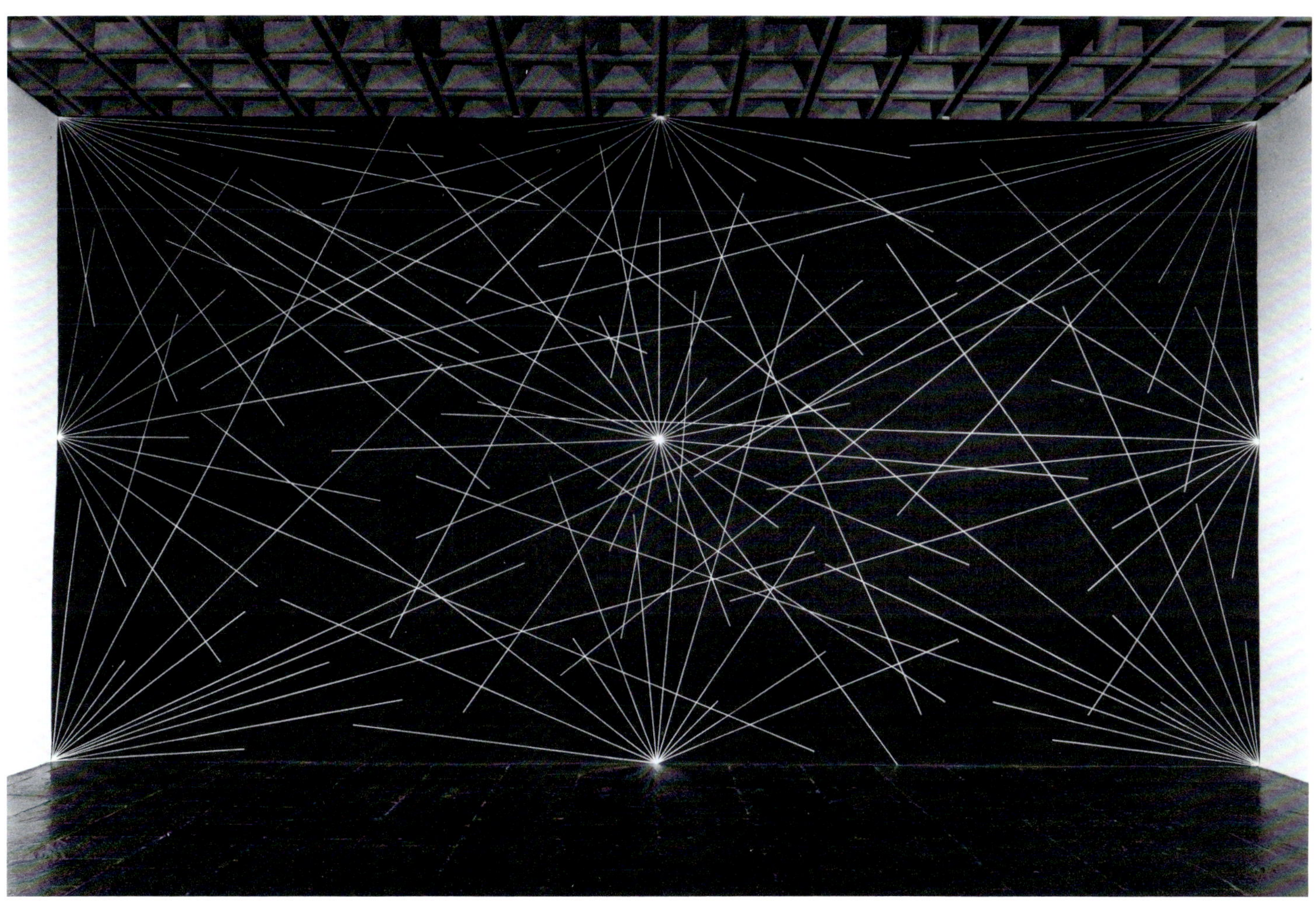

Lines to Points on a Grid: 24 Lines from the Center of the Wall, 12 Lines from the Midpoint of Each Side, 12 Lines from Each Corner, 1976
Six-inch pencil grid and white crayon lines on black painted wall, dimensions variable
Gift of the Gilman Foundation, Inc. 78.1

Kim MacConnel

Born in Oklahoma City, 1946
Studied at the University of California, San Diego (B.A., 1969; M.F.A., 1972)
Lives in Encinitas, California

My paintings are my reactions to things, things that I like or not: spiritual, material and materialistic things. I try to utilize some of my spiritual beliefs in conjunction or in contradiction with other images. . . . In the piece called "Formidable," I put together chemistry bottles, men in top hats, sort of a cliché symbol for the "capitalista," and the hand which is called "Abhaya Mundra," Shiva's right hand in his dance of the universe, which looks like he is signalling "okay" and it means that the universe is simply going where it's going regardless of what we do. That's the mixture of the spiritual, the symbolic and the material—contradictions that correspond. This, to me, expresses some hope for the world.

Quoted in Robert Becker, "Kim MacConnel," *Interview*, 12 (June 1982), p. 54.

One-Artist Exhibitions

1975
Holly Solomon Gallery, New York

1976
La Jolla Museum of Contemporary Art, California
Holly Solomon Gallery, New York

1978
Galerie Bruno Bischofberger, Zurich
Mayor Gallery, London
University Art Museum, University of California, Berkeley

1979
Dart Gallery, Chicago
Holly Solomon Gallery, New York

1980
Holly Solomon Gallery, New York

1982
James Corcoran Gallery, Los Angeles
Holly Solomon Gallery, New York

Selected Group Exhibitions

1971
University of California, San Diego, "Decorations"

1975
Whitney Museum of American Art, New York, "1975 Biennial Exhibition"

1977
Institute of Contemporary Art, University of Pennsylvania, Philadelphia, "Improbable Furniture"
P.S. 1, Institute for Art and Urban Resources, Long Island City, New York, "Pattern Painting"

1978
Contemporary Arts Center, Cincinnati, "Arabesque"

1979
Hirshhorn Museum and Sculpture Garden, Smithsonian Institution, Washington, D.C., "Directions"
Institute of Contemporary Art, University of Pennsylvania, Philadelphia, "The Decorative Impulse" (traveled)
Whitney Museum of American Art, New York, "1979 Biennial Exhibition"

1980
Mannheimer Kunstverein, Mannheim, West Germany, "Dekor" (traveled)

1981
Whitney Museum of American Art, New York, "1981 Biennial Exhibition"

Selected Bibliography

Armstrong, Richard. *Collection Applied Design* (exhibition catalogue). La Jolla, California: La Jolla Museum of Contemporary Art, 1976.
Becker, Robert. "Kim MacConnel," *Interview*, 12 (June 1982), pp. 52–54.
Fox, Howard N. *Directions* (exhibition catalogue). Washington, D.C.: Smithsonian Institution Press, for the Hirshhorn Museum and Sculpture Garden, 1979.
Kardon, Janet. *The Decorative Impulse* (exhibition catalogue). Philadelphia: Institute of Contemporary Art, University of Pennsylvania, 1979.
Meyer, Ruth K. *Arabesque* (exhibition catalogue). Cincinnati: Contemporary Arts Center, 1978.

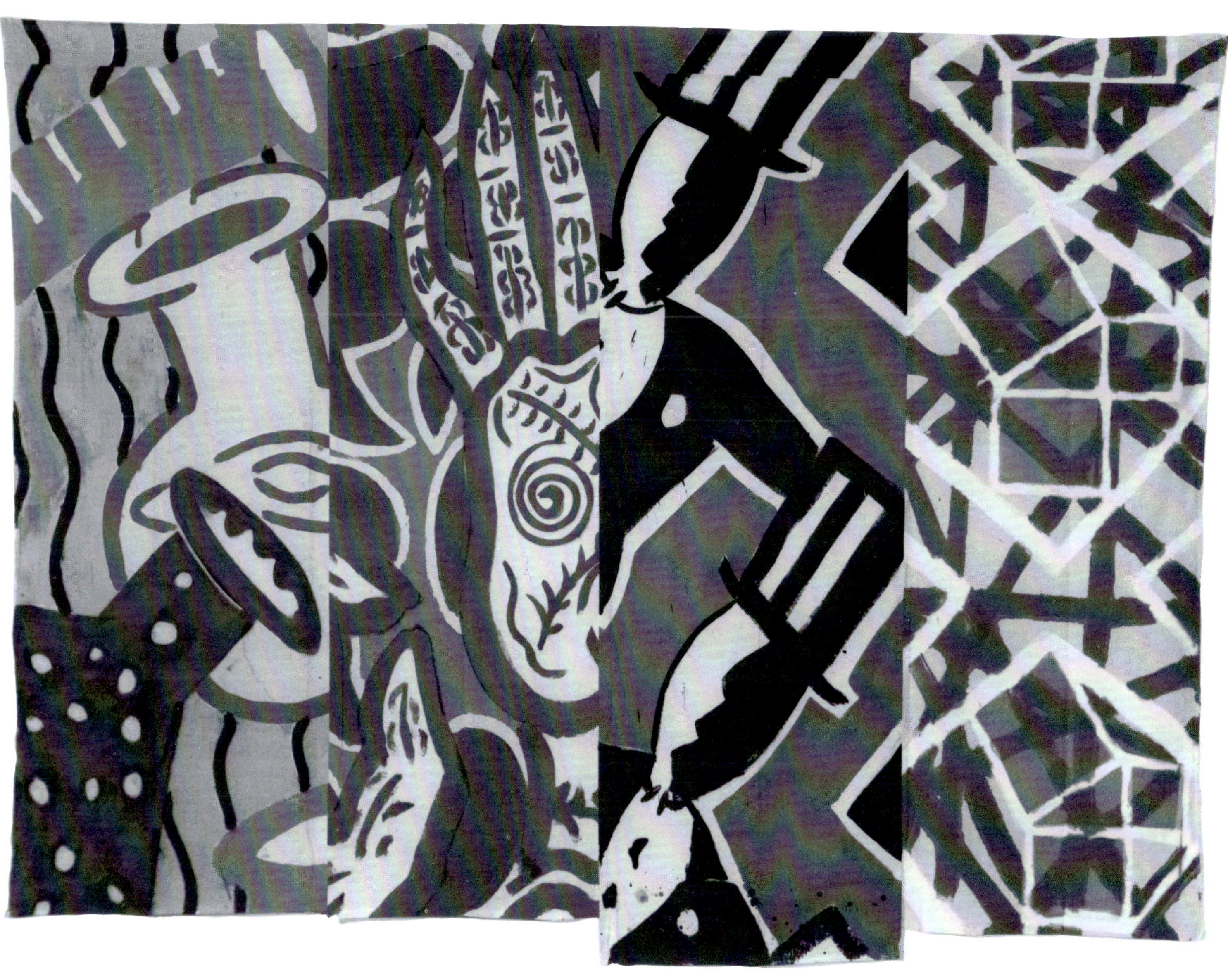

Formidable, 1981
Acrylic on cotton, 97¼ x 129¼″ (247 x 328.3 cm)
Purchase, with funds from the Louis and Bessie Adler Foundation, Inc., Seymour M. Klein, President 82.8

Robert Mangold

I've always had the desire to make the work be a unity, and I wanted nothing to be ahead of anything else. . . . I wanted the elements, which were the periphery line and the internal line, the surface color, etc., to be equal. I wanted them to be so totally locked together that they were inseparable. . . . The importance is on the linkage between idea and process and on the materialization of it, the final object. . . . It should present itself as a unit. In a frontal, in a complete way. It was that whole idea I had about painting—about the uniqueness of flat art, that it could be taken in completely, at once. . . . In other words, one of the reasons people gave for saying that painting was dead seemed like the very thing that made it extremely unique and important.

Quoted in Robin White, "Robert Mangold," *View*, 1 (December 1978), pp. 7–8.

Born in North Tonawanda, New York, 1937
Studied at the Cleveland Institute of Art (1956–59); Yale University, New Haven, Connecticut (B.F.A., 1961; M.F.A., 1963)
Lives in Washingtonville, New York

Selected One-Artist Exhibitions

1964
Thibaut Gallery, New York

1965
Fischbach Gallery, New York

1968
Galerie Müller, Stuttgart, West Germany

1970
Fischbach Gallery, New York

1971
The Solomon R. Guggenheim Museum, New York

1973
Galerie Yvon Lambert, Paris
Galerie Annemarie Verna, Zurich
Daniel Weinberg Gallery, San Francisco

1974
La Jolla Museum of Contemporary Art, California
John Weber Gallery, New York

1976
Galleria D'Alessandro Ferranti, Rome
Galerie Konrad Fischer, Düsseldorf
John Weber Gallery, New York

1977
Kunsthalle Basel, Switzerland
Museum Haus Lange, Krefeld, West Germany

1978
InK. (Halle für Internationale Neue Kunst), Zurich
Galerie Schellmann und Kluser, Munich

1980
Kunsthalle Bielfeld, West Germany
John Weber Gallery, New York

1982
Sidney Janis Gallery, New York
Stedelijk Museum, Amsterdam

Selected Group Exhibitions

1966
The Solomon R. Guggenheim Museum, New York, "Systematic Painting"

1968
Whitney Museum of American Art, New York, "Recent Acquisitions"

1970
Albright-Knox Art Gallery, Buffalo, New York, "Modular Paintings"

1972
Kassel, West Germany, "Documenta 5"

1973
Whitney Museum of American Art, New York, "American Drawings: 1963–1973"

1975
The Baltimore Museum of Art, Maryland, "Fourteen Artists"

1976
The Museum of Modern Art, New York, "Drawing Now" (traveled)

1977
Kassel, West Germany, "Documenta 6"
Museum of Contemporary Art, Chicago, "A View of a Decade"
New York State Museum, Albany, "New York: The State of Art"
The Solomon R. Guggenheim Museum, New York, "American Postwar Painting in the Guggenheim Collection"

1978
Albright-Knox Art Gallery, Buffalo, New York, "American Painting of the 1970s" (traveled)

1979
The Aldrich Museum of Contemporary Art, Ridgefield, Connecticut, "The Minimal Tradition"
Whitney Museum of American Art, New York, "1979 Biennial Exhibition"

1981
Yale University Art Gallery, New Haven, Connecticut, "Twenty Artists: Yale School of Art 1950–1970"

1982
Kassel, West Germany, "Documenta 7"

1983
Whitney Museum of American Art, New York, "1983 Biennial Exhibition"

Selected Bibliography

Heere, Heribert, and Bernhard Kerber. *Robert Mangold: Gemälde* (exhibition catalogue). Bielfeld, West Germany: Kunsthalle Bielfeld, 1980.
Spector, Naomi. *Robert Mangold* (exhibition catalogue). La Jolla, California: La Jolla Museum of Contemporary Art, 1974.
Storck, Gerhard. *Robert Mangold: Four Large Works* (exhibition catalogue). Krefeld, West Germany: Museum Haus Lange, 1977.
van Grevenstein, Alexander. *Robert Mangold* (exhibition catalogue). Amsterdam: Stedelijk Museum, 1982.
Waldman, Diane. *Robert Mangold* (exhibition catalogue). New York: The Solomon R. Guggenheim Museum, 1971.

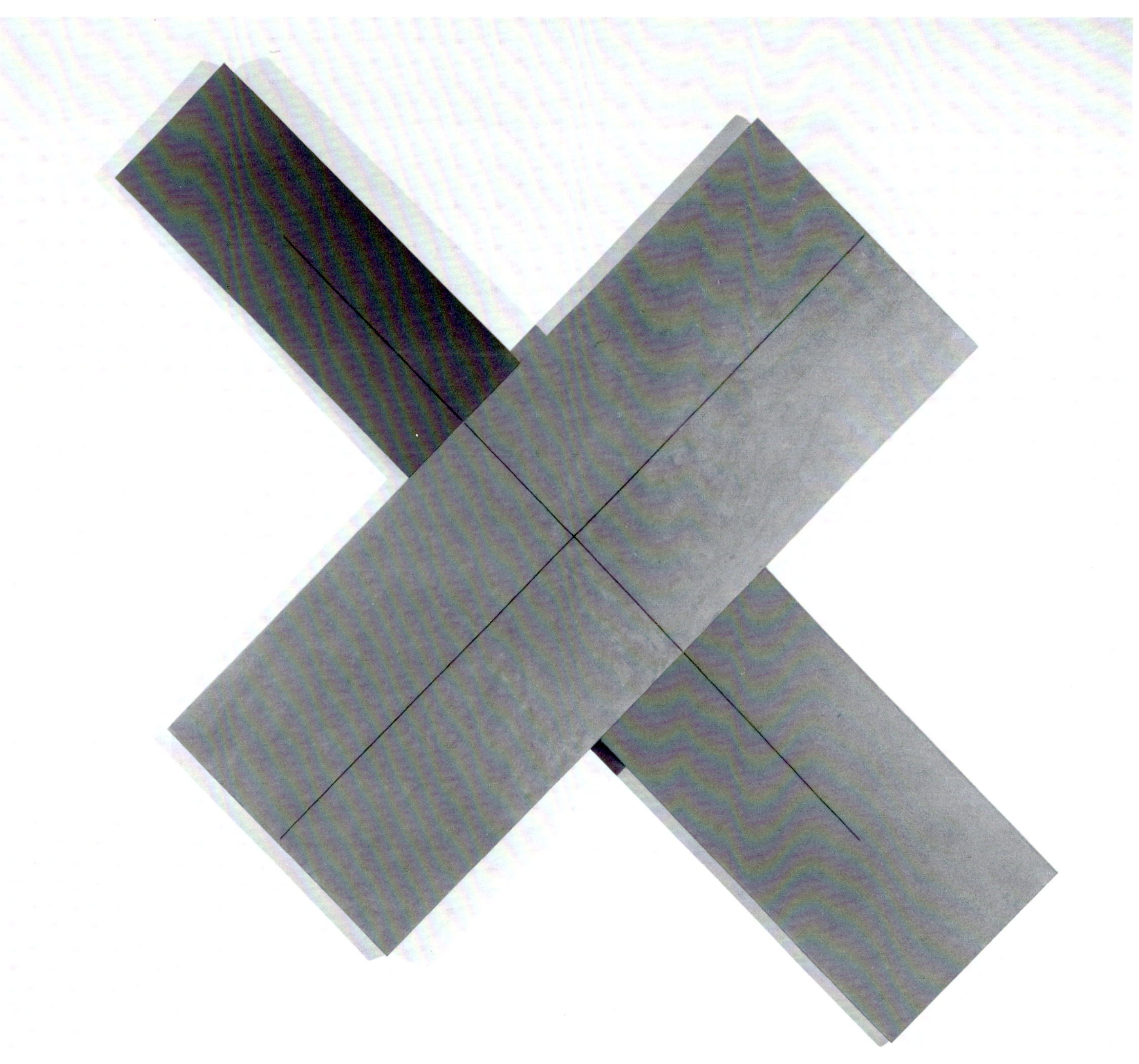

Three Red X Within X, 1981
Acrylic and black pencil on canvas, 109⅞ x 109″
(279.1 x 276.9 cm)
Purchase, with funds from the Painting and Sculpture Committee 83.4 a–c

Brice Marden

Born in Bronxville, New York, 1938
Studied at Florida Southern College, Lakeland (1957–58); Boston University (B.F.A., 1961); Yale University Summer School of Art and Music, Norfolk, Connecticut (1961); Yale University, New Haven, Connecticut (M.F.A., 1963).
Lives in New York

The painting was started from a note to myself that said "a table of glasses of lemonade and Coca-Cola. Interesting color." The painting started with colors that approached those colors from memory. As it progressed that idea became less important than the formal aspects which dealt with creating a strong tension and pull between the outside panels. I also wanted to push the color to a stronger intensity than to which I had been accustomed. After a summer in Greece I felt the light should be intenser, clearer and less shrouded. . . . In Greece I stayed on an island overlooking the sea. I worked in a garden, drawing. I studied light changes and the movements of the sea. I watched light changes change edges . . . the painting deals with a lot of those moments. . . . I did not consciously put that into the painting. It happened.

Quoted from statement dated June 23, 1973, Artists' Files, Whitney Museum of American Art, New York.

Selected One-Artist Exhibitions

1966
Bykert Gallery, New York

1968
Bykert Gallery, New York

1969
Galerie Yvon Lambert, Paris

1971
Galerie Konrad Fischer, Düsseldorf
Galleria Gian Enzo Sperone, Turin, Italy

1972
Bykert Gallery, New York
Locksley Shea Gallery, Minneapolis

1974
Contemporary Arts Museum, Houston

1975
The Solomon R. Guggenheim Museum, New York

1978
Pace Gallery, New York

1979
Kunstraum, Munich, West Germany (traveled)

1981
Whitechapel Art Gallery, London (traveled)

Selected Group Exhibitions

1967
Institute of Contemporary Art, University of Pennsylvania, Philadelphia, "A Romantic Minimalism"

1969
Fort Worth Art Museum, Texas, "Drawings: An Exhibition of American Drawings"
Vassar College Art Gallery, Poughkeepsie, New York, "Concept

1970
Albright-Knox Art Gallery, Buffalo, New York, "Modular Painting"
Whitney Museum of American Art, New York, "1969 Annual Exhibition: Contemporary American Painting"

1971
Whitney Museum of American Art, New York, "The Structure of Color"

1972
Kassel, West Germany, "Documenta 5"
Walker Art Center, Minneapolis, "Painting: New Options"

1973
Whitney Museum of American Art, New York, "1973 Biennial Exhibition: Contemporary American Art"

1974
The Museum of Modern Art, New York, "Eight Contemporary Artists"

1975
Rice Museum & Sewall Gallery, The Institute for Arts, Rice University, Houston, "Brice Marden, David Novros, Mark Rothko"
Stedelijk Museum, Amsterdam, "Fundamental Painting"

1976
The Museum of Modern Art, New York, "Drawing Now" (traveled)

1977
Whitney Museum of American Art, New York, "1977 Biennial Exhibition"

1981
Royal Academy of Arts, London, "A New Spirit in Painting"

Selected Bibliography

Ashton, Dore. *Brice Marden's Drawings, 1963–1973* (exhibition catalogue). Houston: Contemporary Arts Museum, 1974.
Keen, Hermann, and Klaus Kertess. *Brice Marden: Drawings 1964–1978* (exhibition catalogue). Munich: Kunstraum, 1979.
Licht, Jennifer. *Eight Contemporary Artists* (exhibition catalogue). New York: The Museum of Modern Art, 1974.
Serota, Nicholas. *Brice Marden: Paintings, Drawings and Prints 1975–1980* (exhibition catalogue). London: Whitechapel Art Gallery, 1981.
Shearer, Linda. *Brice Marden* (exhibition catalogue). New York: The Solomon R. Guggenheim Museum, 1975.

Untitled #11, 1977
India ink, graphite, and gesso on canvas, 72 x 72″
(182.9 x 182.9 cm)
Gift of the American Art Foundation 77.44

Robert Moskowitz

A lot of the paintings are just about survival—different ways of surviving. . . . I think of the "Swimmer" as like being in New York City—trying to survive. There is an ambiguity in the image—a balance between swimming and drowning, and a balance between a realistic thing and an abstract thing. It has double elements which I think is interesting. . . . The ambiguity is always there, but I do not want it to be mystical. I will usually title the painting in such a way that it is clear. In all good work there is a kind of ambiguity, and I am trying to get the image just over that line.

Quoted in Richard Marshall, *New Image Painting*, exhibition catalogue (New York: Whitney Museum of American Art, 1978), p. 50.

Born in New York, 1935
Lives in New York

Selected One-Artist Exhibitions

1962
Leo Castelli Gallery, New York

1970
French and Company, New York

1971
Hayden Gallery, Massachusetts Institute of Technology, Cambridge

1973
Nancy Hoffman Gallery, New York

1974
Nancy Hoffman Gallery, New York

1977
The Clocktower, Institute for Art and Urban Resources, New York

1979
La Jolla Museum of Contemporary Art, California
Margo Leavin Gallery, Los Angeles
Daniel Weinberg Gallery, San Francisco

1980
Margo Leavin Gallery, Los Angeles
Daniel Weinberg Gallery, San Francisco

1981
Walker Art Center, Minneapolis (traveled)

1983
Blum/Helman Gallery, New York

Selected Group Exhibitions

1961
The Museum of Modern Art, New York, "Art of Assemblage"

1969
Whitney Museum of American Art, New York, "1969 Annual Exhibition: Contemporary American Painting"

1973
Whitney Museum of American Art, New York, "1973 Biennial Exhibition: Contemporary American Art"

1978
Albright-Knox Art Gallery, Buffalo, New York, "American Painting of the 1970s" (traveled)
Whitney Museum of American Art, New York, "New Image Painting"

1979
Grey Art Gallery and Study Center, New York University, "American Painting: The Eighties"
Renaissance Society, University of Chicago, "Visionary Images"
Whitney Museum of American Art, New York, "1979 Biennial Exhibition"

1980
International Pavilion, 39th Venice Biennale, Italy, "Art in the Seventies: Open '80"

1981
Kunsthalle Basel, Switzerland, "Moskowitz/Rothenberg/Schnabel" (traveled)

1982
The Art Institute of Chicago, "74th American Exhibition"

Selected Bibliography

Blum, Peter, and Michael Hurson. *Robert Moskowitz* (exhibition catalogue). Basel, Switzerland: Kunsthalle Basel, 1981.

Cathcart, Linda L. *American Painting of the 1970s* (exhibition catalogue). Buffalo, New York: Albright-Knox Art Gallery, 1978.

Lyons, Lisa. *Robert Moskowitz: Recent Paintings* (exhibition catalogue). Minneapolis: Walker Art Center, 1981.

Marshall, Richard. *New Image Painting* (exhibition catalogue). New York: Whitney Museum of American Art, 1978.

Wechsler, Judith. *Robert Moskowitz: Recent Paintings* (exhibition catalogue). Cambridge, Massachusetts: Hayden Gallery, Massachusetts Institute of Technology, 1971.

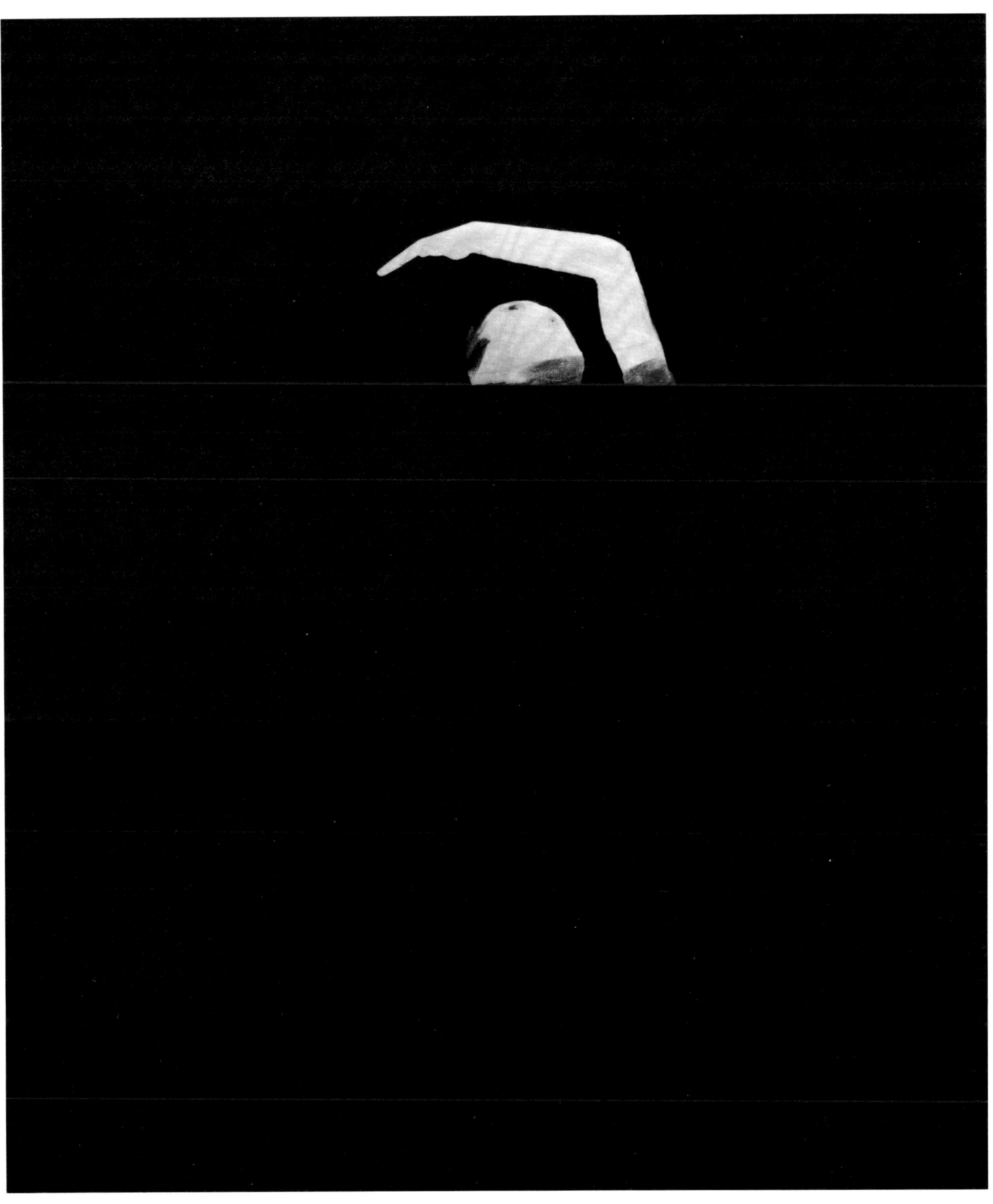

Swimmer, 1977
Oil and pure pigment on canvas, 90 x 74¾″
(228.6 x 189.9 cm)
Gift of Jennifer Bartlett 82.9

Elizabeth Murray

Born in Chicago, 1940
Studied at the School of The Art Institute of Chicago (B.F.A., 1962); Mills College, Oakland, California (M.F.A., 1964)
Lives in New York

I never start a painting from a clear, rational plan or from a complete drawing. I work more impulsively. Often, though, the motivation comes from the desire to make a shape or to get a certain color. The idea is to enact what happens. . . . There are shapes and figures in my paintings which refer to forms in nature and to the human body. It is a figurative space. But the shapes are not identifiable with a specific thing. They feel like transformations. Since they are organic shapes, associations created by the viewer become inevitable. But the shape painted actually belongs to itself. The act of painting, which is a solitary one, ultimately teaches the artist about the complexity of painting.

Quoted in Barbara Rose, *American Painting: The Eighties—A Critical Interpretation* (New York: Vista Press, 1979), unpaginated.

Selected One-Artist Exhibitions

1975
Paula Cooper Gallery, New York
The Jared Sable Gallery, Toronto

1976
Paula Cooper Gallery, New York

1978
Paula Cooper Gallery, New York
Phyllis Kind Gallery, Chicago

1980
Galerie Mukai, Tokyo

1981
Paula Cooper Gallery, New York

1982
Daniel Weinberg Gallery, Los Angeles

Selected Group Exhibitions

1972
Whitney Museum of American Art, New York, "1972 Annual Exhibition: Contemporary American Painting"

1973
Whitney Museum of American Art, New York, "1973 Biennial Exhibition: Contemporary American Art"

1977
The Solomon R. Guggenheim Museum, New York, "Nine Artists: The Theodoron Awards"
Museum of Contemporary Art, Chicago, "A View of a Decade"
The New Museum, New York, "Early Work by Five Contemporary Artists: Ron Gorchov, Elizabeth Murray, Dennis Oppenheim, Dorothea Rockburne, Joel Shapiro"
New York State Museum, Albany, "New York: The State of Art"

1979
Grey Art Gallery and Study Center, New York University, "American Painting: The Eighties"
Hayward Gallery, London, "New Painting/New York"
Whitney Museum of American Art, New York, "1979 Biennial Exhibition"

1981
Haus der Kunst, Munich, "Amerikanische Malerei: 1930–1980"
Whitney Museum of American Art, New York, "1981 Biennial Exhibition"

1982
The Art Institute of Chicago, "74th American Exhibition"
Whitney Museum of American Art, New York, "Abstract Drawings, 1911–1981"

Selected Bibliography

Armstrong, Tom. *Amerikanische Malerei: 1930–1980* (exhibition catalogue). Munich: Prestel-Verlag and Haus der Kunst, 1981.
Kuspit, Donald B. "Elizabeth Murray's Dandyish Abstraction," *Artforum*, 16 (February 1978), pp. 28–31.
Murry, Jesse. "Quintet: The Romance of Order and Tension in Five Paintings by Elizabeth Murray," *Arts Magazine*, 55 (May 1981), pp. 102–105.
1981 Biennial Exhibition (exhibition catalogue). Foreword by Tom Armstrong. Preface by John G. Hanhardt, Barbara Haskell, Richard Marshall, and Patterson Sims. New York: Whitney Museum of American Art, 1981.
Rose, Barbara. *American Painting: The Eighties* (exhibition catalogue). New York: Vista Press, 1979.
Shearer, Linda. *Nine Artists: The Theodoron Awards* (exhibition catalogue). New York: The Solomon R. Guggenheim Museum, 1977.

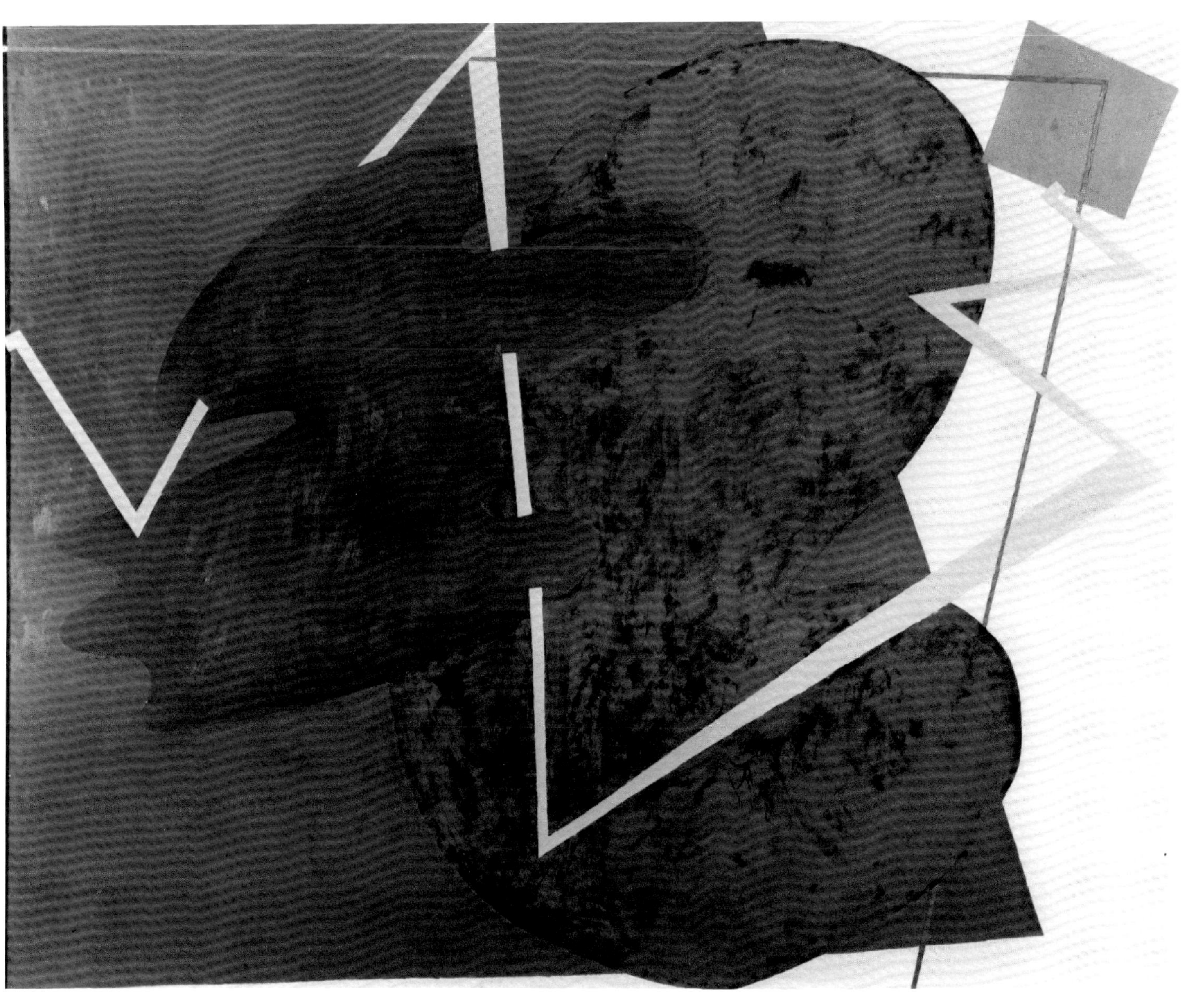

Children Meeting, 1978
Oil on canvas, 101 x 127″ (256.5 x 322.6 cm)
Gift of the Louis and Bessie Adler Foundation, Inc., Seymour M. Klein, President 78.34

Alice Neel

Born in Merion Square, Pennsylvania, 1900
Studied at the Philadelphia School of Design (now Moore College of Art) (1921–25)
Lives in New York

I feel that Andy Warhol is a very interesting character understanding as he does the barometer of advertising in this "country and age" of advertising. He is a phenomenon of our times and believing as I do that people are the greatest and profoundest key to an era (even though our technological society for many years had crossed them out) I felt he was extremely important. Man in a sense is everything. . . . Andy Warhol asked me to paint him. I never got to it until 1970 . . . I found him personally very kind and reticent and even the economy of my technique in the painting tries to convey this along with other things.

Quoted from statement dated August 26, 1971, Artists' Files, Whitney Museum of American Art, New York.

One-Artist Exhibitions

1951
A.C.A. Gallery, New York

1954
A.C.A. Gallery, New York

1963
Graham Gallery, New York

1966
Graham Gallery, New York

1971
Moore College of Art, Philadelphia

1974
Whitney Museum of American Art, New York

1975
Portland Center for the Visual Arts, Oregon
Georgia Museum of Art, Athens

1977
Graham Gallery, New York
Lehigh University, Bethlehem, Pennsylvania

1978
Graham Gallery, New York
Skidmore College, Saratoga Springs, New York

1979
Middendorf Lane Gallery, Washington, D.C.
Akron Art Institute, Ohio

1980
Boston University Art Gallery

1981
Artist Union, Moscow

1982
Robert Miller Gallery, New York

1983
Art Gallery, Loyola Marymount University, Los Angeles

Selected Group Exhibitions

1964
American Federation of Arts, New York, "The Emotional Temperatures of Art"

1972
Whitney Museum of American Art, New York, "1972 Annual Exhibition: Contemporary American Painting"

1975
New York Cultural Center, "Women Choose Women"

1976
Los Angeles County Museum, "Women Artists: 1550–1950"
Pennsylvania State University, University Park, "Portraits 1776–1976"
Wildenstein Gallery, New York, "Portraits of the Self and Others"

1980
Danforth Museum, Framingham, Massachusetts, "Aspects of the 70's: Directions in Realism"
Whitney Museum of American Art, New York, "The Figurative Tradition and the Whitney Museum of American Art: Paintings and Sculpture from the Permanent Collection"

1981
Pennsylvania Academy of the Fine Arts, Philadelphia, "Contemporary American Realism Since 1960" (traveled)
San Antonio Museum of Art, "Real, Really Real and Super Real: Directions in Contemporary American Realism" (traveled)

1982
Contemporary Arts Center, New Orleans, "The Human Figure"
Whitney Museum of American Art, Fairfield County, Stamford, Connecticut, "Five Artists and the Figure"

Selected Bibliography

Goodyear, Frank. *Contemporary American Realism Since 1960* (exhibition catalogue). Philadelphia: Pennsylvania Academy of the Fine Arts, 1981.
Harris, Ann Sutherland, and Linda Nochlin. *Women Artists: 1550–1950* (exhibition catalogue). Los Angeles: Museum Associates of the Los Angeles County Museum of Art, 1976.
Hills, Patricia, and Roberta K. Tarbell. *The Figurative Tradition and the Whitney Museum of American Art: Paintings and Sculpture from the Permanent Collection* (exhibition catalogue). New York: Whitney Museum of American Art, 1980.
Solomon, Elke Morger. *Alice Neel* (exhibition catalogue). New York: Whitney Museum of American Art, 1974.

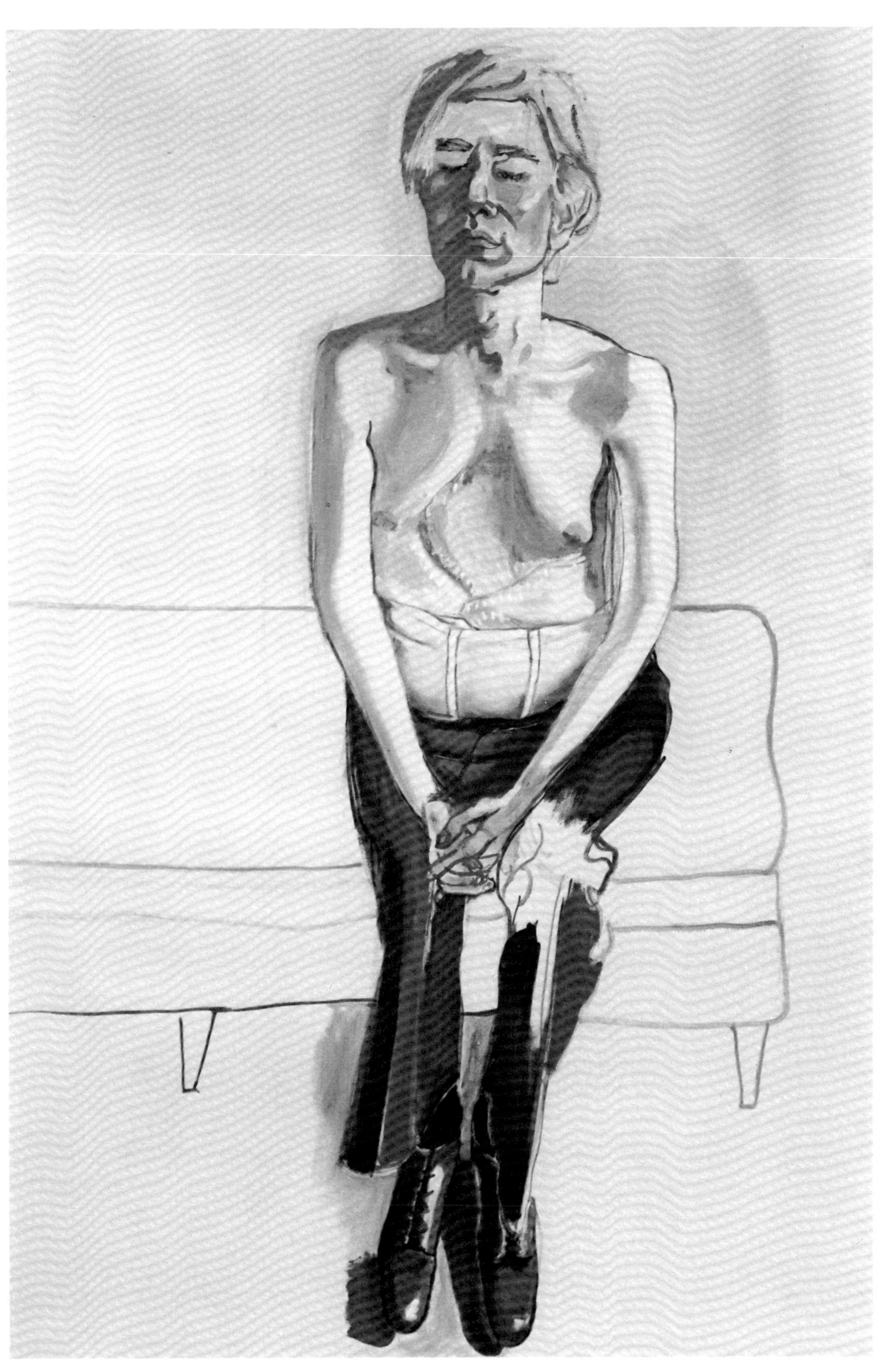

Andy Warhol, 1970
Oil on canvas, 60 x 40″ (152.4 x 101.6 cm)
Gift of Timothy Collins 80.52

Ed Paschke

Born in Chicago, 1939
Studied at the School of The Art Institute of Chicago (B.F.A., 1961; M.F.A., 1970)
Lives in Chicago

Today my paintings relate both conceptually and technically to television—to electronic visual media. . . . Say you just can't get the picture tuned in right and finally you just accept the fact and enjoy the nice green glow around the edge there, or that purple smear over there, or that streak going through every three seconds . . . sometimes looking at the illusion of the picture, the depth of the picture, and at other times being called to the surface of it with those electronic impulses shooting across the screen. It's pretty much the same way in a painting—the idea of the illusion of depth in the picture plane. . . . What I'm trying to do in my paintings is float back and forth, sometimes getting involved with the illusion of depth and at other times calling attention to the fact that we're dealing with a flat surface.

Quoted in Michelle Vishny, "An Interview with Ed Paschke," *Arts Magazine*, 55 (December 1980), p. 147.

Selected One-Artist Exhibitions

1970
Deson-Zaks Gallery, Chicago

1971
Hundred Acres Gallery, New York

1972
Deson-Zaks Gallery, Chicago

1973
Richard DeMarco Gallery, Edinburgh, Scotland
Deson-Zaks Gallery, Chicago

1974
Contemporary Arts Center, Cincinnati
Hundred Acres Gallery, New York
Galerie Darthea Speyer, Paris

1975
Deson-Zaks Gallery, Chicago
Pyramid Gallery, Washington, D.C.

1976
Galerie Darthea Speyer, Paris

1977
Phyllis Kind Gallery, Chicago

1978
Phyllis Kind Gallery, New York
Galerie Darthea Speyer, Paris

1979
Phyllis Kind Gallery, Chicago
Phyllis Kind Gallery, New York

1980
Phyllis Kind Gallery, New York

1981
Galerie Darthea Speyer, Paris

1982
Phyllis Kind Gallery, New York
Renaissance Society, University of Chicago (traveled)

Selected Group Exhibitions

1969
Whitney Museum of American Art, New York, "Human Concern/Personal Torment: The Grotesque in American Art"
Institute of Contemporary Art, University of Pennsylvania, Philadelphia, "Spirit of the Comics"

1972
Museum of Contemporary Art, Chicago, "Chicago Imagist Art"
National Gallery of Canada, Ottawa, "What They're Up To In Chicago"

1973
Whitney Museum of American Art, New York, "1973 Biennial Exhibition: Contemporary American Art"
1973 Bienal of São Paolo, Brazil, "Made in Chicago" (traveled)

1977
E.B. Crocker Art Gallery, Sacramento, California, "The Chicago Connection"
Museum of Contemporary Art, Chicago, "A View of a Decade"

1979
Aspen Center for the Visual Arts, Colorado, "American Portraits of the Sixties and Seventies"

1980
Mayor Gallery, London, "Six Artists from Chicago"
Sunderland Arts Centre, England, "'Who Chicago?' an Exhibition of Contemporary Imagists" (traveled)

1981
Whitney Museum of American Art, New York, "1981 Biennial Exhibition"
Cleveland Museum of Art, Ohio, "Contemporary Artists"
Haus der Kunst, Munich, "Amerikanische Malerei 1930–1980"

1982
Whitney Museum of American Art, New York, "Focus on the Figure: Twenty Years"
Indianapolis Art Museum, "Painting and Sculpture Today"

Selected Bibliography

Armstrong, Tom. *Amerikanische Malerei 1930–1980* (exhibition catalogue). Munich: Haus der Kunst, 1981.
Doty, Robert. *Human Concern/Personal Torment: The Grotesque in American Art* (exhibition catalogue). New York: Whitney Museum of American Art, 1969.
Musgrave, Victor, ed. *Ed Paschke: Selected Works 1967–1981* (exhibition catalogue). Chicago: Renaissance Society, University of Chicago, 1982.
———. *"Who Chicago?" An Exhibition of Contemporary Imagists* (exhibition catalogue). Essays by Dennis Adrian, Russell Bowman, and Roger Brown. England: Sunderland Arts Centre, 1980.
1981 Biennial Exhibition (exhibition catalogue). Foreword by Tom Armstrong. Preface by John G. Hanhardt, Barbara Haskell, Richard Marshall, and Patterson Sims. New York: Whitney Museum of American Art, 1981.
Schultze, Franz. *Chicago Imagist Art* (exhibition catalogue). Chicago: Museum of Contemporary Art, 1972.

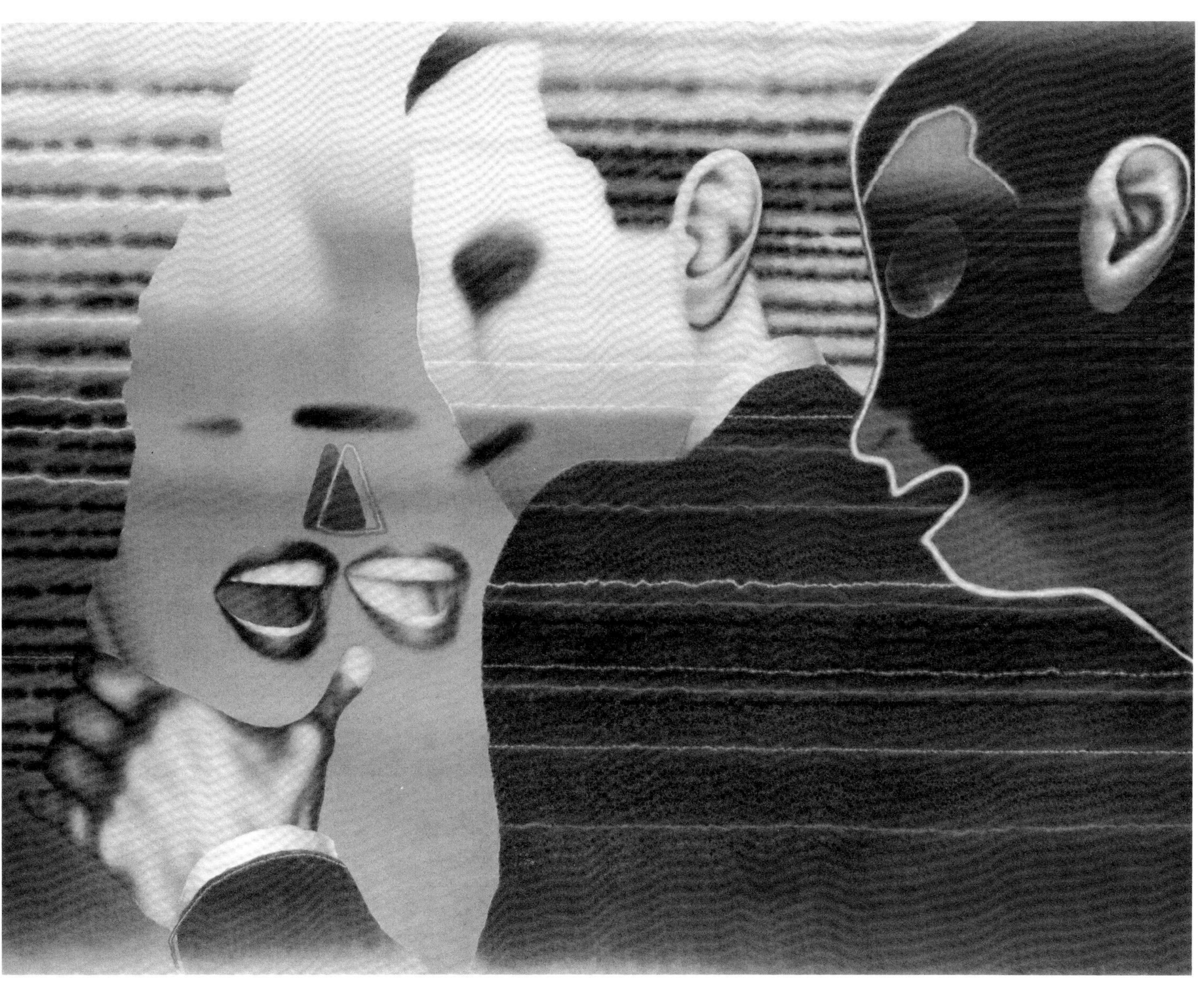

Violencia, 1980
Oil on canvas, 74 x 96″ (188 x 243.8 cm)
Gift of Sherry and Alan Koppel in memory of
Miriam and Herbert Koppel 82.46

Susan Rothenberg

Born in Buffalo, New York, 1945
Studied at Cornell University, Ithaca, New York (B.F.A., 1966); George Washington University, Washington, D.C. (1967); Corcoran Museum School, Washington, D.C. (1967)
Lives in New York

The way the horse image appeared in my paintings was not an intellectual procedure. Most of my work is not run through a rational part of my brain. It comes from a place in me that I don't choose to examine. I just let it come. . . . But I knew that the horse is a powerful, recognizable thing, and that it would take care of my need for an image. For years I didn't give much thought to why I was using a horse. I just thought about wholes and parts, figures and space.

Quoted in Hayden Herrera, "Expressionism Today: An Artists' Symposium," *Art in America*, 70 (December 1982), p. 65.

Selected One-Artist Exhibitions

1975
112 Greene Street Gallery, New York

1976
Willard Gallery, New York

1977
Willard Gallery, New York

1978
Greenberg Gallery, St. Louis
University Art Museum, University of California, Berkeley
Walker Art Center, Minneapolis

1979
Willard Gallery, New York

1980
Galerie Rudolf Zwirner, Cologne
Mayor Gallery, London

1981
Willard Gallery, New York

1982
Stedelijk Museum, Amsterdam

1983
Willard Gallery, New York

Selected Group Exhibitions

1974
A.M. Sachs Gallery, New York, "New Talent"

1976
Fine Arts Gallery, California State University, Los Angeles, "New Work/New York"

1977
The Museum of Modern Art, New York, "Extraordinary Women"
New York State Museum, Albany, "New York: The State of Art"
Sarah Lawrence College, Bronxville, New York, "Painting 75 76 77" (traveled)

1978
Albright-Knox Art Gallery, Buffalo, New York, "American Painting of the 1970s" (traveled)
Vassar College Art Gallery, Poughkeepsie, New York, "Hunt, Jenney, Lane, Rothenberg, Shapiro"
Whitney Museum of American Art, New York, "New Image Painting"

1979
Grey Art Gallery and Study Center, New York University, New York, "American Painting: The Eighties"

1980
Padiglione d'Arte Contemporanea di Milano, Milan, "Pictures in New York Today"
United States Pavilion, 39th Venice Biennale, Italy, "Drawings: The Pluralist Decade" (traveled)

1981
Akron Art Museum, Ohio, "The Image in American Painting and Sculpture 1950–1980"
Kunsthalle Basel, Switzerland, "Moskowitz/Rothenberg/Schnabel" (traveled)

1982
The Art Institute of Chicago, "74th American Exhibition"
Martin-Gropius-Bau, West Berlin, "Zeitgeist"

1983
Whitney Museum of American Art, New York, "1983 Biennial Exhibition"

Selected Bibliography

Blum, Peter. *Susan Rothenberg* (exhibition catalogue). Basel, Switzerland: Kunsthalle Basel, 1981.
Cathcart, Linda L. *American Painting of the 1970s* (exhibition catalogue). Buffalo, New York: Albright-Knox Art Gallery, 1978.
Marshall, Richard. *New Image Painting* (exhibition catalogue). New York: Whitney Museum of American Art, 1978.
Morrin, Peter, ed. *Hunt, Jenney, Lane, Rothenberg, Shapiro* (exhibition catalogue). Poughkeepsie, New York: Vassar College Art Gallery, 1978.
Rosenthal, Mark. "From Primary Structures to Primary Imagery," *Arts Magazine*, 53 (October 1978), pp. 106–107.
van Grevenstein, Alexander. *Susan Rothenberg: Recent Paintings* (exhibition catalogue). Amsterdam: Stedelijk Museum, 1982.

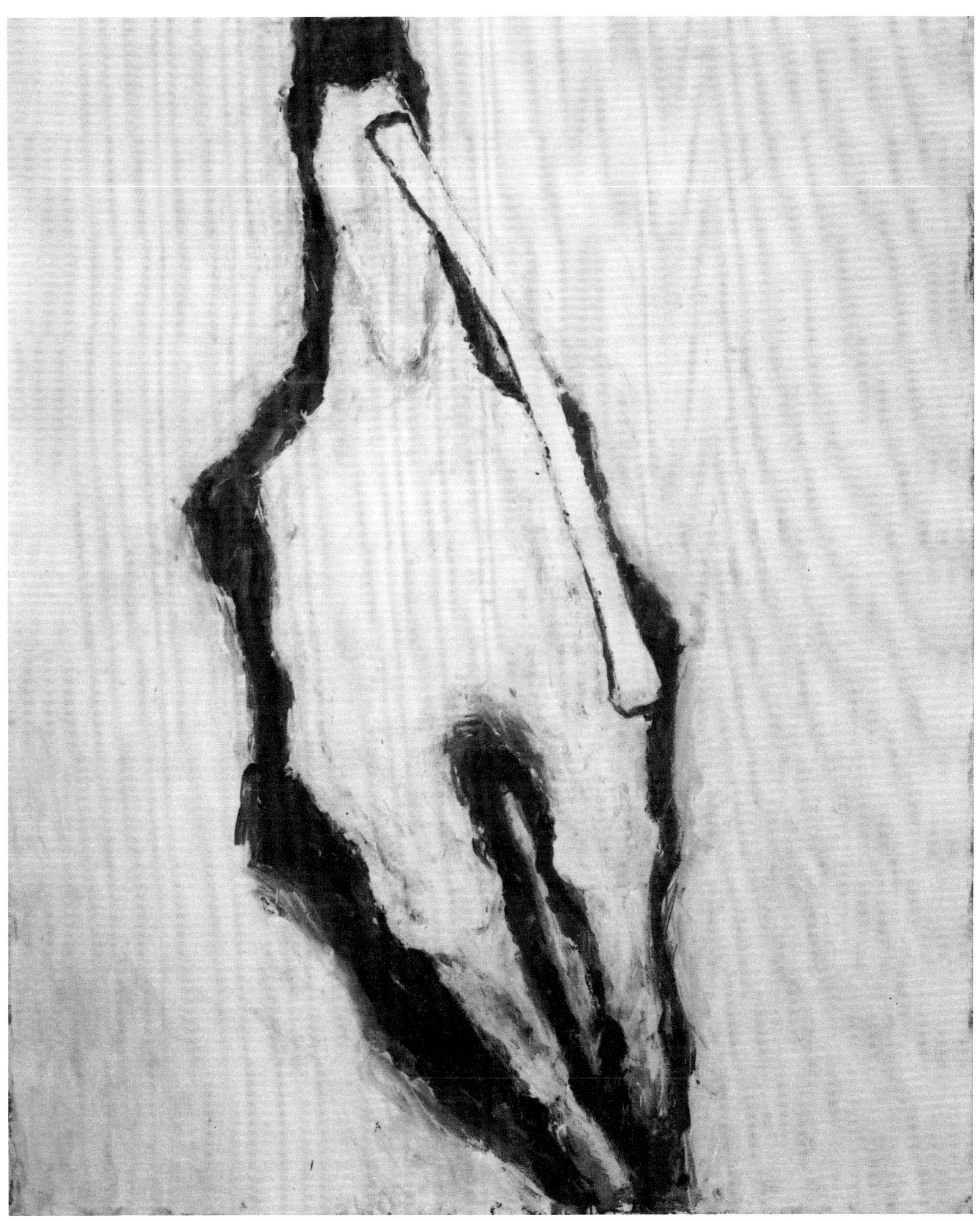

For the Light, 1978–79
Acrylic and flashe on canvas, 105 x 87″ (226.7 x 221 cm)
Purchase, with funds from Peggy and Richard Danziger 79.23

Robert Ryman

I wanted to make a painting without the image isolated within the space, so that the painting itself was an image. . . . I use the white because it's neutral—it's a paint that allows other things to come into focus with the work. The surface, the subtle colors of the surface, the texture, the painting as a whole. . . . A painting of mine consists of the painted surface and the composition, the light reflection and absorption, the edges and structure of the painting itself, whether it's canvas or plastic or whatever the material is that holds the paint, and then the visual composition of the fasteners, which we see, that hold it to the wall and make it part of the wall, which is also brought into our vision. That was partly the consideration with the fasteners. I'm also trying to make very clear that the painting exists only on the wall, and once it's down from the wall, the fasteners are lost and so the composition is lost and the painting is not alive. You know, it doesn't exist until it's in a situation, it's in a room on a wall.

Quoted in Barbaralee Diamonstein, *Inside New York's Art World* (New York: Rizzoli International Publications, Inc., 1979), pp. 332–334.

Born in Nashville, Tennessee, 1930
Studied at the Tennessee Polytechnic Institute (1948–49); George Peabody College for Teachers, Nashville (1949–50)
Lives in New York

Selected One-Artist Exhibitions

1967
Paul Bianchini Gallery, New York

1968
Konrad Fischer Gallery, Düsseldorf

1969
Ace Gallery, Los Angeles
Fischbach Gallery, New York
Galerie Yvon Lambert, Paris

1971
Dwan Gallery, New York

1972
The Solomon R. Guggenheim Museum, New York
John Weber Gallery, New York

1974
Stedelijk Museum, Amsterdam

1975
Kunsthalle Basel, Switzerland

1977
Whitechapel Art Gallery, London

1979
Sidney Janis Gallery, New York

1980
InK. (Halle für Internationale Neue Kunst), Zurich

1981
Sidney Janis Gallery, New York
Kunsthalle, Düsseldorf
Musée National d'Art Moderne, Centre National d'Art et de Culture Georges Pompidou, Paris

Selected Group Exhibitions

1964
Kaymer Gallery, New York, "Eleven Artists"

1966
The Solomon R. Guggenheim Museum, New York, "Systematic Painting"

1969
Kunsthalle Bern, Switzerland, "When Attitudes Become Form" (traveled)
Whitney Museum of American Art, New York, "Anti-Illusion: Procedures/Materials"

1970
Albright-Knox Art Gallery, Buffalo, New York, "Modular Paintings"
Galleria Civica d'Arte Moderna, Turin, Italy, "Conceptual Art/Arte Povera/Land Art"

1972
Kassel, West Germany, "Documenta 5"
Institute of Contemporary Art, University of Pennsylvania, Philadelphia, "Grids"

1973
Whitney Museum of American Art, New York, "American Drawings: 1963–1973"

1975
Institute of Contemporary Art, University of Pennsylvania, Philadelphia, "Painting, Drawing & Sculpture of the 60s and the 70s from the Dorothy and Herbert Vogel Collection" (traveled)

1976
Fine Arts Center Gallery, University of Massachusetts, Amherst, "Critical Perspectives in American Art" (traveled)
The Museum of Modern Art, New York, "Drawing Now"

1977
Kassel, West Germany, "Documenta 6"
Whitney Museum of American Art, New York, "1977 Biennial Exhibition"

1978
Albright-Knox Art Gallery, Buffalo, New York, "American Painting of the 1970s" (traveled)

1981
Haus der Kunst, Munich, "Amerikanische Malerei 1930–1980"
Royal Academy of Arts, London, "A New Spirit in Painting"

1982
Kassel, West Germany, "Documenta 7"
Whitney Museum of American Art, New York, "Painting and Sculpture Acquired Since 1978"

Selected Bibliography

Cathcart, Linda. *American Painting of the 1970s* (exhibition catalogue). Buffalo, New York: Albright-Knox Art Gallery, 1978.
Davies, Hugh M., ed. *Critical Perspectives in American Art* (exhibition catalogue). Amherst: Fine Arts Center Gallery, University of Massachusetts, 1976.
Sauer, Christel. *Robert Ryman Paintings 1958–1980* (exhibition catalogue). Zurich: InK. (Halle für Internationale Neue Kunst), 1980.
Spector, Naomi. *Robert Ryman* (exhibition catalogue). Amsterdam: Stedelijk Museum, 1974.
———. *Robert Ryman* (exhibition catalogue). London: Whitechapel Art Gallery, 1977.
Tucker, Marcia, and James Monte. *Anti-Illusion: Procedures/Materials* (exhibition catalogue). New York: Whitney Museum of American Art, 1969.
Waldman, Diane. *Robert Ryman* (exhibition catalogue). New York: The Solomon R. Guggenheim Museum, 1972.

Carrier, 1979
Oil on cotton with metal brackets, 81½ x 78″
(207 x 198.1 cm)
Purchase, with funds from the Painting and Sculpture Committee, and the National Endowment for the Arts 80.40

David Salle

Born in Norman, Oklahoma, 1952
Studied at California Institute of the Arts, Valencia (B.F.A., 1973; M.F.A., 1975)
Lives in New York

If the work is about anything it's about a certain kind of representation, a certain kind of presentation which is more often found in popular culture than high culture because high culture is about exalted means of presentation—in my mind—and popular culture is about denying you access to the means of presentation, to the mechanics of presentation. . . . In all my images there's a notion of complicity and covertness that makes you think about popular culture—but they're not "pop" in the sense that they are celebrating anything, that they are in love with anything like that. In my work an image is not a "criticism" or a response. Even if it's borrowed, it must feel primary.

Quoted in Peter Schjeldahl, "David Salle Interview," *Journal* (Los Angeles Institute of Contemporary Art), no. 30 (September/October 1981), p. 21.

Selected One-Artist Exhibitions

1975
Claire S. Copley Gallery, Los Angeles

1976
Artists Space, New York
Foundation Corps de Garde, Groningen, Netherlands

1977
Foundation De Appel, Amsterdam
The Kitchen, New York

1979
The Kitchen, New York

1980
Galerie Bruno Bischofberger, Zurich
Annina Nosei Gallery, New York

1981
Mary Boone Gallery, New York
Larry Gagosian Gallery, Los Angeles

1982
Mary Boone Gallery and Leo Castelli Gallery, New York

Selected Group Exhibitions

1975
Long Beach Museum of Art, California, "Southland Video Anthology"

1979
Joseloff Gallery, Hartford Art School, Connecticut, "Imitation of Life"
Padiglione d'Arte Contemporanea, Milan, "Pictures in New York Today"
Studio Cannaviello, Milan, "Recognizable Images"

1980
Brooke Alexander Gallery, New York, "Illustration and Allegory"
Palazzo Triennale, Milan, "Nuova Immagine" (traveled)

1981
Albright-Knox Art Gallery, Buffalo, New York, "Figures: Forms and Expressions"
Allen Memorial Art Museum, Oberlin College, Ohio, "Young Americans"
California Institute of the Arts, Valencia, "Tenth Anniversary Exhibition"
Museen der Stadt, Cologne, "Westkunst: Heute"

1982
Kassel, West Germany, "Documenta 7"
Martin-Gropius-Bau, West Berlin, "Zeitgeist"
Renaissance Society, University of Chicago, "Art and Mass Media"
Walker Art Center, Minneapolis, "Eight Artists: The Anxious Edge"
Whitney Museum of American Art, New York, "Focus on the Figure: Twenty Years"

1983
Whitney Museum of American Art, New York, "1983 Biennial Exhibition"

Selected Bibliography

Kotik, Charlotta, and Susan Krane. *Figures: Forms and Expressions* (exhibition catalogue). Buffalo, New York: Albright-Knox Art Gallery, 1981.
Lawson, Thomas. "Last Exit: Painting," *Artforum*, 20 (October 1981), pp. 40–47.
Lyons, Lisa. *Eight Artists: The Anxious Edge* (exhibition catalogue). Minneapolis: Walker Art Center, 1982.
Ratcliff, Carter. *Illustration and Allegory* (exhibition catalogue). New York: Brooke Alexander Gallery, 1980.
Schjeldahl, Peter. "David Salle Interview," *Journal* (Los Angeles Institute of Contemporary Art), 30 (September/October 1981), pp. 15–21.

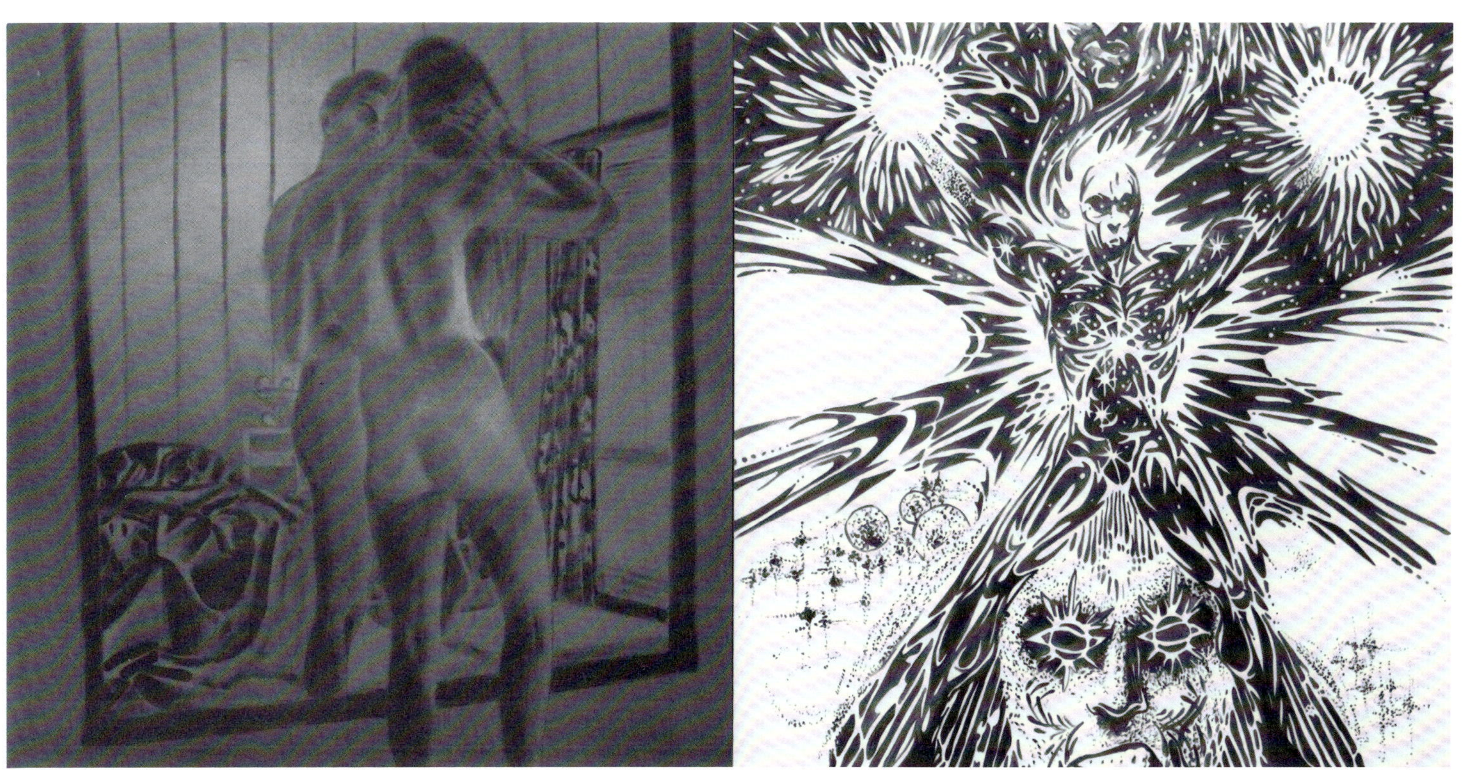

Splinter Man, 1982
Oil and acrylic on canvas: each of two panels, 98 x 98″ (248.9 x 248.9 cm); overall, 98 x 196″ (248.9 x 497.8 cm)
Purchase, with funds from Mr. and Mrs. Charles M. Diker 82.12 a-b

Julian Schnabel

Born in New York, 1951
Studied at the University of Houston (B.F.A., 1972); Whitney Museum of American Art Independent Study Program, New York (1973–74)
Lives in New York

My painting comes out of the continuum of art that has been. It's not antiart in any way. It's just an art that can get up and stick its head out of the window and do things that were maybe impossible before. . . . I'm not distorting things in my paintings. I'm selecting things that have already been distorted in life, and painting them pretty true to their contour. It's not interpretive. My brushstrokes are not emotional. It's the way they configure together that becomes emotional. . . . My painting is more about what I think the world is like than what I think I'm like. I'm aiming at an emotional state, a state that people can literally walk into and let themselves be engulfed by.

Quoted in Hayden Herrera, "Expressionism Today: An Artists' Symposium," *Art in America*, 70 (December 1982), pp. 66–67.

Selected One-Artist Exhibitions

1976
Contemporary Arts Museum, Houston

1979
Mary Boone Gallery, New York
Daniel Weinberg Gallery, San Francisco

1980
Galerie Bruno Bischofberger, Zurich
Young/Hoffman Gallery, Chicago

1981
Mary Boone Gallery and Leo Castelli Gallery, New York

1982
Margo Leavin Gallery, Los Angeles
Los Angeles County Museum of Art
Stedelijk Museum, Amsterdam
Tate Gallery, London

1983
Leo Castelli Gallery, New York

Selected Group Exhibitions

1977
Holly Solomon Gallery, New York, "Surrogate/Self Portraits"

1979
Hallwalls Gallery, Buffalo, New York, "Four Artists"
Renaissance Society, University of Chicago, "Visionary Images"

1980
International Pavilion, 39th Venice Biennale, Italy, "Art in the Seventies: Open '80"

1981
Akron Art Museum, Ohio, "The Image in American Painting and Sculpture 1950–1980"
Kunsthalle Basel, "Moskowitz/Rothenberg/Schnabel" (traveled)
Royal Academy of Arts, London, "A New Spirit in Painting"
Whitney Museum of American Art, New York, "1981 Biennial Exhibition"

1982
The Art Institute of Chicago, "74th American Exhibition"
Martin-Gropius-Bau, West Berlin, "Zeitgeist"
Whitney Museum of American Art, New York, "Focus on the Figure: Twenty Years"

1983
Whitney Museum of American Art, New York, "1983 Biennial Exhibition"

Selected Bibliography

Ammann, Jean-Christophe, and Carter Ratcliff. *Julian Schnabel* (exhibition catalogue). Basel, Switzerland: Kunsthalle Basel, 1981.
Joachimides, Christos M., ed. *A New Spirit in Painting* (exhibition catalogue). London: Royal Academy of Arts, 1981.
Pincus-Witten, Robert. "Julian Schnabel: Blind Faith," *Arts Magazine*, 56 (February 1982), pp. 152–155.
Ratcliff, Carter. *Visionary Images* (exhibition catalogue). Chicago: Renaissance Society, University of Chicago, 1979.
Ricard, Rene. "Not About Julian Schnabel," *Artforum*, 19 (Summer 1981), pp. 74–80.
van Gevenstein, Alexander, and Rene Ricard. *Julian Schnabel* (exhibition catalogue). Amsterdam: Stedelijk Museum, 1982.

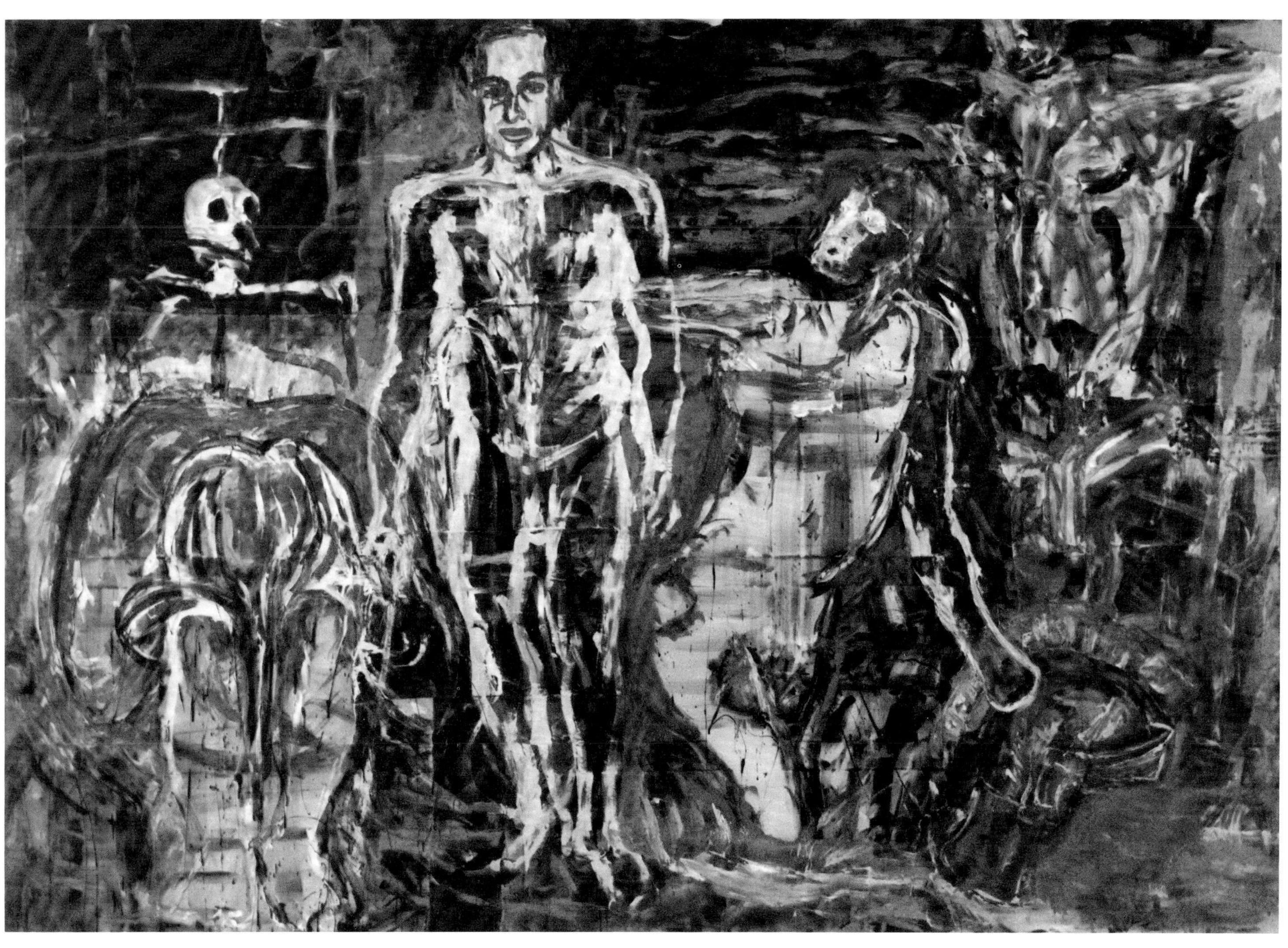

Hope, 1982
Oil on velvet, 108 x 156″ (274.3 x 396.2 cm)
Purchase, with funds from an anonymous donor
82.13

Richard Serra

The . . . drawings, from 1972–73, are still involved with line or shape on paper, so there's a figure-ground acceptance there. I hadn't worked my way to the shape being in itself the integrated structure of the drawing. I began making those drawings as a form of meditation—a form of concentration. I no longer wanted to make markings on a piece of paper: I wanted to make the drawing integral to its structure and properties. What I continually find to be true is that the concentration I apply to drawing is a way of tuning, or honing, my eye. The more I draw, the better I see and the more I understand.

Quoted in Lizzie Borden, "Richard Serra," in *Richard Serra: Drawings 1971–1977*, exhibition catalogue (Amsterdam: Stedelijk Museum, 1977), unpaginated.

Born in San Francisco, 1939
Studied at the University of California, Santa Barbara (B.A., 1961); Yale University, New Haven, Connecticut (M.F.A., 1964)
Lives in New York

Selected One-Artist Exhibitions

1968
Galerie Ricke, Cologne

1969
Leo Castelli Gallery, New York
Galerie Lambert, Milan

1970
Ace Gallery, Los Angeles
Pasadena Art Museum, California

1974
Ace Gallery, Los Angeles
Leo Castelli Gallery, New York
Visual Arts Gallery, School of Visual Arts, New York

1975
Galerie de Gestlo, Hamburg, West Germany
Portland Center for the Visual Arts, Oregon

1977
Galerie Daniel Templon, Paris
Stedelijk Museum, Amsterdam (traveled)

1978
Blum/Helman Gallery, New York
Museum of Modern Art, Oxford, England

1979
University Art Museum, University of California, Berkeley

1980
The Hudson River Museum, Yonkers, New York
Museum Boymans-van Beuningen, Rotterdam

1981
Blum/Helman Gallery, New York
Leo Castelli Gallery, New York

1982
Leo Castelli Gallery, New York
The Saint Louis Art Museum

Selected Group Exhibitions

1967
Richard Bellamy/Noah Goldowsky Gallery, New York, "From Arp to Artschwager I"

1968
Whitney Museum of American Art, New York, "1968 Annual Exhibition: Contemporary American Sculpture"

1969
Kunsthalle Bern, Switzerland, "When Attitudes Become Form"

1970
Galleria Civica d'Arte Moderna, Turin, Italy, "Conceptual Art/Arte Povera/Land Art"
The Museum of Modern Art, New York, "Information"
Whitney Museum of American Art, New York, "1970 Annual Exhibition: Contemporary American Sculpture"

1971
Los Angeles County Museum of Art, "Art and Technology"
Louisiana Museum, Humlebaek, Denmark, "Amerikanische Kunst 1950–1970"
Walker Art Center, Minneapolis, "Works for New Spaces"

1972
Kassel, West Germany, "Documenta 5"

1973
Whitney Museum of American Art, New York, "1973 Biennial Exhibition: Contemporary American Art"

1974
The Art Museum, Princeton University, New Jersey, "Line as Language: Six Artists Draw"

1976
The Museum of Modern Art, New York, "Drawing Now" (traveled)

1977
Kassel, West Germany, "Documenta 6"
Renaissance Society, University of Chicago, "Ideas in Sculpture 1965–77"
Whitney Museum of American Art, New York, "1977 Biennial Exhibition"

1980
The Corcoran Gallery of Art, Washington, D.C., "37th Biennial of Contemporary American Painting"
Hayden Gallery, Massachusetts Institute of Technology, Cambridge, "Mel Bochner/Richard Serra"

1981
Whitney Museum of American Art, New York, "1981 Biennial Exhibition"

1982
Kassel, West Germany, "Documenta 7"
The Solomon R. Guggenheim Museum, New York, "New York School: Four Generations"
Whitney Museum of American Art, New York, "Abstract Drawings 1911–1981: Selections from the Permanent Collection"

Selected Bibliography

Halbreich, Kathy. *Mel Bochner/Richard Serra* (exhibition catalogue). Cambridge, Massachusetts: Hayden Gallery, Massachusetts Institute of Technology, 1980.
Krauss, Rosalind. *Line as Language: Six Artists Draw* (exhibition catalogue). Princeton, New Jersey: The Art Museum, Princeton University, 1974.
———. *Passages in Modern Sculpture*. New York: Viking Press, 1977.
Szeeman, Harald. *When Attitudes Become Form* (exhibition catalogue). Bern: Kunsthalle Bern, 1969.
Weyergraf, Clara, ed. *Richard Serra: Interviews, Etc. 1970–1980* (exhibition catalogue). Yonkers, New York: The Hudson River Museum, 1980.

Untitled, 1972
Lithographic crayon on paper, 37¾ x 49¾″
(95.9 x 126.4 cm)
Gift of Susan Morse Hilles 74.10

Joel Shapiro

I took the metaphor of the house and isolated it. I took a house and plopped it in the middle of a field—not a grassy, green field—I mean an area. This house is not engaged so much with the space that it actually occupies, but functions in a much more psychologically determined space instead. It is removed. It is very sentimental. It gives a real sense of isolation. This small, longing house is removed from you, but you can feel it.

Quoted in Richard Marshall and Roberta Smith, *Joel Shapiro*, exhibition catalogue (New York: Whitney Museum of American Art, 1982), p. 98.

Born in New York, 1941
Studied at New York University (B.A., 1964; M.F.A., 1969)
Lives in New York

Selected One-Artist Exhibitions

1970
Paula Cooper Gallery, New York

1972
Paula Cooper Gallery, New York

1973
The Clocktower, Institute for Art and Urban Resources, New York

1974
Paula Cooper Gallery, New York

1975
Paula Cooper Gallery, New York

1976
Paula Cooper Gallery, Los Angeles
Museum of Contemporary Art, Chicago

1977
Albright-Knox Art Gallery, Buffalo, New York
Paula Cooper Gallery, New York

1979
Paula Cooper Gallery, New York

1980
Bell Gallery, List Art Center, Brown University, Providence, Rhode Island (traveled)
Paula Cooper Gallery, New York
Whitechapel Art Gallery, London (traveled)

1981
The Israel Museum, Jerusalem
Daniel Weinberg Gallery, San Francisco
Young-Hoffman Gallery, Chicago

1982
Whitney Museum of American Art, New York (traveled)

Selected Group Exhibitions

1969
Whitney Museum of American Art, New York, "Anti-Illusion: Procedures/Materials"

1970
Whitney Museum of American Art, New York, "1970 Annual Exhibition: Contemporary American Sculpture"

1973
Whitney Museum of American Art, New York, "American Drawings: 1963–1973"

1974
The Art Institute of Chicago, "71st American Exhibition"

1976
Fine Arts Center Gallery, University of Massachusetts, Amherst, "Critical Perspectives in American Art" (traveled)
Akademie der Künste, West Berlin, "New York—Downtown Manhattan: Soho"

1977
Kassel, West Germany, "Documenta 6"
The New Museum, New York, "Early Work by Five Contemporary Artists: Ron Gorchov, Elizabeth Murray, Dennis Oppenheim, Dorothea Rockburne, Joel Shapiro"
Walker Art Center, Minneapolis, "Scale and Environment: 10 Sculptors"
Whitney Museum of American Art, New York, "1977 Biennial Exhibition"

1979
The Museum of Modern Art, New York, "Contemporary Sculpture: Selections from the Collection of The Museum of Modern Art"
Whitney Museum of American Art, New York, "The Decade in Review: Selections from the 1970s"
Whitney Museum of American Art, New York, "1979 Biennial Exhibition"

1980
United States Pavilion, 39th Venice Biennale, "Drawings: The Pluralist Decade" (traveled)

1981
Akron Art Museum, Ohio, "The Image in American Painting and Sculpture, 1950–1980"
Whitney Museum of American Art, New York, "1981 Biennial Exhibition"

1982
The Art Institute of Chicago, "74th American Exhibition"
Kassel, West Germany, "Documenta 7"
San Francisco Museum of Modern Art, "Twenty American Artists: Sculpture 1982"

Selected Bibliography

Critical Perspectives in American Art (exhibition catalogue). Introduction by Hugh M. Davies. Texts by Sam Hunter, Rosalind Krauss, and Marcia Tucker. Amherst, Massachusetts: Fine Arts Center Gallery, University of Massachusetts, 1976.
Early Work by Five Contemporary Artists: Ron Gorchov, Elizabeth Murray, Dennis Oppenheim, Dorothea Rockburne, Joel Shapiro (exhibition catalogue). Introduction by Marcia Tucker. Interviews by Susan Logan, Allan Schwartzman, and Marcia Tucker. New York: The New Museum, 1977.
Joel Shapiro (exhibition catalogue). Foreword by Stephen Prokopoff. Text by Rosalind Krauss. Chicago: Museum of Contemporary Art, 1976.
Joel Shapiro: Sculpture and Drawing (exhibition catalogue). Foreword by Nicholas Serota. Text by Roberta Smith. London: Whitechapel Art Gallery, 1980.
Marshall, Richard, and Roberta Smith. *Joel Shapiro* (exhibition catalogue). New York: Whitney Museum of American Art, 1982.
Scale and Environment: 10 Sculptors (exhibition catalogue). Introduction by Martin Friedman. Texts by Michael R. Klein, Laurence Shopmaker, Lisa Lyons, and Judith Hoos Fox. Minneapolis: Walker Art Center, 1977.
Tucker, Marcia, and James Monte. *Anti-Illusion: Procedures/Materials* (exhibition catalogue). New York: Whitney Museum of American Art, 1969.

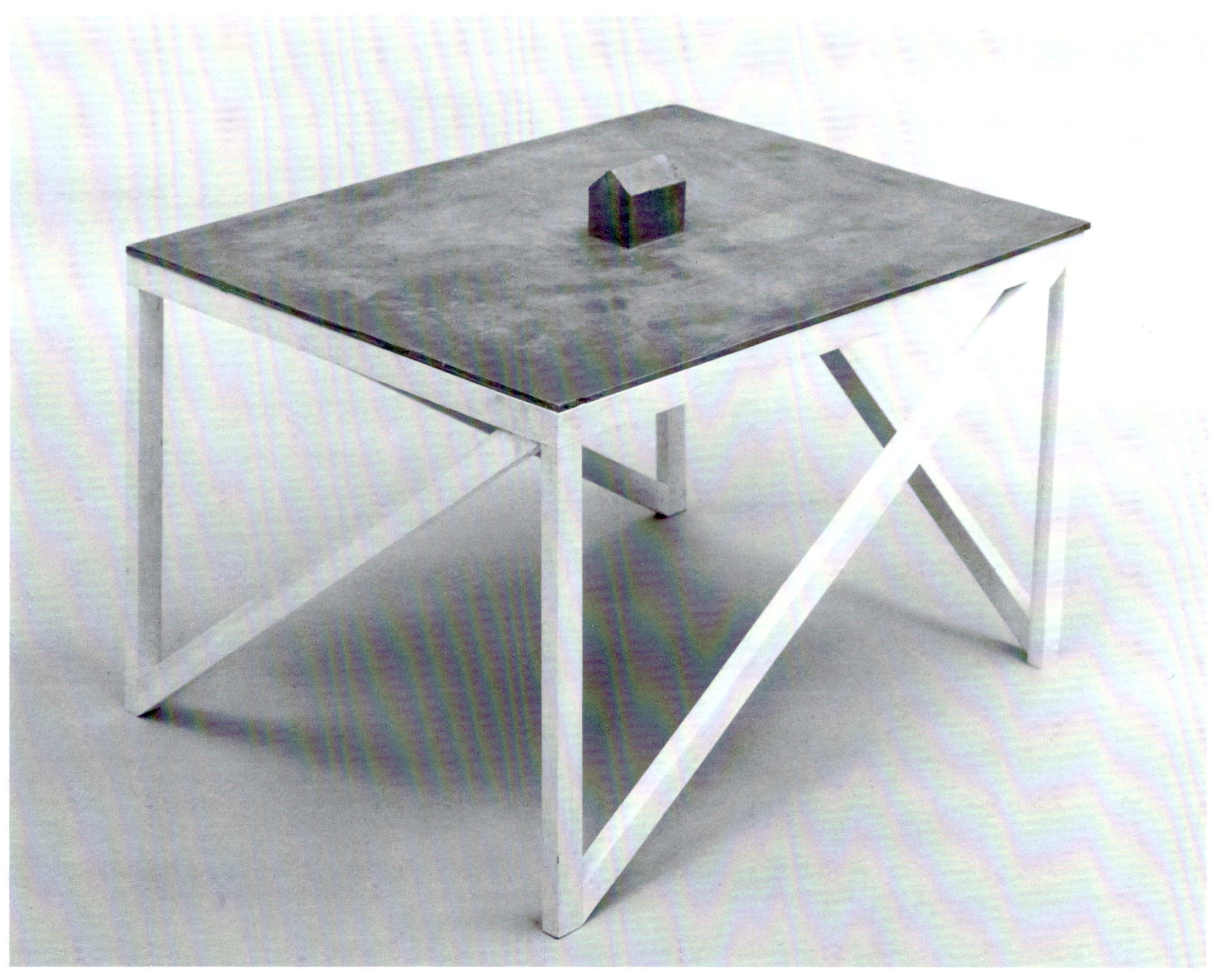

Untitled, 1975–76
Bronze on wood base: 3½ x 28¾ x 21½″ (8.9 x 73 x 54.6 cm); base, 17½ x 28¾ x 21½″ (44.5 x 73 x 54.6 cm)
Gift of Mrs. Oscar Kolin 76.22

Alexis Smith

The text for the piece is in two parts: the first part, the preface, is a quote from Jean Cocteau's Diary, which he wrote while he was making the movie "Beauty and the Beast." This quote alludes to the function and means of work of the artist; the second part of the text is his brief synopsis of the plot of Beauty and the Beast, slightly edited with one character deleted, so that it corresponds more closely to the original version of the fairy tale.

Fragments of this text are illustrated with a series of collage images on blue paper; in addition to the obvious content of the images and their illustrative relationship to the text, they were specifically chosen for their color and tactile/form relationships to one another. The entire piece is predominantly red, black and white, and brown. There are two pages, typewritten text from the "Beauty and the Beast" screenplay on flimsy white typing paper, with no visual metaphors which are more powerful than any actual image could be.

Quoted from statement dated July 28, 1978, Artists' Files, Whitney Museum of American Art, New York.

Born in Los Angeles, California, 1949
Studied at the University of California, Irvine (B.A., 1970)
Lives in Venice, California

Selected One-Artist Exhibitions

1974
Riko Mizuno Gallery, Los Angeles

1975
Art Gallery, University of California, Santa Barbara
Whitney Museum of American Art, New York

1977
Holly Solomon Gallery, New York
Nicholas Wilder Gallery, Los Angeles

1978
Rosamund Felsen Gallery, Los Angeles
Holly Solomon Gallery, New York

1979
De Appel, Amsterdam
Holly Solomon Gallery, New York

1980
Rosamund Felsun Gallery, Los Angeles

1981
Los Angeles Contemporary Exhibitions
Holly Solomon Gallery, New York

1982
Rosamund Felsen Gallery, Los Angeles
Margo Leavin Gallery, Los Angeles

Selected Group Exhibitions

1972
Pasadena Museum of Modern Art, California, "Southern California Attitudes"

1975
La Jolla Museum of Contemporary Art, California, "University of California, Irvine: 1965–75"
Visual Arts Gallery, School of Visual Arts, New York, "Four Los Angeles Artists: Foulkes, Goode, Smith, Wheeler" (traveled)
Whitney Museum of American Art, New York, "1975 Biennial Exhibition"

1976
Portland Center for the Visual Arts, Oregon, "Via Los Angeles"

1977
Contemporary Arts Museum, Houston, "American Narrative/Story Art"
Los Angeles Institute of Contemporary Art, "Narrative Themes/Audio Works"
Musée d'Art Moderne de la Ville de Paris, "10e Biennale de Paris"

1978
Institute of Contemporary Art, Boston, "Narration"

1979
San Francisco Museum of Modern Art, "Paper on Paper"
Whitney Museum of American Art, New York, "The Decade in Review: Selections from the 1970s"
Whitney Museum of American Art, New York, "1979 Biennial Exhibition"

1980
Los Angeles Institute of Contemporary Art, "Tableau"

1981
Los Angeles County Museum of Art, "Art in Los Angeles—The Museum as Site: Sixteen Projects"
Renaissance Society, University of Chicago, "Words as Images"
Whitney Museum of American Art, New York, "1981 Biennial Exhibition"

Selected Bibliography

Barron, Stephanie. *Art in Los Angeles—The Museum as Site: Sixteen Projects* (exhibition catalogue). Los Angeles: Los Angeles County Museum of Art, 1981.
Leja, Michael. *Narration* (exhibition catalogue). Boston: Institute of Contemporary Art, 1978.
Schimmel, Paul. *American Narrative/Story Art* (exhibition catalogue). Houston: Contemporary Arts Museum, 1977.
Wortz, Melinda. *University of California, Irvine: 1965–75* (exhibition catalogue). La Jolla, California: La Jolla Museum of Contemporary Art, 1975.

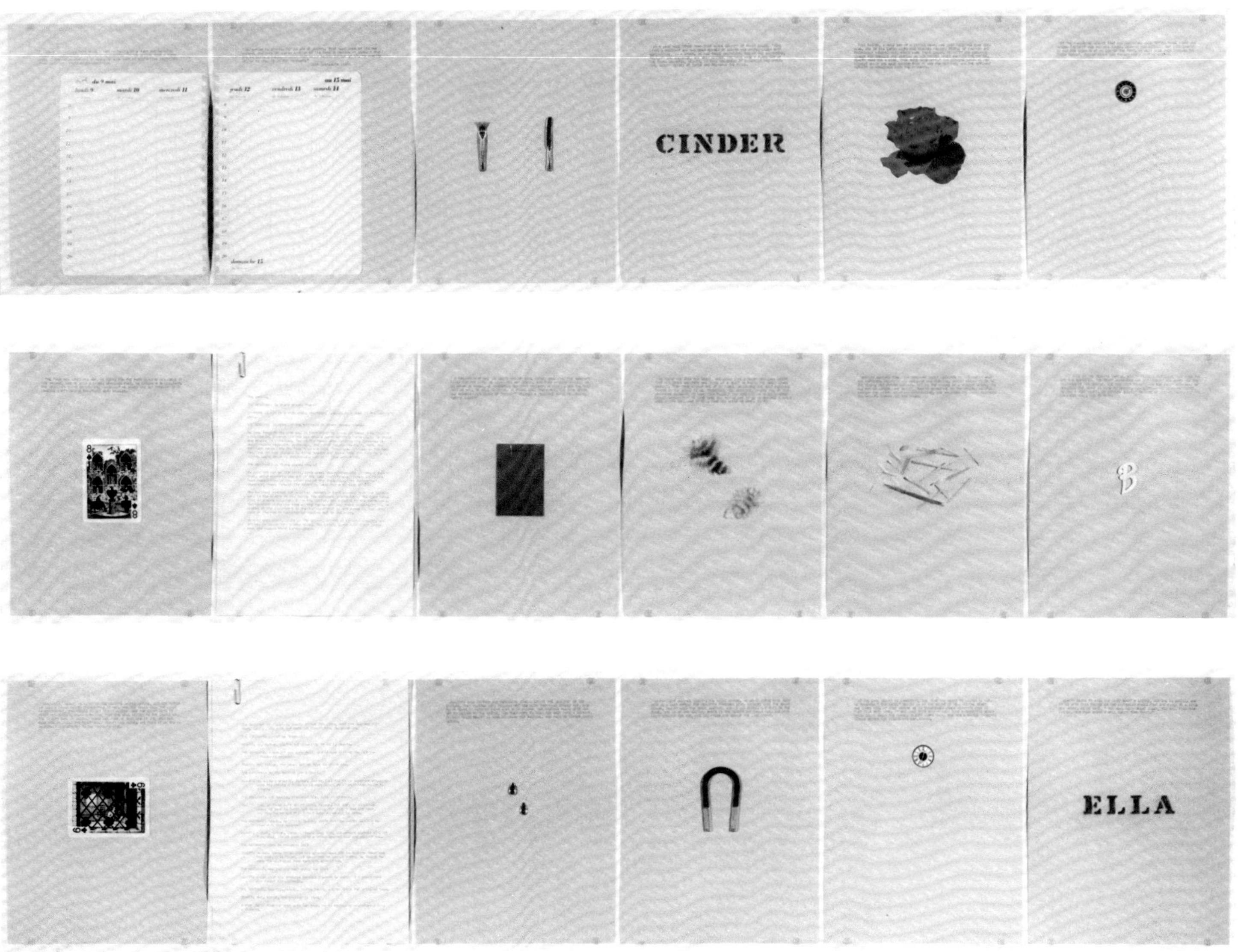

Beauty and the Beast, 1977
Collage on paper: each of three panels, 12½ x 53¾ x 1″ (31.8 x 136.5 cm); overall, 12½ x 161¼″ (31.8 x 409.6 cm)
Gift of Mr. and Mrs. William A. Marsteller
78.30

Pat Steir

What I really want to say about my work . . . is that it's a research rather than a statement. It's research about connections. The connections are about the components of everything in the universe, whatever that question is that makes us remain religious in a way. Awe, I think the word is awe. I hope that my investigations appear to be an expression of the awe that I feel about all the chaos that is life. And when I say chaos, I mean it really in every expression of the word: in a scientific way, in a personal way and in an art way. I'm taking pieces out of the chaos to investigate them, so they can be seen. . . . I feel that art and art history and nature are all the same thing. It's always been the same for me: art is an expression of the life of humans.

Quoted in Kathan Brown and Pat Steir, *Pat Steir Etchings and Drawings*, exhibition catalogue (Oakland, California: Crown Point Press, 1981), unpaginated.

Born in Newark, New Jersey, 1938
Studied at Boston University (B.A., 1960); Pratt Institute, Brooklyn, New York (B.F.A., 1962)
Lives in New York

Selected One-Artist Exhibitions

1971
Graham Gallery, New York

1972
Paley & Lowe, Inc., New York

1973
Corcoran Gallery of Art, Washington, D.C.

1975
Fourcade, Droll, Inc., New York

1976
The Art Gallery, University of Maryland, College Park
Galerie Farideh Cadot, Paris
Otis Art Gallery, Los Angeles

1977
Carl Solway Gallery, Cincinnati

1978
Droll/Kolbert Gallery, New York
Galerie Marilena Bonomo, Bari, Italy

1980
Droll/Kolbert Gallery, New York

1981
Bell Gallery, List Art Center, Brown University, Providence, Rhode Island
Crown Point Press Gallery, Oakland, California
Max Protetch Gallery, New York

1982
Nina Freudenheim Gallery, Buffalo, New York
Galerie Annemarie Verna, Zurich
Galerie Farideh Cadot, Paris

1983
Contemporary Arts Museum, Houston
Helen Foresman Spencer Museum of Art, University of Kansas, Lawrence (traveled)

Selected Group Exhibitions

1972
Corcoran Gallery of Art, Washington, D.C., "Seven Young Artists: Works on Paper"
Whitney Museum of American Art, New York, "1972 Annual Exhibition: Contemporary American Painting"

1973
Whitney Museum of American Art, New York, "American Drawings: 1963–1973"
Whitney Museum of American Art, New York, "1973 Biennial Exhibition: Contemporary American Art"

1974
Institute of Contemporary Art, Boston, "Joan Snyder and Pat Steir"

1976
Indianapolis Museum of Art, "Painting and Sculpture Today 1976"

1977
Archer M. Huntington Gallery, University Art Museum, University of Texas, Austin, "New in the Seventies"
Museum of Contemporary Art, Chicago, "A Survey of Prints (1970–1977)"
P.S. 1, Institute for Art and Urban Resources, Long Island City, New York, "A Painting Show"
Whitney Museum of American Art, New York, "1977 Biennial Exhibition"

1978
Albright-Knox Art Gallery, Buffalo, New York, "American Painting of the 1970s" (traveled)
University Art Museum, University of California, Santa Barbara, "Contemporary Drawing/New York"

1980
The Brooklyn Museum, New York, "American Drawings in Black & White: 1970–1980"

1981
Weatherspoon Art Gallery, University of North Carolina, Greensboro, "Art on Paper, 1981"

1982
Crown Point Press Gallery, Oakland, California, "Representing Reality: Fragments from the Image Field—An Exhibition of Etchings and Woodblock Prints by Gunter Brus, Francesco Clemente, Joel Fisher, Robert Kushner, Pat Steir, William T. Wiley"

Selected Bibliography

Baker, Kenneth. *Joan Snyder and Pat Steir* (exhibition catalogue). Boston: Institute of Contemporary Art, 1974.
Broun, Elizabeth. *Form, Illusion, Myth: Prints and Drawings of Pat Steir* (exhibition catalogue). Lawrence, Kansas: Helen Foresman Spencer Museum of Art, University of Kansas, 1983.
Brown, Kathan. *Pat Steir: Etchings and Paintings* (exhibition catalogue). Oakland, California: Crown Point Press, 1981.
Cathcart, Linda. *American Painting of the 1970s* (exhibition catalogue). Buffalo, New York: Albright-Knox Art Gallery, 1978.
Mayo, Marti. *Arbitrary Order: Paintings by Pat Steir* (exhibition catalogue). Houston: Contemporary Arts Museum, 1983.
Solomon, Elke. *American Drawings: 1963–1973* (exhibition catalogue). New York: Whitney Museum of American Art, 1973.

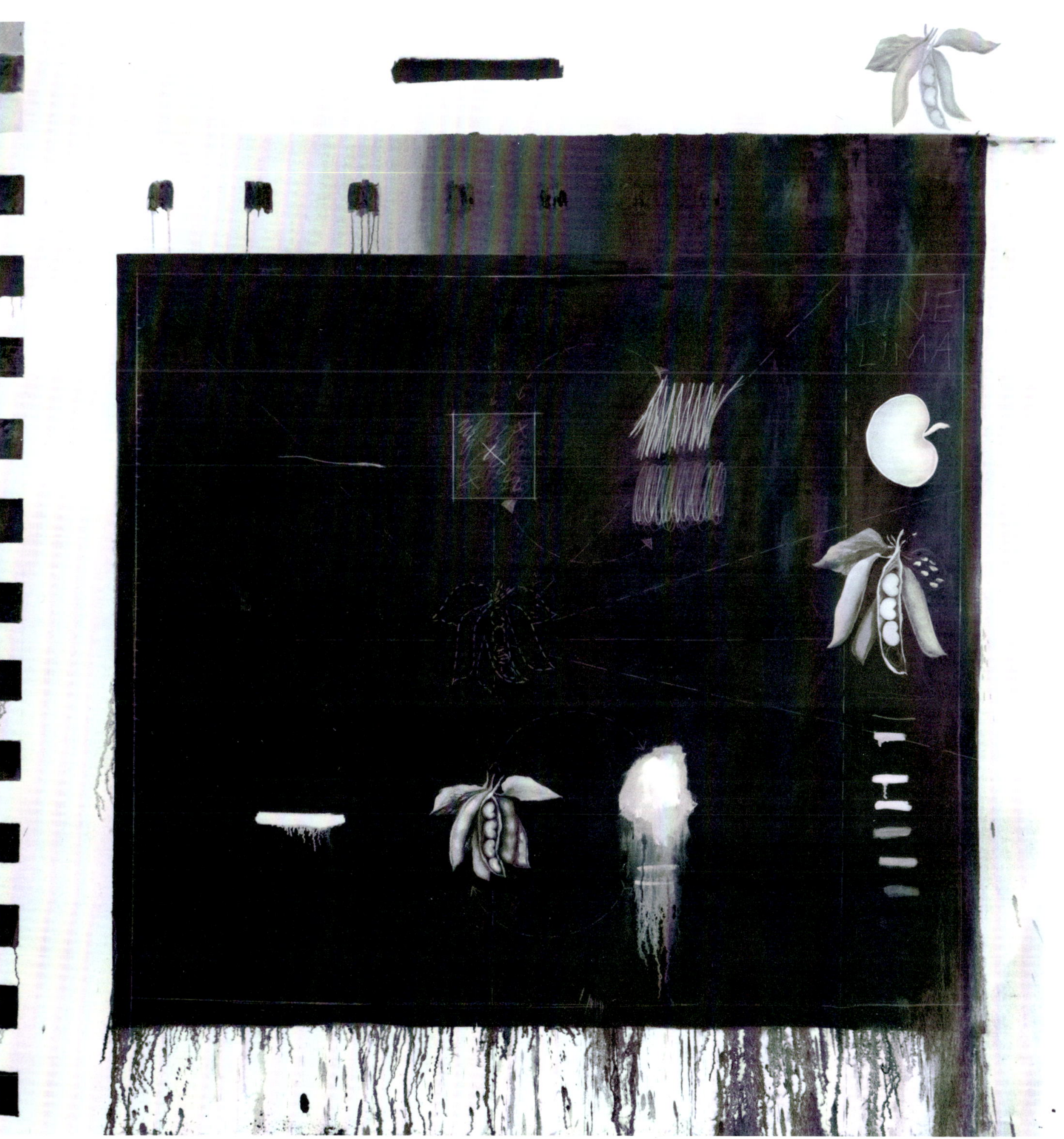

Line Lima, 1973
Oil and pencil on canvas, 84 x 84″ (213.4 x 213.4 cm)
Anonymous gift 74.44

Frank Stella

Born in Malden, Massachusetts, 1936
Studied at Princeton University, New Jersey (B.A., 1958)
Lives in New York

I call the series "Circuits"—which means it's named after auto-racing circuits . . . like Hockenheim in Germany and Silverstone in England. . . . They reflect chicanes, or the curves that drivers talk about all the time. . . . They all have associative meanings for me. My painting is nonrepresentational. Actually, the only thing I choose not to do is to use representational techniques, per se, toward a representational end. . . . The one limit that abstract painting doesn't have and that almost all representational painting is bound by is fixed focus, the fixed perspective; it's a one-shot. Your vision is always held in, which isn't anything like real vision. In that sense, abstract painting is more real, because it allows you to look around; you move in it, and things aren't all conventionally related.

Quoted in Emile de Antonio, "Frank Stella: A Passion for Painting," *GEO*, 4 (March 1982), pp. 15–16.

Selected One-Artist Exhibitions

1960
Leo Castelli Gallery, New York

1963
Ferus Gallery, Los Angeles

1966
Pasadena Art Museum, California

1967
Seattle Art Museum, Washington
Leo Castelli Gallery, New York

1969
Rose Art Museum, Brandeis University, Waltham, Massachusetts

1970
The Museum of Modern Art, New York
Hayward Gallery, London
Stedelijk Museum, Amsterdam

1971
Pasadena Art Museum, California
Art Gallery of Ontario, Canada

1973
Knoedler Contemporary Art, New York
The Phillips Collection, Washington, D.C.

1976
Kunsthalle Basel, Switzerland

1977
The Baltimore Museum of Art
Kunsthalle Bielefeld, Bielefeld, West Germany (traveled)

1978
Fort Worth Art Museum, Texas (traveled)

1979
Leo Castelli Gallery, New York
The Museum of Modern Art, New York

1981
M. Knoedler & Co., Inc., New York

1982
The University of Michigan Museum of Art, Ann Arbor, and The American Federation of Arts (traveled)

Selected Group Exhibitions

1960
The Museum of Modern Art, New York, "Sixteen Americans"

1962
Whitney Museum of American Art, New York, "Geometric Abstraction in America"

1963
Whitney Museum of American Art, New York, "Annual Exhibition 1963: Contemporary American Painting"

1965
The Museum of Modern Art, New York, "The Responsive Eye"
Whitney Museum of American Art, New York, "1965 Annual Exhibition: Contemporary American Painting"

1966
The Art Institute of Chicago, "68th American Exhibition"
The Solomon R. Guggenheim Museum, New York, "Systematic Painting"

1968
Kassel, West Germany, "Documenta 4"
The Museum of Modern Art, New York, "The Art of the Real: USA 1948–1968"

1969
The Metropolitan Museum of Art, New York, "New York Painting and Sculpture: 1940–1970"

1976
The Art Institute of Chicago, "The Seventy-Second American Exhibition"
The Solomon R. Guggenheim Museum, New York, "Twentieth Century American Drawing: Three Avant-Garde Generations"

1977
Museum of Contemporary Art, Chicago, "A View of a Decade"
New York State Museum, Albany, "New York: The State of Art"

1978
Albright-Knox Art Gallery, Buffalo, New York, "American Painting of the 1970's" (traveled)

1979
Whitney Museum of American Art, New York, "1979 Biennial Exhibition"

1980
Fine Arts Center, University of Massachusetts, Amherst, "Sculpture on the Wall: Relief Sculpture of the Seventies"
Hirshhorn Museum and Sculpture Garden, Smithsonian Institution, Washington, D.C., "The Fifties: Aspects of Painting in New York"
The Museum of Modern Art, New York, "Printed Art: A View of Two Decades"

1981
The Corcoran Gallery of Art, Washington, D.C., "37th Biennial Exhibition of Contemporary American Painting"

Selected Bibliography

Axsom, Richard H. *Frank Stella Prints: 1967–1982* (exhibition catalogue). Ann Arbor: The University of Michigan Museum of Art, 1982.
Leider, Philip. *Stella Since 1970* (exhibition catalogue). Fort Worth: Fort Worth Art Museum, 1978.
Richardson, Brenda. *Frank Stella: The Black Paintings* (exhibition catalogue). Baltimore: The Baltimore Museum of Art, 1977.
Rosenblum, Robert. *Frank Stella*. New York: Penguin Books, 1971.
Rubin, William S. *Frank Stella* (exhibition catalogue). New York: The Museum of Modern Art, 1970.

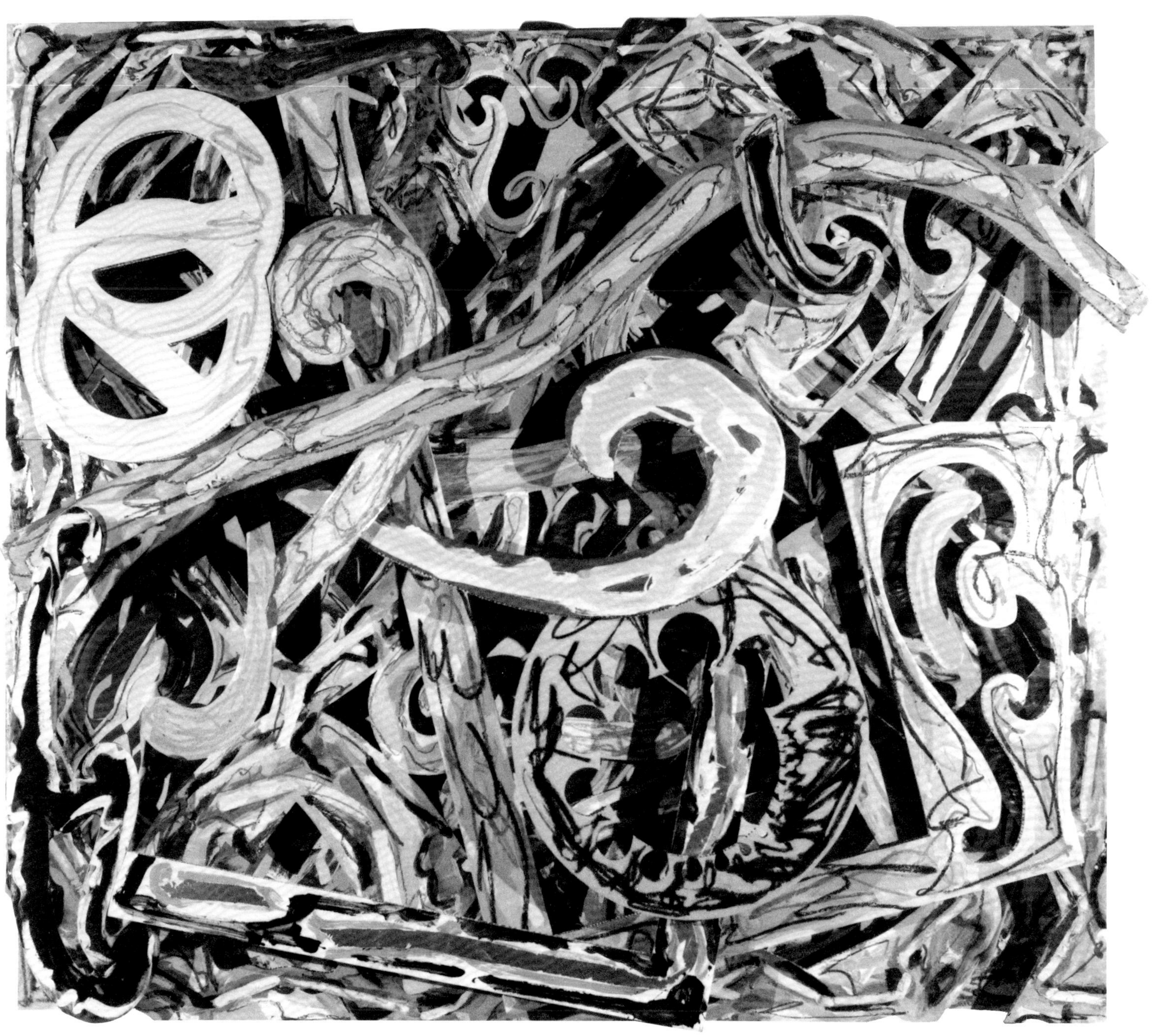

Silverstone, 1981
Mixed media on aluminum and fiberglass, 105½ x 122 x 22″ (268 x 310 x 56 cm)
Purchase, with funds from the Louis and Bessie Adler Foundation, Inc., Seymour M. Klein, President; the Sondra and Charles Gilman, Jr., Foundation, Inc.; Mr. and Mrs. Robert M. Meltzer; and the Painting and Sculpture Committee 81.26

James Surls

Born in Terrell, Texas, 1943
Studied at Sam Houston State College, Huntsville, Texas (B.S., 1966); Cranbrook Academy of Art, Bloomfield Hills, Michigan (M.F.A., 1969)
Lives in Splendora, Texas

I'm not a gunslinger; I'm not trying to kill the art of the past decade, but I think it's gone. To me minimalism is nothing more than good design . . . there is a total absence of personality. I want art to look back at me. . . . I want my art to engage the spectator in a mental conversation. I want people to work at it. I want it to exist on as many levels as it can; I want it to test the limits, to push past the extremes.

Quoted in Carolyn Kinder Carr, "James Surls: Sculpture and Drawings," *Dialogue: The Ohio Arts Journal* (January-February 1982), p. 24.

One-Artist Exhibitions

1974
Delahunty Gallery, Dallas
Tyler Museum of Art, Texas

1975
Contemporary Arts Museum, Houston

1977
Contemporary Arts Museum, Houston
Delahunty Gallery, Dallas

1979
Delahunty Gallery, Dallas

1980
Allan Frumkin Gallery, New York

1981
Allan Frumkin Gallery, New York
Daniel Weinberg Gallery, San Francisco

Selected Group Exhibitions

1973
Fort Worth Art Museum, Texas, "Tarrant County Annual"

1975
Fort Worth Art Museum, Texas, "Exchange: DFW/SFO" (traveled)
Fort Worth Art Museum, Texas, "Tarrant County Annual"

1977
The Solomon R. Guggenheim Museum, New York, "Nine Artists: The Theodoron Awards"

1979
Whitney Museum of American Art, New York, "1979 Biennial Exhibition"

1982
San Francisco Museum of Modern Art, "20 American Artists: Sculpture 1982"

Selected Bibliography

Kutner, Janet. *James Surls: Sculpture* (exhibition catalogue). Dallas: Delahunty Gallery, 1977.
Neubert, George, W. *20 American Artists: Sculpture 1982* (exhibition catalogue). San Francisco: San Francisco Museum of Modern Art, 1982.
1979 Biennial Exhibition (exhibition catalogue). Preface by Tom Armstrong. Foreword by John G. Hanhardt, Barbara Haskell, Richard Marshall, Mark Segal, and Patterson Sims. New York: Whitney Museum of American Art, 1979.
Schimmel, Paul. *James Surls: New Sculpture* (exhibition catalogue). New York: Allan Frumkin Gallery, 1980.
Shearer, Linda. *Nine Artists: The Theodoron Awards* (exhibition catalogue). New York: The Solomon R. Guggenheim Museum, 1977.

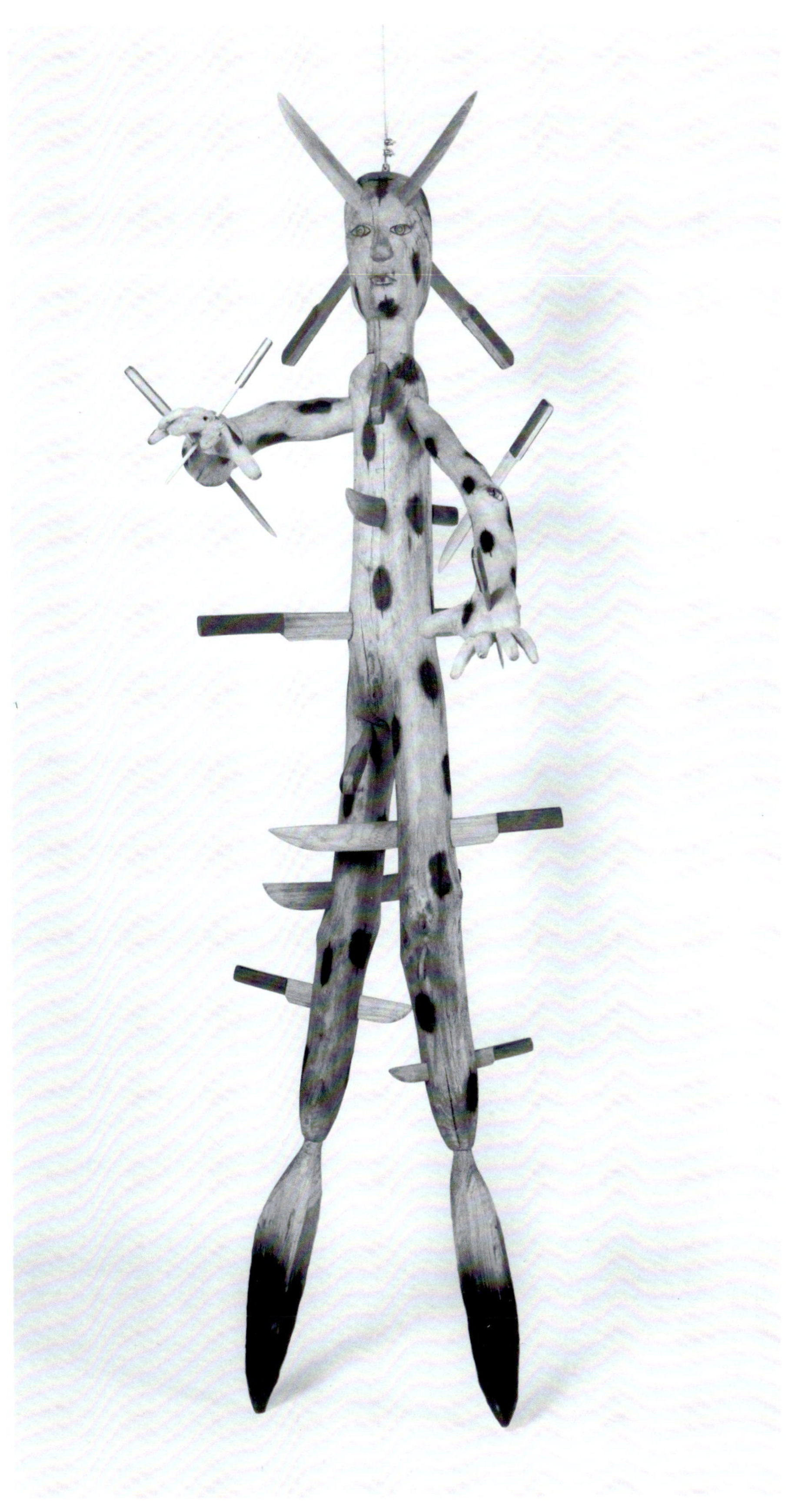

Me and the Butcher Knives, 1982
Oak and mahogany, 101 x 37 x 39″ (256.5 x 94 x 99.1 cm)
Purchase, with funds from an anonymous donor
82.14

John Torreano

Born in Flint, Michigan, 1941
Studied at Cranbrook Academy of Art, Bloomfield, Michigan (B.F.A., 1961); Ohio State University, Columbus (M.A., 1967)
Lives in New York

The column was a solution to the problem of frontality in painting. It was against the idea of painting as a "window," a view into another world or a space. It was my way of dealing with the question of point-of-view. In other words, the column in combination with the jewels makes explicit the issue of particularity of "point-of-view," the question of where one is and what one sees.

Quoted from statement dated April 12, 1983, Artists' Files, Whitney Museum of American Art, New York.

Selected One-Artist Exhibitions

1971
Reese Paley Gallery, San Francisco

1974
Artists Space, New York

1976
Bykert Gallery, New York

1977
Droll/Kolbert Gallery, New York
Nancy Lurie Gallery, Chicago

1979
Droll/Kolbert Gallery, New York
Nancy Lurie Gallery, Chicago

1980
Joslyn Art Museum, Omaha

1981
Hamilton Gallery, New York
Young/Hoffman Gallery, Chicago

1982
Suzanne Hilberry Gallery, Birmingham, Michigan

1983
Hamilton Gallery, New York

Selected Group Exhibitions

1970
Whitney Museum of American Art, New York, "1970 Annual Exhibition: Contemporary American Painting"

1971
Whitney Museum of American Art, New York, "Lyrical Abstraction"

1972
Madison Art Center, Wisconsin, "New American Abstract Painting"

1974
Paula Cooper Gallery, New York, "Three Artists"

1976
Alessandra Gallery, New York, "Ten Approaches to the Decorative"

1977
P.S. 1, Institute for Art and Urban Resources, Long Island City, New York, "A Painting Show"

1978
Fine Arts Galleries, University of South Florida, Tampa, "Two Decades of Abstraction"
The Queens Museum, Flushing, New York, "Private Myths: Unearthings of Contemporary Art"
Renaissance Society, University of Chicago, "Thick Paint"
Whitney Museum of American Art, New York, "American Art 1950 to the Present"

1979
Neuberger Museum, State University of New York, College at Purchase, "10 Artists/Artists Space"
Palazzo Reale, Milan, "Pittura Ambiente"

1980
Galerie Gillespie-Laage-Salomon, Paris, "Trois Dimensions—Sept Américains"
Museum of Contemporary Art, Chicago, "3 Dimensional Painting"
P.S. 1, Institute for Art and Urban Resources, Long Island City, New York, "Watercolor Exhibition"
Whitney Museum of American Art, New York, Downtown Branch, "Painting in Relief"

1981
Oscarsson Hood Gallery, New York, "The New Spiritualism"

1982
Contemporary Arts Museum, Houston, "The Americans: Collage"
Wave Hill, Bronx, New York, "New Perspectives"

Selected Bibliography

Baur, John I.H., and Larry Aldrich. *Lyrical Abstraction* (exhibition catalogue). New York: Whitney Museum of American Art, 1971.
Day, Holliday T. *I-80 Series: John Torreano* (exhibition catalogue). Omaha: Joslyn Art Museum, 1980.
Delehanty, Suzanne. 10 *Artists/Artists Space* (exhibition catalogue). Purchase, New York: Neuberger Museum, State University of New York, 1979.
Owens, Craig. *New Perspectives* (exhibition catalogue). Bronx, New York: Wave Hill, 1982.
Tannenbaum, Judith. *3 Dimensional Painting* (exhibition catalogue). Chicago: Museum of Contemporary Art, 1980.

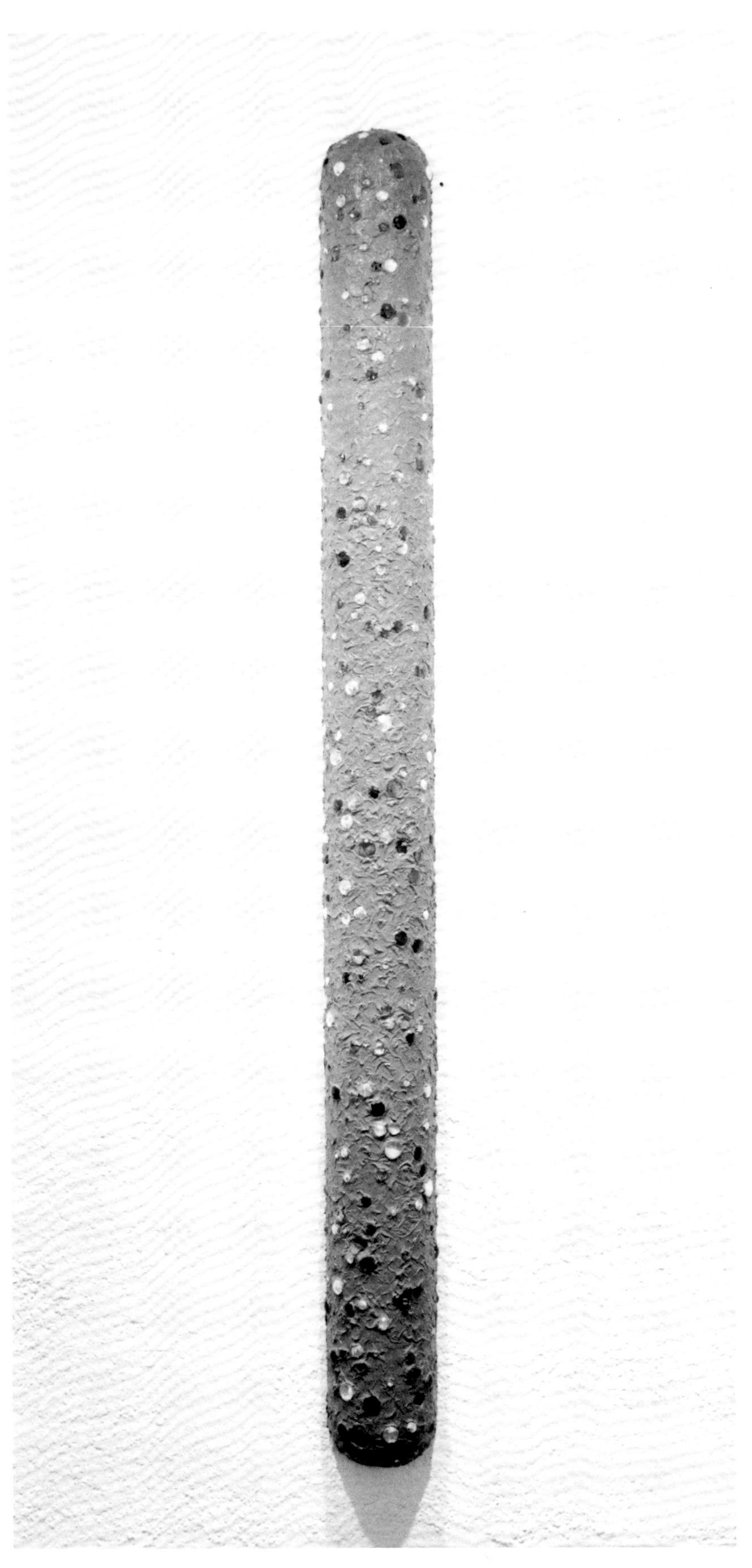

Red Column, 1974
Oil, acrylic, and glass jewels on wood, 96 x 8″
(243.8 x 20.3 cm)
Gift of the Larry Aldrich Foundation (by
exchange) 78.7

William T. Wiley

Born in Bedford, Indiana, 1937
Studied at the San Francisco Art Institute (B.F.A., 1961; M.F.A., 1962)
Lives in Forest Knolls, California

"Harpoon for the Dreamer" was started after a very strong, vivid dream. It is the only work that I ever consciously started from a dream. It was very mysterious and had a powerful aftertaste. Some of the images, and the harpoon, come directly from the dream. I was 3 or 4 days into the painting when I got word of Cliff Westermann's death. It all seemed to echo together, and became a form to pay homage to Cliff and to the mystery that surrounds our life, death, and dreams. And I often wonder who can show the line between what we call dreaming and what we call awake.

Quoted from statement dated April 26, 1983, Artists' Files, Whitney Museum of American Art, New York.

Selected One-Artist Exhibitions

1960
Richmond Art Center, California
San Francisco Museum of Art
Staempfli Gallery, New York

1964
Staempfli Gallery, New York

1968
Allan Frumkin Gallery, New York
Hansen Fuller Gallery, San Francisco

1969
Hansen Fuller Gallery, San Francisco
San Francisco Art Institute

1971
Hansen Fuller Gallery, New York
University Art Museum, University of California, Berkeley (traveled)

1972
Allan Frumkin Gallery, New York
Hansen Fuller Gallery, San Francisco
Margo Leavin Gallery, Los Angeles

1973
Allan Frumkin Gallery, New York
Stedelijk Museum, Amsterdam

1974
Allan Frumkin Gallery, Chicago
Hansen Fuller Gallery, San Francisco

1975
Hansen Fuller Gallery, San Francisco
Portland Center for the Visual Arts, Oregon

1976
Allan Frumkin Gallery, New York
Margo Leavin Gallery, Los Angeles
The Museum of Modern Art, New York

1978
Hansen Fuller Gallery, San Francisco
Morgan Gallery, Shawnee Mission, Kansas

1979
The Baltimore Museum of Art (traveled)
Allan Frumkin Gallery, Chicago
Allan Frumkin Gallery, New York
Walker Art Center, Minneapolis (traveled)

1980
San Jose Museum of Art, California

1981
University Fine Arts Galleries, Florida State University, Tallahassee (traveled)

Selected Group Exhibitions

1960
Whitney Museum of American Art, New York, "Young America 1960"

1962
Whitney Museum of American Art, New York, "Fifty California Artists"

1966
Whitney Museum of American Art, New York, "Annual Exhibition 1966: Contemporary Sculpture and Prints"

1967
Los Angeles County Museum of Art, "American Sculpture of the Sixties"
University Art Museum, University of California, Berkeley, "Funk"
Whitney Museum of American Art, New York, "1967 Annual Exhibition of Contemporary Painting"

1968
Whitney Museum of American Art, New York, "1968 Annual Exhibition: Contemporary American Sculpture"

1969
Institute of Contemporary Art, University of Pennsylvania, Philadelphia, "Spirit of the Comics"
Whitney Museum of American Art, New York, "Human Concern/Personal Torment"

1973
Whitney Museum of American Art, New York, "Extraordinary Realities".
Whitney Museum of American Art, New York, "1973 Biennial Exhibition: Contemporary American Art"

1976
Whitney Museum of American Art, New York, "200 Years of American Sculpture" (traveled)

1978
Albright-Knox Art Gallery, Buffalo, New York, "American Painting of the 1970s" (traveled)

1980
Montgomery Museum of Fine Arts, Alabama, "American Painting of the 60s and 70s: The Real, The Ideal, The Fantastic"

1981
Akron Art Museum, Ohio, "The Image in American Painting and Sculpture, 1950–1980"
Neuberger Museum, State University of New York, College at Purchase, "Soundings"

1982
San Francisco Museum of Modern Art, "20 American Artists: Sculpture 1982"

1983
Whitney Museum of American Art, New York, "1983 Biennial Exhibition"

Selected Bibliography

Beal, Graham J., and John Perreault. *Wiley Territory* (exhibition catalogue). Minneapolis: Walker Art Center, 1979.
Richardson, Brenda. *William T. Wiley Graphics 1967–1979* (exhibition catalogue). Chicago: Landfall Press, 1980.
———. *Wizdumb: William T. Wiley* (exhibition catalogue). Berkeley: University Art Museum, University of California, 1971.
Selz, Peter. *Funk* (exhibition catalogue). Berkeley: University Art Museum, University of California, 1967.
William T. Wiley (exhibition catalogue). Essays by Beth Coffelt, Matthew Kangas, John Perreault, Brenda Richardson, Albert Stewart. Tallahassee, Florida: University Fine Arts Galleries, Florida State University, 1981.

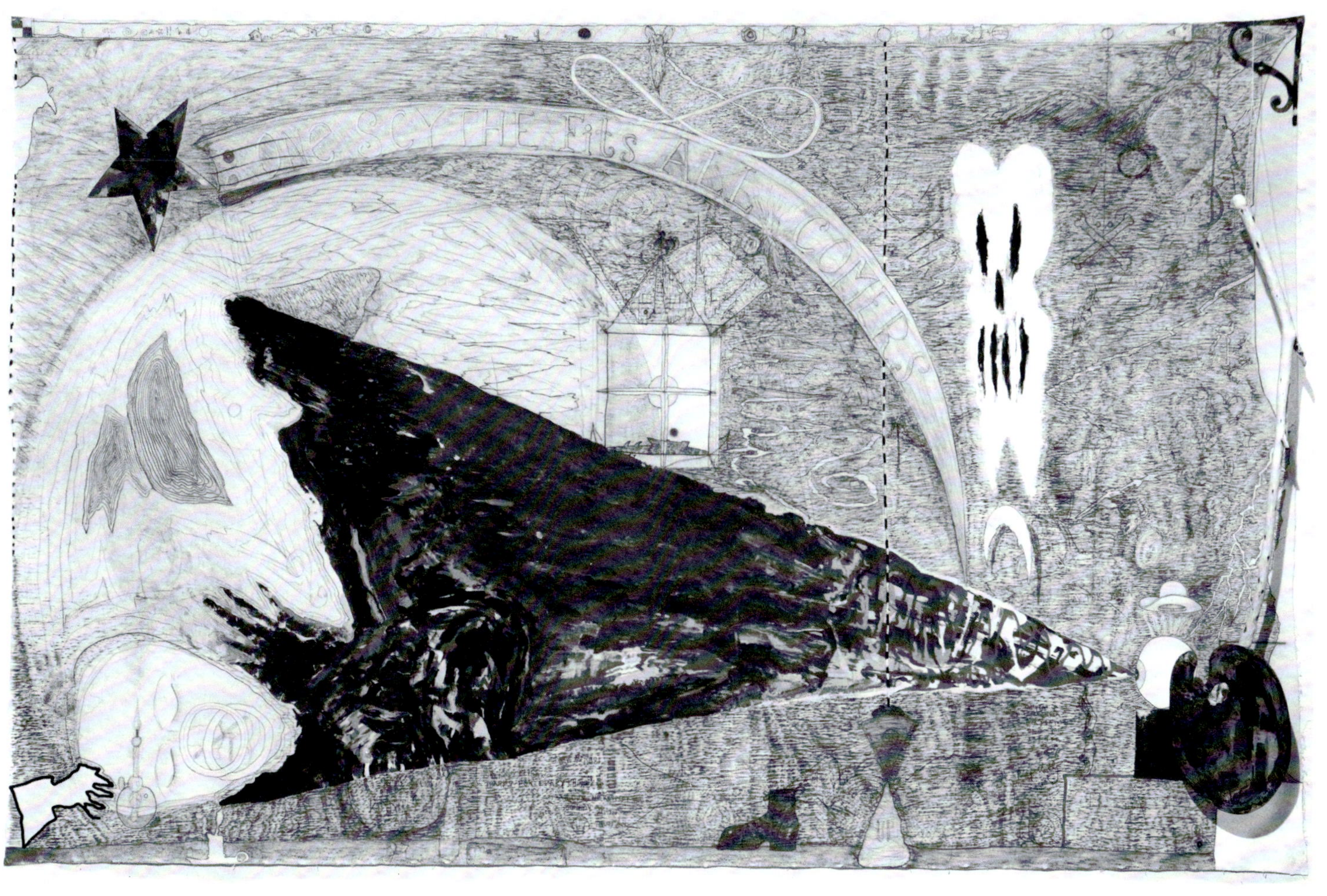

Harpoon for the Dreamer, 1981
Acrylic, charcoal, and pastel on canvas; construction of bay laurel with steel wire and plywood with acrylic, graphite, and colored pencil: canvas, 96¾ x 153″ (245.7 x 388.6 cm) (irregular); wood construction, 75 x 14 x 8″ (190.5 x 35.6 x 20.3 cm)
Purchase, with funds from the Painting and Sculpture Committee 83.9 a–b

Jackie Winsor

I selected a cube to work with. I wanted the focus to be on what went on within the form. . . . You get to participate in the form, you get to see through it, while it marks off space, while it marks it off solidly and intangibly. It's there and it's not there . . . the interior space is physically inaccessible to you but it is accessible in that you can project mentally into it. . . . Yet your initial experience of the piece, kinesthetically, is about solidity, density, weight. Only as you enter into a more subtle participation with the piece, do you become intrigued with its core. I like the idea of a window into a space and the fact that the space is both revealed and concealed. . . . The pieces have a quietness to them, they have their own energy. . . . You sense a space much greater than the volume actually used up.

Quoted in Jackie Winsor and Ellen Phelan, "A Conversation Between Two Sculptors," in *Jackie Winsor/Sculpture*, exhibition catalogue (Cincinnati: Contemporary Arts Center, 1977), pp. 7–8.

Born in Newfoundland, Canada, 1941
Studied at Yale Summer School of Art and Music, Norfolk, Connecticut (1964); Massachusetts College of Art, Boston (B.F.A., 1965); Rutgers University, New Brunswick, New Jersey (M.F.A., 1967)
Lives in New York

Selected One-Artist Exhibitions

1968
Douglass College Gallery, New Brunswick, New Jersey

1971
Nova Scotia College of Art and Design, Halifax, Nova Scotia, Canada

1973
Paula Cooper Gallery, New York

1976
Contemporary Arts Center, Cincinnati (traveled)
Paula Cooper Gallery, New York

1978
Wadsworth Atheneum, Hartford, Connecticut

1979
The Museum of Modern Art, New York (traveled)

1981
Virginia Museum, Richmond

1982
Akron Art Museum, Ohio

Selected Group Exhibitions

1968
American Federation of Artists, "Soft Sculpture"

1969
The Riverside Museum, New York, "American Abstract Artists"

1970
Whitney Museum of American Art, New York, "1970 Annual Exhibition: Contemporary American Sculpture"

1971
Aldrich Museum of Contemporary Art, Ridgefield, Connecticut, "Twenty-six Contemporary Women Artists"

1972
The Detroit Institute of the Arts, "Twelve Statements Beyond the 60s"

1973
Allen Memorial Art Museum, Oberlin College, Ohio, "Four Young Americans"
Musée d'Art Moderne de la Ville de Paris, "8e Biennale de Paris"
Whitney Museum of American Art, New York, "1973 Biennial Exhibition: Contemporary American Art"

1974
The Art Institute of Chicago, "71st American Exhibition"
Indianapolis Museum of Art, "Painting and Sculpture Today 1974"
The Museum of Modern Art, New York, "Recent Acquisitions"
Whitney Museum of American Art, New York, "Recent Acquisitions"

1975
Hayward Gallery, London, "The Condition of Sculpture"

1977
Museum of Contemporary Art, Chicago, "A View of a Decade"
Renaissance Society, University of Chicago, "Ideas in Sculpture: 1965–1977"
The Vancouver Art Gallery, British Columbia, Canada, "Strata: Nancy Graves, Eva Hesse, Michelle Stuart, Jackie Winsor"
Whitney Museum of American Art, New York, "1977 Biennial Exhibition"

1978
Kunsthaus, Zurich, "Soft Sculpture"

1979
Whitney Museum of American.Art, New York, "1979 Biennial Exhibition"

1981
Visual Arts Gallery, School of Visual Arts, New York, "Sculptural Density"

1982
Margo Leavin Gallery, Los Angeles, "Works in Wood"
Whitney Museum of American Art, Fairfield County, Stamford, Connecticut, "Surveying the Seventies: Selections from the Permanent Collection"

1983
Whitney Museum of American Art, New York, "1983 Biennial Exhibition"

Selected Bibliography

Bear, Liza. "An Interview with Jackie Winsor," *Avalanche*, Spring 1972, pp. 10–17.
Boulton, Jack. *Jackie Winsor: Sculpture* (exhibition catalogue). Text by Jackie Winsor and Ellen Phelan. Cincinnati: Contemporary Arts Center, 1976.
Johnson, Ellen. *Jackie Winsor* (exhibition catalogue). New York: The Museum of Modern Art, 1979.
Kolbert, Frank. *Twelve Statements Beyond the 60s* (exhibition catalogue). Detroit: The Detroit Institute of the Arts, 1972.
Lippard, Lucy R. *Twenty-six Contemporary Women Artists* (exhibition catalogue). Ridgefield, Connecticut: Aldrich Museum of Contemporary Art, 1971.
———. "Jackie Winsor," *Artforum*, 12 (February 1974), pp. 56–58.
Pincus-Witten, Robert. "Winsor Knots: The Sculpture of Jackie Winsor," *Arts Magazine*, 51 (June 1977), pp. 127–133.

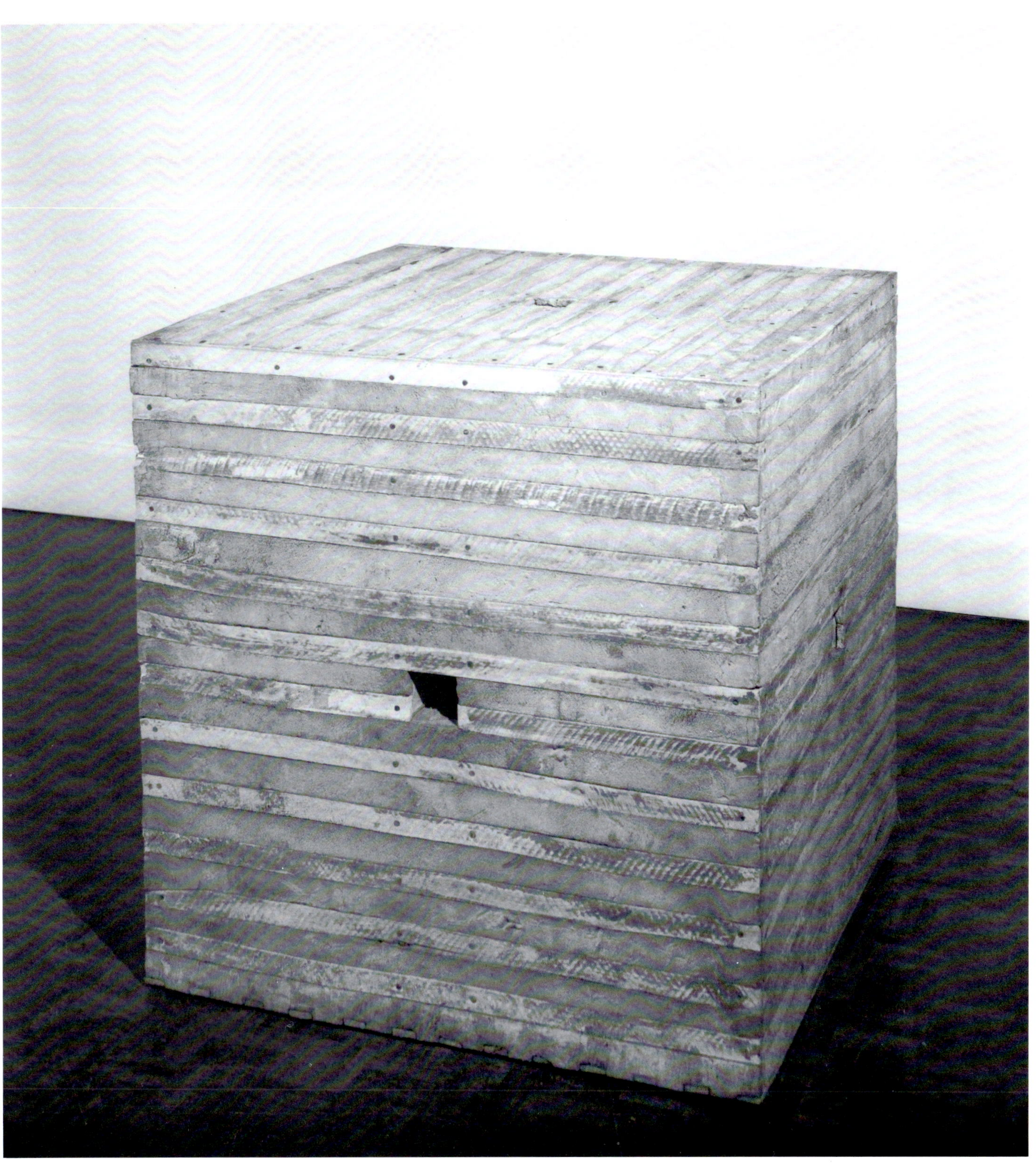

Cement Piece, 1976–77
Cement, wood, and wire, 36 x 36 x 36″ (91.4 x 91.4 x 91.4 cm)
Purchase, with funds from the Louis and Bessie Adler Foundation, Inc., Seymour M. Klein, President; Mr. and Mrs. Robert M. Meltzer; and Mrs. Nicholas Millhouse 80.7

Robert S. Zakanitch

Painting had become too cerebral and I wanted it to become more physical, more touchable (but still intelligent), and I wanted to reach a broader audience and not just the art historian, artist sect. . . . What started to happen was that the marks began to be patterns, and the patterns referential images once again. . . . What was becoming evident and wonderfully ironic was that although I was now using referential imagery (which gave me the feeling of freshness, newness, unlimitedness and excitement), it was through the use of abstraction, the emphases on the paint and surface that the dynamics began to happen and what made it art. But what had radically changed was the content and my attitude, which was now interested in additive and not reductive ideas. Modern Art, as I knew it, would never be the same for me.

Quoted from statement dated March 1983, Artists' Files, Whitney Museum of American Art, New York.

Born in Elizabeth, New Jersey, 1935
Studied at Newark School of Fine and Industrial Art, New Jersey (1955–57)
Lives in New York

Selected One-Artist Exhibitions

1968
Stable Gallery, New York

1970
Reese Paley Gallery, New York

1971
Reese Paley Gallery, New York

1973
Cunningham Ward Gallery, New York

1974
Cunningham Ward Gallery, New York

1977
Holly Solomon Gallery, New York

1978
Robert Miller Gallery, New York

1979
Robert Miller Gallery, New York
Galerie Rudolf Zwirner, Cologne

1980
Galerie Bruno Bischofberger, Zurich
Robert Miller Gallery, New York
Galerie Daniel Templon, Paris

1981
Akira Ikeda Gallery, Nagoya, Japan
Institute of Contemporary Art, University of Pennsylvania, Philadelphia
Mayor Gallery, London
Robert Miller Gallery, New York

1982
Asher Faure Gallery, Los Angeles
Makler Gallery, Philadelphia

Selected Group Exhibitions

1967
Whitney Museum of American Art, New York, "1967 Annual Exhibition of Contemporary Painting"

1968
Philadelphia Museum of Art, "The Pure and the Clear: American Innovations"

1969
Whitney Museum of American Art, New York, "1969 Annual Exhibition: Contemporary American Painting"

1971
Whitney Museum of American Art, New York, "Lyrical Abstraction"
Whitney Museum of American Art, New York, "The Structure of Color"

1972
Indianapolis Museum of Art, "Painting and Sculpture Today 1972"
Vassar College Art Gallery, Poughkeepsie, New York, "New American Abstract Painting"

1974
Whitney Museum of American Art, New York, Downtown Branch, "Continuing Abstraction in American Art"

1977
P.S. 1, Institute of Art and Urban Resources, Long Island City, New York, "Pattern Painting"
Museum of American Foundation for the Arts, Miami, Florida, "Patterning and Decoration" (traveled)

1979
Institute of Contemporary Art, University of Pennsylvania, Philadelphia, "The Decorative Impulse" (traveled)

1980
Mannheimer Kunstverein, Mannheim, West Germany, "Dekor" (traveled)
National Gallery of Art, Washington, D.C., "The Morton G. Neumann Family Collection: Selected Works" (traveled)
United States Pavilion, 39th Venice Biennale, Italy, "Drawings: The Pluralist Decade" (traveled)

1981
The Squibb Art Gallery, Princeton, New Jersey, "Aspects of Post-Modernism: Decorative and Narrative Art"
Whitney Museum of American Art, New York, "1981 Biennial Exhibition"

1982
Galerie Civica, Modena, Italy, "Transavanguardia: Italia/America"
Museum of Fine Arts, Boston, "A Private Vision: Contemporary Art From the Graham Gund Collection"

Selected Bibliography

Baur, John I.H., and Larry Aldrich. *Lyrical Abstraction* (exhibition catalogue). New York: Whitney Museum of American Art, 1971.
Hunter, Sam. *Aspects of Post-Modernism: Decorative and Narrative Art* (exhibition catalogue). Princeton, New Jersey: The Squibb Art Gallery, 1981.
Kardon, Janet. *The Decorative Impulse* (exhibition catalogue). Philadelphia: Institute of Contemporary Art, University of Pennsylvania, 1981.
———. *Robert S. Zakanitch* (exhibition catalogue). Philadelphia: Institute of Contemporary Art, University of Pennsylvania, 1981.
Oliva, Achille Bonito. *Transavanguardia: Italia/America* (exhibition catalogue). Modena, Italy: Galeria Civica, 1982.
Tucker, Marcia. *The Structure of Color* (exhibition catalogue). New York: Whitney Museum of American Art, 1971.

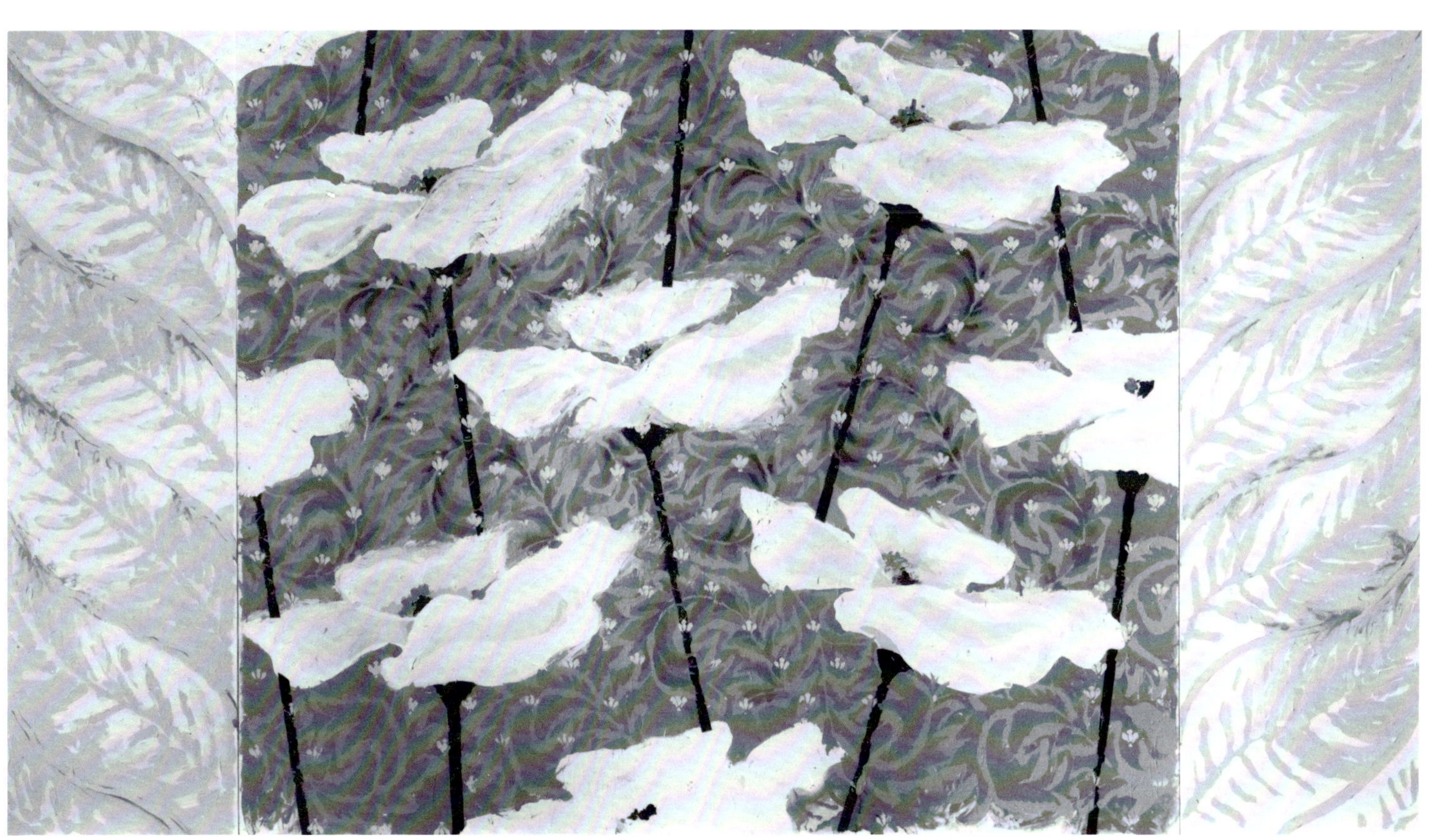

Angel Feet, 1978
Acrylic on canvas, 94 x 174″ (238.8 x 442 cm)
Promised gift of an anonymous donor P.26.83

Joe Zucker

My selection of subject matter in relation to kinds of surfaces is important. Pictorial content becomes an iconography to discuss the topography of the painting. . . . The subjects I paint—plantations, sailing ships, alchemists, etc.—are metaphors. They have many implications, which are left to what the viewer brings to them. . . . Merlyn . . . is a magician traveling in time from the future to the past. "Merlyn's Lab" depicts the wizard surrounded by various creatures and the instruments of his alchemic science—a badger, an owl, bats, an alligator, a retort, etc. Again in terms of the surface, fashioning an alligator skin offers a lot of tactile opportunities for a painter, as does the tutor himself, bedecked in his robes with scepter and vials of magical liquid. Merlyn's alchemy is analogous to the situation of the artist—he is a metaphor for process. I do not look to the future for what I am painting now. I work with the past and the present.

Quoted in Richard Marshall, *New Image Painting*, exhibition catalogue (New York: Whitney Museum of American Art, 1978), p. 68.

Born in Chicago, 1941
Studied at the School of The Art Institute of Chicago (B.F.A., 1964; M.F.A., 1966)
Lives in East Hampton, New York

Selected One-Artist Exhibitions

1965
Heistand Hall Art Gallery, Miami University, Oxford, Ohio

1966
Adele Rosenberg Gallery, Chicago

1968
Walker Art Center, Minneapolis

1971
University of Montana, Missoula

1974
Bykert Gallery, New York
Texas Gallery, Houston

1975
Bykert Gallery, New York
Daniel Weinberg Gallery, San Francisco

1976
The Baltimore Museum of Art
Bykert Gallery, New York

1978
Holly Solomon Gallery, New York
Young/Hoffman Gallery, Chicago

1979
Galerie Bruno Bischofberger, Zurich
Mayor Gallery, London
Holly Solomon Gallery, New York

1980
Holly Solomon Gallery, New York

1981
Dart Gallery, Chicago
Holly Solomon Gallery, New York
University Art Museum, University of California, Berkeley

1982
Albright-Knox Art Gallery, Buffalo, New York
La Jolla Museum of Contemporary Art, California

Selected Group Exhibitions

1964
The Art Institute of Chicago, "67th Annual Exhibition by Artists of Chicago and Vicinity"

1965
Walker Art Center, Minneapolis, "Twelve Chicago Painters" (traveled)

1968
Walker Art Center, Minneapolis, "1968 Biennial of Painting and Sculpture: Iowa, Minnesota, North Dakota, South Dakota, Wisconsin"

1972
Madison Art Center, Wisconsin, "New American Abstract Painting"

1976
Akademie der Künste, West Berlin, "Soho: Downtown Manhattan"
Fort Worth Art Museum, "The Great American Rodeo" (traveled)
Daniel Weinberg Gallery, San Francisco, "Richard Artschwager, Chuck Close, Joe Zucker" (traveled)

1977
Whitney Museum of American Art, New York, "1977 Biennial Exhibition"

1978
Pace Gallery, New York, "Grids"
Whitney Museum of American Art, New York, "New Image Painting"

1979
Hayward Gallery, London, "New Painting/New York"
Whitney Museum of American Art, New York, "1979 Biennial Exhibition"

1980
Mannheimer Kunstverein, Mannheim, West Germany, "Dekor" (traveled)
Neue Galerie, Sammlung Ludwig, Aachen, West Germany, "Les Nouveaux Fauves—Die Neuen Wilden"
United States Pavilion, 39th Venice Biennale, "Drawings: The Pluralist Decade" (traveled)

1983
Whitney Museum of American Art, New York, "1983 Biennial Exhibition"

Selected Bibliography

Belloli, Jay. *The Great American Rodeo* (exhibition catalogue). Fort Worth: Fort Worth Art Museum, 1976.
Kardon, Janet, ed. *Drawings: The Pluralist Decade* (exhibition catalogue). Texts by John Hallmark Neff, Rosalind Krauss, Richard Lorber, Edit deAk, John Perreault, Howard N. Fox, and Nancy Foote. Philadelphia: Institute of Contemporary Art, University of Pennsylvania, 1980.
Krane, Susan. *Surfacing Images: The Painting of Joe Zucker 1969–1982* (exhibition catalogue), Buffalo, New York: Albright-Knox Art Gallery, 1982.
Marshall, Richard. *New Image Painting* (exhibition catalogue). New York: Whitney Museum of American Art, 1978.
Richardson, Brenda. *Joe Zucker: New Paintings* (exhibition catalogue). Baltimore: The Baltimore Museum of Art, 1976.

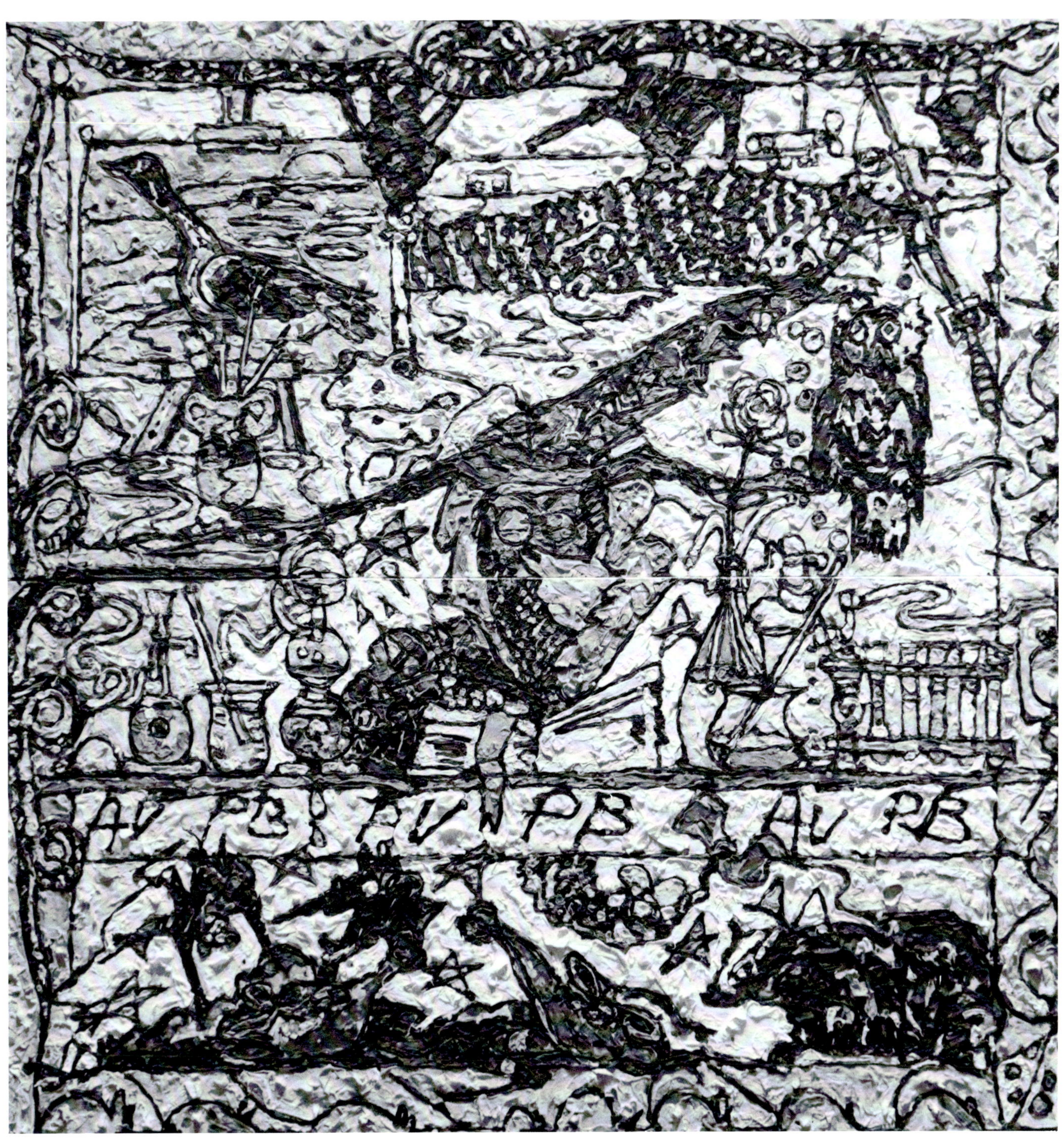

Merlyn's Lab, 1977
Acrylic, cotton, and rhoplex on canvas, 96 x 96″
(243.8 x 243.8 cm)
Gift of the Louis and Bessie Adler Foundation,
Inc., Seymour M. Klein, President 78.16

National Committee of the Whitney Museum of American Art

"American Art Since 1970" was approved for funding by the members of the 1981–82 National Committee:

Mr. Edward R. Hudson, Jr., *Chairman*

Mr. and Mrs. Douglas Auchincloss
New York, New York

Mrs. Grace Belt
New York, New York

Mr. and Mrs. Edwin A. Bergman
Chicago, Illinois

Mr. and Mrs. Sydney F. Biddle
New York, New York

Mr. Winton M. Blount
Montgomery, Alabama

The Honorable Anne Cox Chambers
Atlanta, Georgia

Mr. and Mrs. Thomas B. Coleman
New Orleans, Louisiana

Mr. and Mrs. Kenneth N. Dayton
Wayzata, Minnesota

Mr. and Mrs. Walter B. Ford II
Warren, Michigan

Mr. and Mrs. Brendan Gill
New York, New York

Mr. Graham Gund
Cambridge, Massachusetts

Mr. and Mrs. Gordon Hanes
Winston-Salem, North Carolina

Mr. and Mrs. S. Roger Horchow
Dallas, Texas

Mr. and Mrs. Edward R. Hudson, Jr.
Fort Worth, Texas

Mr. and Mrs. R. Crosby Kemper
Kansas City, Missouri

Mr. Seymour H. Knox
Buffalo, New York

Mr. and Mrs. Robert P. Kogod
Bethesda, Maryland

Mr. and Mrs. George P. Kroh
Mission Hills, Kansas

Mr. and Mrs. Richard E. Lang
Seattle, Washington

Mr. and Mrs. Leonard A. Lauder
New York, New York

Mr. and Mrs. Sydney Lewis
Richmond, Virginia

Mrs. Robert B. Mayer
Chicago, Illinois

Mr. and Mrs. Robert E. Meyerhoff
Phoenix, Maryland

Mr. and Mrs. Nicholas Millhouse
New York, New York

Mr. and Mrs. S. I. Morris
Houston, Texas

Mrs. John D. Murchison
Addison, Texas

Mr. and Mrs. Harold C. Price
Bartlesville, Oklahoma

Mr. and Mrs. C. Lawson Reed
Cincinnati, Ohio

Mr. and Mrs. Richard M. Ross
Columbus, Ohio

Mr. and Mrs. Clinton Swingle
Elverson, Pennsylvania

Mr. A. Alfred Taubman
Troy, Michigan

Mrs. Louise Talbot Trigg
Santa Fe, New Mexico

Mr. and Mrs. Cornelius Vanderbilt Whitney
New York, New York

Mr. and Mrs. Robert Woods
Los Angeles, California

The following members have joined the National Committee since 1981-82

Mr. and Mrs. Anthony Ames
Atlanta, Georgia

Mr. Lee Bass
Fort Worth, Texas

Mrs. Kenyon C. Bolton
Cleveland, Ohio

Mr. and Mrs. James S. DeSilva, Jr.
La Jolla, California

Mr. and Mrs. Herbert E. Jones, Jr.
Charleston, West Virginia

Mr. and Mrs. Donald S. MacNaughton
Nashville, Tennessee

Mr. and Mrs. Raymond Mason
Jacksonville, Florida

Mr. Byron R. Meyer
San Francisco, California

Mr. and Mrs. A.J.F. O'Reilly
Pittsburgh, Pennsylvania

Mr. and Mrs. Paul C. Schorr III
Lincoln, Nebraska

Rev. and Mrs. Alfred R. Shands III
Louisville, Kentucky

Mr. and Mrs. Donald R. Scutchfield
Woodside, California

Mrs. Nellie Taft
Cincinnati, Ohio

Mr. Leslie Wexner
Columbus, Ohio

Mr. and Mrs. David M. Winton
Wayzata, Minnesota